The Awkward Questions in Education

Schools and systems face unprecedented challenges, such as falling attendance, recruitment, and retention issues; the validity of external monitoring of schools; and the advent of artificial intelligence (AI). In *The Awkward Questions in Education*, Al Kingsley tackles the tough, often-avoided issues plaguing the sector today.

Drawing on over 35 years of experience, Kingsley explores the deep-seated challenges that many in education encounter daily and opens critical conversations that we need to have if we're to enact real, sustainable change. Chapters address key questions such as the following:

- Are we teaching students the right skills for the future?
- Do we need more and different spaces to improve attendance and engagement?
- Is the system truly inclusive?
- How should we handle the integration of AI in classrooms?
- What can be done to solve the ongoing teacher recruitment and retention crisis?

Featuring interviews with key stakeholders, including school leaders, policy-makers, teachers, and governors, this is a must-read for school leaders, multi-academy trusts (MATs), teachers, governors, trustees, and anyone passionate about the future of education.

Al Kingsley MBE has spent the last 30 years in the EdTech space and nearly two decades as a school trustee and governor. He was awarded the 2023 "Edufuturist of the Year," the Education Resources Awards "Outstanding Achievement" award, and the British Education Suppliers Association "Inspiring Leaders" awards in 2023. He is the group CEO of NetSupport, an internationally acclaimed EdTech vendor and chair of a MAT, and on the Department for Education (DfE) advisory board for the East of England. He was awarded an MBE (Member of the Order of the British Empire) in the King's 2025 New Year's Honours, for services to education.

"The world is progressing at unprecedented speed, and our education system struggles to keep pace. *The Awkward Questions in Education* confronts the consequential 'Elephants in the Room'—those pivotal questions that stir debate and ignite our shared passion for a better future. Al Kingsley is sounding out a rallying call for educators, policymakers and parents to co-create an offering that prepares our children for success. This book challenges us to move beyond comfort zones, ultimately leading us to empower students to actively shape the future they envision. [...] An important book for those who, deep down, know there is another way."

Dan Fitzpatrick, *The AI Educator*

"A much-needed dose of honesty and insight.... With decades of experience in education, Al Kingsley is uniquely qualified to address the most pressing issues facing our schools today: Are schools doing enough? Are teachers being asked to do too much? Is the system fit for purpose? [...] Kingsley challenges the status quo and offers a roadmap for a better future for education."

Sugata Mitra, *Professor Emeritus, NIIT University*

"What's so impressive about Al Kingsley's way of working is that he draws from his wide and deep knowledge across the educational landscape, not just in the UK but internationally. Quite how he manages to be all over the data from different systems and also synthesise and share it is remarkable! *The Awkward Questions in Education* provides important provocations and considerable research for us to reframe how we currently conceive of and improve the experiences and outcomes for our young people, together with an engaged, committed and fulfilled community of professionals. This engaging book will provide the stimulus for many a deep conversation across the sector. It's written from a place of great experience and deep generosity and I'm sure readers will enjoy it as much as I do."

Mary Myatt, *Education Writer and Speaker*

"Al Kingsley's *The Awkward Questions in Education* is an insightful exploration of critical issues shaping education today. With clarity and conviction, Al tackles the pressing challenges and complexities educators, policymakers, and leaders face, highlighting the conversations that are essential for meaningful change. This book serves as a powerful resource for those committed to reshaping the future of education, prompting us to ask the difficult, yet necessary, questions. This is an indispensable guide for anyone invested in creating a more inclusive, innovative, and responsive education system."

Matt Pitman, *Head of Secondary, Global Village Learning, and Author of The Connection Curriculum*

""*The Award Questions in Education*" dares to talk about the Taboo issues and are addressed, refreshingly, head-on. It's what many (most?) of us in education have been thinking/wondering, maybe at times afraid to say or address, but Al has skilfully articulated it all in one place.

This book is written with transparency, integrity and with an excellent understanding of the educational system. Al doesn't just challenge what's going on but essentially offers possible solutions/options/areas to become even better.

The Awkward Questions in Education is engaging to read – really interesting – drawn from Al's wealth of experience."

Mark Farmer, *CEO, Bridge Academy Trust & East of England (DFE) Regional Board Member*

"Asking better questions is the best way to get better answers. It might sound obvious but it is books like Al's that help us frame these questions. As someone who likes to 'poke the bear' in education, I hugely value Al's approach to **The Awkward Questions in Education**.

I was particularly drawn to long-term thinking for the future of education – hybrid environments, accessibility, AI, professionalism of teachers – as is to be expected, **Al knows his stuff and articulates it in a way that resonates**. Another important investment in our sector from the OG."

Ben Whitaker, *Author of The Ideas Guy and co-host of the Edufuturists podcast*

"Al is a breath of fresh air – constantly sharing learning, always offering a supportive hand and continually pushing out his positivity!"

Drew Povey*, Leadership Specialist*

"I love how Al encourages and inspires the next generation. My pupils have benefitted so much over the years from his generosity, enthusiasm and opportunities offered."

Martin Bailey*, Digital Enrichment Leader*

"I have worked with Al since 2013 when I joined Hampton Academies Trust. It is an absolute privilege to work with Al who is beyond dedicated to not only our trust but supporting, challenging and improving the delivery of education across the board."

Emily Culpin, *Governance Professional, Hampton Academies Trust*

"Al is a shining light of the EdTech world. He is a fantastic advocate of EdTech collaboration between school leaders, education systems and the industry. Al champions and creates opportunities for teachers, school leaders and EdTech suppliers to work-together constructively to share knowledge and best-practice."

Caroline Wright, *Director General, British Educational Suppliers Association*

"I first met Al in 2020 when he provided support to our failing MAT. From the start he gave me invaluable assistance allowing for a successful transfer to a new MAT. Al has a clear vision of child focused education, and his depth of knowledge in all things educational was priceless."

Paul Rout, *Previous Chair of KWEST Multi-Academy Trust*

The Awkward Questions in Education

The Elephants in the Room from AI to Teacher Retention

Al Kingsley

LONDON AND NEW YORK

Designed cover image: Getty Images

First published 2025
by Routledge
4 Park Square, Milton Park, Abingdon, Oxon OX14 4RN

and by Routledge
605 Third Avenue, New York, NY 10158

Routledge is an imprint of the Taylor & Francis Group, an informa business

© 2025 Al Kingsley

The right of Al Kingsley to be identified as author of this work has been asserted in accordance with sections 77 and 78 of the Copyright, Designs and Patents Act 1988.

All rights reserved. No part of this book may be reprinted or reproduced or utilised in any form or by any electronic, mechanical, or other means, now known or hereafter invented, including photocopying and recording, or in any information storage or retrieval system, without permission in writing from the publishers.

Trademark notice: Product or corporate names may be trademarks or registered trademarks, and are used only for identification and explanation without intent to infringe.

British Library Cataloguing-in-Publication Data
A catalogue record for this book is available from the British Library

Library of Congress Cataloging-in-Publication Data
Names: Kingsley, Al, author.
Title: The awkward questions in education : the elephants in the room from AI to teacher retention / Al Kingsley.
Description: Abingdon, Oxon ; New York, NY : Routledge, 2025. | Includes bibliographical references and index.
Identifiers: LCCN 2024051972 | ISBN 9781032883175 (hardback) | ISBN 9781032883144 (paperback) | ISBN 9781003537168 (ebook)
Subjects: LCSH: Education--Aims and objectives. | Educational technology. | Teachers--Recruiting. | Education and state. | Educational change.
Classification: LCC LB41 .K495 2025 | DDC 370.11--dc23/ eng/20250207
LC record available at https://lccn.loc.gov/2024051972

ISBN: 978-1-032-88317-5 (hbk)
ISBN: 978-1-032-88314-4 (pbk)
ISBN: 978-1-003-53716-8 (ebk)

DOI: 10.4324/9781003537168

Typeset in Melior
by KnowledgeWorks Global Ltd.

Contents

About the Author ... viii
Preface ... ix

1. What makes a good school, and how do we measure that? ... 1
2. The shifting need for skills versus current curriculum offers ... 29
3. When it comes to system growth, is leadership always putting the children first? ... 56
4. Does AI change the role of the teacher? ... 82
5. Improving attendance in education – do we need more and different "spaces"? ... 123
6. Is the future of education going to become hybrid or online? ... 141
7. Recruitment and retention – do we undersell the profession? ... 152
8. Why can't we have a long-term plan for education? ... 170
9. The barriers to growth in our education systems (are they within)? ... 192
10. Wrapping up ... 214

Acknowledgements ... 216
Bibliography ... 218
Index ... 235

About the Author

Al Kingsley MBE

Al has spent the last 35 years in the educational technology space, and 20 of those have been spent as a school trustee and governor. He was awarded an MBE (Member of the Order of the British Empire) in the King's 2025 New Year's Honours, for services to education.

He is chair of Hampton Academies Trust in the East of England. Al also sits on the Department for Education's Regional Schools Directors Advisory Board for the East of England and is the independent chair of the County's SEND Board.

He is also group CEO of NetSupport, an internationally acclaimed EdTech vendor, and has lived and worked in both the United Kingdom and the United States.

An active writer about all things education, Al is a member of the Forbes Technology Council and speaks nationally and internationally on educational reform, technology, and best practises.

You can find out more about Al at www.AlKingsley.com

Preface

Why this book and why now?

Firstly, hi, and thanks for taking the time to take a dip into my book. After writing each book, I have a knack for concluding that it will definitely be my last, but as this is my fourth, you will realise I am not so good at sticking to that. I am in a very fortunate position to be invited to travel and speak with other schools and school systems around the world, and now, more than ever, the pressure is really building. So many amazing people are doing their best to deliver the broadest and richest possible experience for our children, despite an ever-growing list of challenges. It seems perfect timing to consolidate and articulate them as best I can and provide a voice to many peers across the sector.

This book is really my overspill of our trust's current risk register. What are the real pressures right now? Are the phonics screening tests, GCSEs (General Certificate of Secondary Education), post 16 outcomes, and league tables our focus? Well, they certainly create pressures and stress for all concerned but our more significant pressures are financial, staff recruitment and retention, pay awards, attendance, the growing mental health needs of our children, the widening gap in terms of skills acquisition, artificial intelligence (AI) being presented as the panacea to everything .... ooh the list goes on. We all have ideas, but being friendly folks, we are not always so quick to criticise or challenge.

What can you expect to unpick while reading the book?

Well, there are some questions that seem to be very much "out there" for discussion, and others that perhaps play more on our sensitivities, or perhaps we might feel are awkward to raise. These are very much my "elephant in the room" topics

I wanted to research, share some evidence on, and then tackle a few related questions within that topic.

We are going to reflect on what really makes a school "good," not just an external judgement, but based on what we all hold most dear as practical and pragmatic measures. Skills is a hot topic but often gets shaped into a critique of current classroom practice and curriculum, so we will reflect on perspectives around the world, try and find the balance between skills and content, as well as look to embrace soft kills for the future workplace.

I wanted to tackle growth, too, the system, be that multi-academy trusts (MATs), international schools, reflect on the changing landscape, perceptions, and the bureaucracy that often drives change. You'll hopefully not be shocked to see AI gets a chapter for discussion: does it change the role of the teacher, the importance of the human, the ethics, and plenty more?

Most of the above is irrelevant if we can't get our children into school, so I take a deep dive on attendance, looking at some of the underlying causes and, of course, the role of parents. Taking a different view on the school setting, we take a look at the discussion around the move to hybrid and online learning, how we ensure equity in our system, pressures on the system, and much more.

Another huge topic is around the growing pressures on teacher retention and recruitment, respect for the profession, compensation, expectations, and more. Linked nicely with this we will also take a look and critical eye to the barriers in creating a long-term plan for education, the curse of politics, finding some common ground, and looking for a way forward.

And then to wrap things up, we will ask the questions about the barriers to growth and change in our education systems, and how many are from within? Is there a fear of change, simple funding, and capacity limitations, and are we closing the gap on an equitable and accessible curriculum?

Just to be clear

This isn't a book that claims to provide you with a checklist of answers. It aims to highlight the conversations we need to bring to the fore; share insights and opinions from others; and, in places, challenge the government to quit tinkering and empower sustained, system-led change.

This book has taken far longer than my previous publications. I have spent months reading research and articles to help shape and inform, speaking to peers, and capturing insights. It's been a labour of love, but I have learnt a lot along the way. We might not always agree, and that's healthy. I absolutely highlight that one size never fits all. All I ask is that you read with an open mind and with a shared intention to help support change where it's needed in our education system.

Figure 0.1 Montage of Al Kingsley speaking

A bit about me

In my previous books, I have included a fairly extensive section on my journey over the last 35 years, and whilst I am proud of the roles and achievements along the way, somehow, I want to steer away from that in this book; it's not about me, nor at any point individuals.

So, let's go for a very succinct who I am today, I'm the proud chair of Hampton Academies Trust in Peterborough, England; I am the independent chair of our regional SEND board; and am serving my third term on the Department for Education's regional advisory board for the East of England. I have supported many MATs, infant, primary, specialist, alternative, and secondary schools on their journeys to improvement or growth. I have written three previous books covering educational technology, governance, and growth strategies, and I speak and write regularly for many educational events and publications.

I do have a second hat, with 30 years of working with educational technology as an EdTech CEO at NetSupport. I also sit on the boards of the Cambridgeshire and Peterborough Combined Authority and the Oxford to Cambridgeshire Partnership, advocating skills and economic growth across my region. I'm a firm believer you support change by getting your sleeves rolled up, even if you have to push against the system. I continue to do my best.

I've won a few awards and recognition in education over the years. Some of the most recent include the 2022 EdTech Leadership Awards winner from *EdTech Digest*, being awarded the 2023 Edufuturist of the Year, winning the 2023 Outstanding Achievement award at the Educational Resources Awards (ERA) Awards, and the 2023 Inspiring Leader winner from the British Educational Suppliers Association (BESA) Awards. In the United States, I was very kindly recognised as one of the 2024 top 100 Influencers in Education by *District Administration* magazine (US) and top 25 Education Technology Influencers by *Feedspot,* alongside on an international basis, being one of the Independent Schools Council (ISC) top ten education disruptors, "Edrupters," of 2023.

That's plenty enough for this introduction. You can find me online at all of the places listed below and I'm always happy to connect and have a chat.

My final request: If you enjoy the book and if it aligns with you, please give it a share and leave a nice review. If it's not for you, let's keep that to ourselves, and sorry ☺.

Find my website and blog at www.AlKingsley.com
For social media contact, you can connect with me on
LinkedIn: www.linkedin.com/in/alkingsley1
X: www.x.com/AlKingsley_Edu
Instagram: www.instagram.com/alkingsley
Published articles: www.authory.com/AlKingsley

What makes a good school, and how do we measure that?

Well, as you will have seen from the chapters of this book, I've picked ten topics that I thought we really needed to open the conversation up on, and of all of them, this first one seems to be the most consistent topic for debate and discussion. Perhaps that's because there isn't one answer, and that's actually at the heart of the problem. Wherever we are in the world, we try to create a template, a framework, and ensure every school within that jurisdiction fits. Daft idea? Well, not if you want an easy way to ensure consistency, an easy way to measure conformity, and, I guess, an easy way to ensure equality across the system. This is the point where many will say, hang on a second, every child is different, so how can one size, no matter how good, be a fit for all children? Now you can hopefully see where this chapter's discussion is going to head!

I see this discussion all the time, not explicitly answering the question "What makes a good school?" but within the context of either a disconnect (or frankly, gulf at times) between what I would say to you about my trust and schools and what Ofsted summarises in their letter after a visit. The third consideration of course, the one that for me is key, is looking ahead to what a good school could or should be for the future, including all the variables of inclusivity, our measures of success, and the gaps we know exist right now.

Setting the scene

I'm not sure this is going to be the most exciting introduction, but I think we should start with a bit of a state of the nation, reflecting on the main factors that typically are used as part of that measure, a Litmus test, of a good school. I'll expand that to a good, or "high-performing," school system on a wider level, too. You might have to bear with me while we go through these familiar measures to start with, but I think it sets the scene.

The most common measure that is held up is the school's **Ofsted** rating (the Office for Standards in Education, Children's Services and Skills), [1] where a good school is one that consistently delivers high standards across a range of categories, which I'm going to incorporate in my groupings below. I am not intentionally taking deep dives into specifics in the curriculum, but it hopefully helps focus the mind and might also highlight any gaps for discussion.

There is long-held view that the best way to influence school performance, culture, and practice is through having some form of accountability framework. In practice, this applies across most sectors, so it is not something new or unique to the world of education. For those not familiar with the history, the aforementioned Ofsted was created in 1992 in response to criticism around school standards. The framework and judgements themselves have been on a journey over the years, originally with a seven-point scale of assessments (excellent–very poor) and something I think we would all probably appreciate, a six-week notice period.

Now I know if you take a look at a school Ofsted report, you will be presented with a summary based on the Quality of Education, Behaviour and Attitudes, Personal Development, and Leadership and Management, as well as an assessment of any early years or post-16 provision, but I wanted to summarise in a slightly more sectional approach of the primary (and very high-level) areas that are covered in a more structured, and hopefully accessible way, that can translate to a school no matter where in the world it is located.

Let's set some context

Below is a summation of those key topics measured during an inspection of a school.

Teaching quality

Without diving into too much detail on any of these categories, the current measures of teaching quality include:

a. Classroom observations to assess various aspects of teaching, including instructional techniques, classroom management, and student engagement.
   Research from the **Bill and Melinda Gates Foundation**'s MET (**Measures of Effective Teaching**) [2] highlighted the importance of high-quality classroom observations in evaluating teaching effectiveness.

b. Looking at student achievement and progress data gathered by both formative and summative tests, which provide insights on the impact of teaching on learning outcomes.

c. Undertaking student surveys so they can provide feedback on their learning experiences, from the broader classroom environment through to the supportiveness of staff.

d. Effective teacher self-assessment and reflection, which is exactly what it says but is key, given the driver for setting professional development goals.

e. This continues from the last item, which is professional development and associated qualifications. I think now more than ever, this is one that doesn't always get the support it should.

The Sutton Trust's "**What Makes Great Teaching?**" [3] report underscores the link between high-quality teaching and student outcomes. It cites the "six components of great teaching" as the key pillars: pedagogical content knowledge, quality of instruction, classroom climate, classroom management, teacher beliefs, and professional behaviours. Perhaps unsurprisingly, the first two were referenced as having the strongest evidence of impact on student outcomes.

If you look at the "**Teaching and Learning Toolkit**" from the **Education Endowment Foundation** [4], you can refine the evidence, impact, and cost measures to see supporting data on specific activities to refine your potential priorities. I'm really conscious of a book intended to encourage debate and discussion at the macro level, not to head down a path of detailing every minutia at the micro level, so where I can, I'll signpost resources that you may wish to expand your reading with.

Let's continue on those core topics influencing an inspection. After teaching quality, we have leadership and management.

Leadership and management

These can often feel a bit woolly, not in terms of significance or importance, but in the variability of how this is assessed and the potential for nuance to be entirely overlooked. The leadership tick list features include the following:

a. The leadership's vision and strategic direction, which includes setting those key expectations and behaviours for staff and students.

b. The school's culture and ethos are important when we think about our values, covering everything from respect and resilience to behaviour, community, and wellbeing. I'll come back to this as there is a disconnect between our priorities around our values and how that is (or isn't) captured in our current assessment of a good school.

c. Quality of teaching and learning with a focus on leaders ensuring high-quality teaching and learning across their schools. This also includes facilitating and enabling professional development for staff.

   Ofsted provided a report in May 2024, **"Independent review of teachers' professional development in schools: phase 1 findings"** [5], which cited that *"teachers and leaders want more time dedicated to professional development, including follow-up, but workload pressures often prevent this"* and that *"in around half the schools visited, it was clear that the staff's understanding of planning and designing a curriculum remained limited, even though they had received some training and development."*

d. Use of data and self-evaluation—how leadership uses data to monitor student progress and school performance. Does the leadership regularly evaluate their own practices and, where appropriate, make data-informed (not data-driven) decisions?

e. Safeguarding—do leaders ensure the school has robust policies and practices in place to protect all students' welfare?

f. Good parental and community engagement—do leaders engage with parents and the wider community to support student learning and wellbeing?

Next up on the list is the breadth of the curriculum offers.

Breadth of the curriculum offers

I think we would ascribe to the fact that a broad and balanced curriculum is essential, which means offering a range of subjects that provide students with a comprehensive education. Clause 2 of the **Education Reform Act 1998** [6], which established the National Curriculum in England and Wales and introduced the terminology describing it as *"a balanced and broadly based curriculum which (a)* *promotes the spiritual, moral, cultural, mental and physical development of pupils at the school and of society; and (b) prepares such pupils for the opportunities, responsibilities and experiences of adult life.*" From an Ofsted perspective, they followed down the path of an "ambitious" curriculum and frankly both are vague and somewhat rhetorical.

The guidance here is that schools should find the balance between those core subjects, i.e., maths, English, the sciences and Modern Foreign Languages, the arts, humanities, physical education, and vocational courses. In theory, a well-rounded curriculum helps develop diverse skills and interests, preparing students for their future pathways. In practice, the challenge with "broad" is its indeterminate nature; it is far from a fixed value, and a measure of broad is both a matter of judgement and context.

All of that said, the scope to offer a broad set of options is not always possible, often not within the capacity or control of the school itself, and probably contradicts aspirations around measures such as the EBacc (**English Baccalaureate**) [7], which tends to steer us back towards a one-size-fits-all expectation for our children and certainly doesn't benefit all of our learners. With a requirement for a student to study English literature and language, mathematics, the three sciences (or combined), a language, and either history or geography, this focus has had a negative impact on uptake of many other subjects.

It is also worth noting that General Certificate of Secondary Education (GCSE) subject choices often shape our A-level choices, which has a ripple effect on those subjects as well. An article published by the **NAHT (National Association of Head Teachers)** in 2019 titled "**The EBacc 10 years on: should it stay or should it go?**" [8] stated

> EBacc has had a significant impact on the choice of A levels, as the majority of KS4 students choose to take subjects that they studied at GCSE. Consequently, in terms of the percentage of entrants at A level in 2019, subjects such as music (-6.4%), performing and expressive arts (-16.9%), theatre studies (-9.2%), design and technology (-5%) and media/film and tv studies (-13.8%) have declined.

I am really not sure why anyone would be surprised about this outcome or not see the natural contradiction when also encouraging a broad curriculum.

There are differing views on this, but **Pepe Di'Iasio,** general secretary of the **Association of School and College Leaders,** also said in an August 2024 article, "**ASCL analysis shows collapse in creative arts A-level entries**" [9]: "*It is clear that the English Baccalaureate has had a devastating effect on creative arts & technology subjects ... The EBacc must be scrapped and more done to champion the importance of subjects that have been sidelined.*"

This feels like a handy segue onto an interlinked topic next in our checklist, which is inclusivity for all learners.

Inclusivity for all learners

In a nutshell, inclusivity ensures that all students, regardless of their background or abilities, have access to a quality education. This includes supporting students with special educational needs and disabilities (SEND), promoting equality, and addressing any barriers to learning. As someone who has been the independent chair of two regional SEND boards, I can confirm that while the intent is there, the capacity, resources, and plan to deliver the aforementioned support is certainly not.

I suspect many of you reading will be familiar with the "Green paper" or, to give it its official title, the "**SEND review: right support, right place, right time**" [10], which was published in March 2022, and in their own words *"sets out our proposals for a system that offers children and young people the opportunity to thrive, with access to the right support, in the right place, and at the right time, so they can fulfil their potential and lead happy, healthy and productive adult lives."* The SEND review was created as a response to the widespread recognition that the system is failing to deliver for children, young people, and their families. I discuss this more in subsequent chapters, as right now we are beyond a crisis. Let's set it at DEFCON 10.

Personal development

This is another section which has a few subtle overlaps on my virtual Venn diagram of topics overall, but the key ones from within it that should be on your checklist (depending on where in the world you are) will be:

a. SMSC (spiritual, moral, social, and cultural development) measures how well a school supports broader personal development beyond academics. I'm not sure how much time is left for this, but that is the aim anyway, and you can do it either through your whole school curriculum or with specific lessons.

   The recently updated 2024 resource, **"SMSC in Education: Everything You Need to Know,"** by **Votes for Schools** [11] provides guidance for all stages and settings.

b. Citizenship and British Values [12]—democracy, rule of law, liberty, respect, and tolerance of those with different faiths and beliefs.

c. Extracurricular Activities—opportunities for students to participate in activities beyond the classroom. The 2024 case study by the **Huntingdon Research School, "The Vital Role of Extracurricular Activities for SEND Pupils"** [13], highlighted *"extracurricular involvement offers a break from the rigors of academic work, allowing students to explore their passions and interests in a relaxed and enjoyable atmosphere. This balance is crucial for maintaining motivation and preventing burnout, particularly for SEND pupils who may face additional academic or sensory challenges."*

d. And finally, Careers Education, which I will cover in the next section.

I hope you are keeping up, only three more to go....

Measures of pupil outcomes

I know this is a divisive topic and we are going to really unpick and challenge this in a bit, but let's start with the obvious checklist.

a. Academic Achievement—think Phonics, SATs, GCSE's/A Levels etc.

b. Progress Measures—from a student's starting point, joining the school, and the Progress 8 measure (albeit we won't have that or an equivalent for a while).

c. Attendance and Behaviour—a significant challenge right now, but as a rule, consistent attendance and good behaviour indicate a positive learning environment. Within this entry, think of observations of behaviour in lessons and around school, students' attitudes to learning, attendance (and punctuality), your exclusion data, and other strategies to manage behaviour.

You'll also see later in the book I have a chapter on improving attendance in education and looking in more detail at the underlying causes. Oh, and no, you won't find increasing fines a credible strategy. Just saying 😊.

d. Preparation for the Next Stages of Education, Training, or Employment.

A useful guide around careers and the next steps is the **"Good Career Guide"** report from the **Gatsby Foundation** [14]. The eight Gatsby benchmarks defined in this report are used as a framework for best quality careers provision and have been adopted as part of the Department for Education's Careers Strategy and their statutory guidance for schools and colleges.

e. Closing Gaps in Achievement—assessing achievement gaps between different cohorts of students. This is presented as an indicator of equity in education provision with all children having an equal opportunity to succeed.

The Sutton Trust shared a **"10-point plan for closing the Attainment Gap"** [15] in February 2024 as a policy briefing, which provided a good summary of key priorities. Perhaps unsurprisingly, some of the levers needed by schools for interventions require change and funding at a national level (national funding formula, extend pupil premium funding, and so on).

We can all support the next category as part of our school values.

Parental and community involvement

I don't suspect there will be any surprises here for anyone reading this, but bear in mind, my hope is that some reading this book will not necessarily come from the frontline of education.

a. Parental Engagement —covers how well the school communicates with parents, involves them in their child's education, and, when appropriate, how they respond to concerns and feedback.

The **Department for Education** undertook a "**review of best practice in parental engagement**" in 2011 [16], citing that "*The evidence confirms the importance of a parental needs analysis, along with understanding what parents already do with their children and how they are most likely to respond positively to attempts to engage them (further) in their children's learning. Programmes should, therefore, be targeted at particular groups of parents, showing sensitivity to cultural norms and expectations, and including specific, detailed and directive advice and guidance.*" The landscape post-pandemic, with an ever-increasing hybrid workplace for parents and greater social, emotional, and mental health challenges, has added new factors for consideration on this topic, which we will discuss in more detail later.

The **Education Endowment Foundation's Parental Engagement Toolkit** [17] is based on 97 individual studies, and it found that "*Parental engagement has a positive impact on average of 4 months' additional progress*" that said, they also state, "*The evidence about how to improve attainment by increasing parental engagement is mixed and much less conclusive.*"

The **Nuffield Foundation**, in its 2013 report "**Do parental involvement interventions increase attainment?**" [18], also suggested that "*There is no good-quality evidence that parental involvement interventions result in improved educational outcomes, in most age groups and for most approaches.*" They identified 68 studies but felt none were sufficiently high quality and had flaws in their methodology.

b. Community Links—where we are evaluated on our extended connections with the local community, including partnerships with local businesses, organisations, and other schools in our vicinity.

I think we would all concur that strong community links, used effectively, can enhance learning opportunities, potentially provide additional resources, as well as supporting student wellbeing. Thinking of the bigger picture also has the potential as a by-product of closer engagement, perhaps adding representation to our governing bodies and ensuring our schools represent and reflect our communities as much as possible.

c. Support for Parents—school takes proactive approaches to providing parents with support to help them engage with their child's learning, such as workshops, information sessions, and digital/physical resources.

d. Feedback Mechanisms —all schools should have effective mechanisms for collecting and acting on feedback from parents and the community, and of course, ensuring their voices are heard and valued. As a rule, responsive and accessible feedback systems help build trust and cooperation between the school and parents.

Evidence of continuous improvement

Okay, we are at home right now regarding our checklist. This final category focuses on the school's ongoing efforts to enhance all aspects of the school, from teaching and learning to leadership and management.

We could call this the "non-coasting" list or just that there is always a need to show evidence of reflection and continuous improvement. For some of these, there is an area of crossover with earlier sections if we were to create a virtual Venn diagram.

a. Self-Evaluation and Development Planning—I think it's fair to say that good schools regularly evaluate their own performance and create detailed development plans to address areas for improvement. I've also yet to encounter a school that doesn't do this to some degree.

b. Professional Development for Staff—We can never have enough CPD (continuous professional development) opportunities for our staff. As the old adage goes, there is only one thing worse than losing highly skilled staff, and that's keeping poorly skilled staff.

c. Monitoring and Assessment Systems—As I shared earlier, schools should have robust systems in place for monitoring and assessing both student progress and the effectiveness of teaching.

d. Innovation and Best Practice—Is the school and leadership open to innovation or adopting research-informed best practices? Is it outward-looking?

e. Stakeholder Involvement—Does the school engage with and/or co-produce with all relevant and appropriate stakeholders as part of any improvement process?

I've reeled off quite a long list there, and most will align neatly with your inspection framework and are fairly common across international education systems, Naturally there are a few nuances, but hopefully I haven't missed anything significant. The intention was to pull together the key topics so they are framed when we talk about our own schools (or a school system) as being measured as good. Which aspects do we emphasise or hold dearest, and which are there just because they are on the list?

Is it a true reflection of the school?

As with any measure, the question will always be whether it is fair, whether it is consistent, and, of course, whether it accurately reflects the school as a whole. That, of course, is where the Ofsted inspection has raised significant criticism. In a ***Schools Week*** article in 2019 for example, titled **"Schools with deprived pupils**

'still less likely to be judged good', admits Ofsted" [19], it highlighted that a year after Amanda Spielman insisted that the latest inspection framework would *"reward schools in challenging circumstances"* **Sean Harford**, Ofsted's national director said, *"Some will be disappointed to see that, so far, schools with more pupils from deprived backgrounds are still less likely to be judged 'good' than those from more affluent backgrounds under the EIF [education inspection framework], just as they were under the last framework"* also saying *"It's unrealistic to think that a new inspection framework is suddenly going to result in a huge leap upwards in inspection grades for schools in disadvantaged areas."*

More recently, **Rt Hon Lord Knight of Weymouth Jim Knight** agreed to chair an Ofsted inquiry into school inspection because he believed that the current system of school inspection is inconsistent, creates staff stress, and distorts behaviour away from better outcomes for children and towards better inspection outcomes. The **Beyond Ofsted** [20] inquiry into the future of school inspection report was published in 2023 [21], and stated that *"Ofsted is in need of major reform. Our research found that it is currently seen as not fit for purpose, and as having a detrimental impact on schools which some perceive as toxic. We acknowledge the need for quality assurance of schools as any institution in receipt of public money should be subject to accountability. However, we need to build trust back into the system so that it can work. The need for change is compelling and urgent."*

They concluded and were persuaded by other international comparisons that self-evaluation through a long-term relationship with an advisor is the best approach for sustained school improvement, which would be best achieved by using a school improvement partner for external validation of the school performance review.

To add an international flavour, Denmark, Estonia, Italy, and Japan are examples of countries that have no regular external school inspections (but do, of course, require self-evaluation). Singapore, often highly regarded as an education system, has inspection as a compulsory part of self-evaluation, but no overall grade is given. Depending on the outcomes, support is then given to the school to help achieve the changes recommended by the inspection.

Let's just pause for a second, because this is often missed; if any process or system identifies areas in need of improvement, surely the best ones would also provide the resources and funds to help drive those changes. In most cases, that just doesn't happen, which misses the point that schools want to improve but often don't have the resources and capacity to do so.

Hopefully, you will appreciate that this is about scene setting and defining the frameworks against which we are currently measured. Is it OK, for example, for me to take the concept of "good schools" within a country and align that directly alongside a measure of a collective **"High-Performing School Systems"** that falls under the **OECD** [22] (Organisation for Economic Co-operation and Development) PISA [23] rankings. I am choosing to be contentious here, but surely the country with the highest number of good schools will naturally sit proudly at the top of the international list of high-performing school systems. (Note: I don't in any way agree that this is a conclusion that could or should be drawn, but it's raised for challenge only in this context.)

So, the **Programme for International Student Assessme**nt (PISA) is, in their own words, *"the OECD's Programme for International Student Assessment. PISA measures 15-year-olds' ability to use their reading, mathematics and science knowledge and skills to meet real-life challenges."* Since 2000, PISA has involved more than 100 countries and around 3.7 million students, so it's well established and, of course, depending on where your country sits on the list, is a measure the government likes to highlight. I wanted to include this because, for me, the PISA rankings fall much more into the concept of the Progress 8 model, with a very tight focus on core subjects, not the breadth of the curriculum or about the child's own personal development. But that aside, is, like it or not, held up there as a measure of great education systems.

It's worth noting for those unfamiliar that the PISA tests are much more scenario based and typically relate to practical situations. For example, the first example maths question from PISA 2022 related to the price of purchasing a car, fuel consumption, and fuel and maintenance costs in the format of a cost estimator set of questions.

They continue to evolve the scope of their assessment, so in 2025, the PISA framework is being refined to include a new assessment of foreign languages and a broader measure of science education rather than science literacy as well as including a focus on education for sustainability and environmental education, which is built around the concept of "Agency in the Anthropocene." I'm probably going a bit off piste here, but I'll share a brief explanation as I was on a learning journey with this phrase myself. *"Agency in the Anthropocene requires understanding that human impacts have already significantly altered Earth's systems, and they continue to do so. It refers to ways of being and acting within the world that position people as part of (rather than separate from) ecosystems, acknowledging and respecting all species and the interdependence of life."*

So, the question throughout this chapter is, what makes a good school, and how do we measure it? So, does PISA give us the answer when looking through a wider lens? Is their measure (and process) sufficiently broad and accessible that it presents a true reflection? I'm not convinced.

In a January 2024 article published by the **National Education Association (NEA)** [24] on **neaToday,** titled "**What can we really learn from the 2022 PISA Test results?**" [25], **Harry Feder**, executive director of the **National Center for Fair and Open Testing (FairTest)** [26], said, *"PISA is a scaled score, norm-referenced, multiple-choice test. Two-thirds of all test takers globally score between 400 and 600 on a section (math, reading and science). Only 2% score over 700. In general, these kinds of tests are set up so results will go down over a longer time frame because, as explained by Professor Andy Hargreaves of Boston College, 'once a* *metric is widely used and has a competitive ranking element, gaming the system leads to overall declines in performance after an early lift, and also has negative side-effects on well-being.'"* So, it is not surprising that during the last two decades, student performance in those core areas of maths, reading, and science have all significantly declined in most OECD countries.

In a separate December 2023 article by FairTest, **"Interpreting PISA Results: It's Poverty, Stupid (With a bit of the iPhone)"** [27], they concluded, *"By scrutinizing the performance of the United States versus other OECD countries, the unshocking conclusion should be that the PISA test is largely a measure of childhood poverty rates rather than academic achievement."* This resonated with my on-the-ground discussions here in our UK schools on the broader topic of the key challenges and underlying drivers.

If we roll back a few years to 2014, in an open letter to **Dr. Andreas Schleicher**, director of the OECD's Programme for International Student Assessment, academics from around the world expressed deep concern about the impact of PISA tests and called for a halt to the next round of testing [28]. They shared that PISA results are anxiously viewed by governments and ministers and are cited as a de facto measure in many subsequent policy reports, and, *"as a result of PISA, countries are overhauling their education systems in the hopes of improving their rankings."* In essence, it has been the catalyst for more and more standardised testing, and as the open letter shared, *"with its three-year assessment cycle, has caused a shift of attention to short-term fixes designed to help a country quickly climb the rankings, despite research showing that enduring changes in education practice take decades, not a few years, to come to fruition."* Sounds quite a lot like "teach to the test," but on a national level.

Are national and international rankings actually helpful?

As with any measure, there is a challenge as to how beneficial these rankings are, let alone if they are an indicator of a system full of "good" schools. The OECD is constantly reviewing and reflecting on this topic and I had the pleasure to co-chair a workstream with the **Foundation for Educational Development (FED)** [29] supporting the OECD research and work on **"Education for Human Flourishing"** under the umbrella of their **"PISA High Performing Systems for Tomorrow (HPST)"** [30] project.

The **High Performing Systems for Tomorrow (HPST) project** has an aim to establish an international framework for the future development of education systems, enabling, as they state, *"countries to reorient their education systems toward new purposes, policies and practices, while considering the implications of artificial intelligence for the purposes of education."*

I include this because it shows a significant shift in mindset from our traditional and somewhat rigid metrics of success to one that very much encompasses the whole child or could, at least, go a long way towards that. The key is that at the heart of the project are a set of crucial questions that I think are worthy of much more significant focus, including:

- What does it mean for humans to flourish in the 21st century?
- How could/should education support human flourishing at every stage of life?
- How should our education systems be designed better to promote human flourishing for all?
- What learning goals and competencies (skills) should people strive for?
- What learning environments would best support them?
- How should the teaching profession evolve to facilitate learning?

And probably the evolution of what I have covered in the last few paragraphs,

- What metrics would enable measurement and benchmarking at the student and system level?

Their research between 2018 and 2021 on the HPST led to the **"Education for Human Flourishing"** [31] work, which set an ambitious vision based on **Aristotle:** *"The flourishing life consists of moral, reason-infused activities that are meaningful for the individual and have a significance in the world; contemplation; and awe-struck enchantment."* The report (pp. 7–8) also considers a key aspect for me, that *collective* flourishing is an integral factor, stating, *"The emphasis on individual flourishing should not suggest that the flourishing of others does not matter. Looking at three non-European approaches to flourishing, Kristjánsson [32] underlines the central importance of caring for and about others. [...] Education for human flourishing concerns one's own flourishing and the flourishing of others."*

One area that feeds in strongly is that the project assessed three core competencies, recognising that competencies contribute to positive outcomes for individuals and society. The three covered are adaptive problem solving, ethical decision making, and aesthetic perception. I'm not going to dive deep into these, as this summary is intended to consolidate our thinking of where we are now with measures and what we might consider for the future. However, in the spirit of immediate contradiction, I want to highlight the latter competency: aesthetic perception. In simple terms, this refers to developing an appreciation of beauty. Or, as **Howard Gardner** quoted [33], to count as beautiful *"an experience must be interesting enough to behold, have a form that is memorable and invite revisiting,"* and for me, this is something we absolutely need to embrace.

I wanted to be clever and highlight the increasing relevance of this in a new technology and AI (artificial intelligence)-centric world, but conveniently in the 2023 **Finnish Ministry of Education and Culture** report, **"Reflections on Competences for Human Flourishing"** [34], they shared a quote, written by ChatGPT 3.5 itself in response to the prompt provided: *"Create a short, aphorism-like philosophical statement on what the most important human skill will be in a future* *dominated by AI."* The resulting quote was *"In the age of artificial intelligence, the most vital human skill is not in competing with machines, but in mastering the art of unscripted creativity—a dance of innovation and imagination that transcends the algorithms of automation."* I think that is a pretty good summation.

As I do my best to reflect on the current measures of assessing an individual school's performance alongside those wider measures of national school systems, you can quickly see an ever-increasing tension between the delivery of our traditional and core academic competencies and, in a rapidly changing and more skills-centric world, the growing recognition that the measures of the development of the whole person are equally important.

Looking further afield

Across "the pond" in the United States of America, responsibility for inspections and measuring school performance falls at the state level, creating a very diverse set of approaches. These were largely shaped by the 2015 **"Every Student Succeeds Act (ESSA)"** [35], introduced by President Obama, which replaced the previous **"No Child Left Behind (NCLB) Act"** [36] enacted in 2002. In summary, ESSA aims to improve educational success by advancing equity for disadvantaged students, mandating high academic standards nationwide, and providing progress data through assessments. It also supports local improvements while managing accountability for low-performing schools to help "drive positive change."

Plenty of the research and data on the U.S. education system is shared by the **National Centre for Education and the Economy (NCEE)** [37], which is a not-for-profit education research, advocacy, and professional learning organisation. The 2018 policy report, **"Inspection Systems: How Top-Performing Nations Hold Schools Accountable"** [38], reviewed assessment systems and approaches by governments around the world. They noted that in responding to ESSA requirements, *"States have proposed adding additional measures of school quality, such as school climate and attendance rates; moved away from a single school rating by providing a 'dashboard' of indicators of school quality."* Following a similar theme to those findings by **Beyond Ofsted,** they also noted, *"inspection systems by themselves do not improve schools; schools need the capacity to implement the recommendations and strengthen instruction and school operations."* They also acknowledged that countries are increasingly focusing on building school capacity by mandating schools conduct self-evaluations and forming teams to develop improvement plans. There is nothing particularly new there, but alongside that, they argue that when done right, inspection systems demonstrate that accountability can drive improvements in school performance, rather than merely assessing it.

Given that every country loves a league table and some national tests, it is not surprising that in the United States they have the **National Assessment of Educational Progress (NAEP)** tests, also referred to as **"The Nation's Report Card"** [39]. This was first introduced in 1969, and it's not a test students study specifically for or get a personal grade as a result (in fact, they are randomly selected to participate). Still, it is used to produce a national litmus test of educational performance across the country for children in the fourth (9–10 years old), eighth (13–14), and twelfth grades (17–18) in various subjects.

NAEP is well established as a benchmark and is recognised as the nation's most influential source of data on K–12 achievement, but as with every national measure of proficiency, it is not without challenge or criticism. Focusing specifically on the NAEP "proficiency" measure, the 2016 article by the Brookings Institute, **"The NAEP proficiency myth"** [40], stated that *"Scholarly panels have reviewed the NAEP achievement standards and found them flawed. The highest scoring nations of the world would appear to be mediocre or poor performers if judged by the NAEP proficient standard."* It is worth noting that there is a difference between a grade-level performance in a subject and proficiency, which is significantly above that.

Supported by the **Carnegie Corporation**, the book *Assessing the Nation's Report Card* [41] by **Chester E. Finn Jr**, a prominent advocate for NAEP, is much more supportive (albeit proposing areas for future development), stating, *"No matter whether your foremost concern is international economic competitiveness or domestic equity, the excellence of our workforce or the upward mobility of children born into poverty and discrimination, the performance of our education system or the return on taxpayer dollars, you won't get the information you need without NAEP."*

I wrote an article for *Education Week* in 2022, challenging this view with a very subtly titled piece, **"Ignore NAEP. Better Yet, Abolish It"** [42]; I know, I was being very bold that day! I suggested that national (and international) tests aren't going to "fix" education. My suggestion, intended to spark discussion and challenge was that if we really want to measure educational success, then first decide what kind of adults we want. Then, measure that. However, this takes time and patience—two things parents and politicians seldom indulge. Parents and politicians alike want fast fixes for obvious reasons, impulses only exacerbated by random scorecards of progress. It caused quite a furore at the time, but I was pleasantly surprised by how many people also agreed.

Travel across to Australia and similar discussions rage around the **NAPLAN** result, or to provide the full name, **National Assessment Program–Literacy and Numeracy** [43], which is an annual assessment for all students in years 3,4,7, and 9. Very much akin to the UK SATS [44], it is designed to measure whether or not Australian school students are developing the literacy and numeracy skills that provide the critical foundation for other learning. Like many national measures, there has been significant turbulence post-pandemic in the outcomes captured. The 2024 results were prominent in the media, with concerns over what was described as a bleak picture. **Sally Larson**, senior lecturer in education at the **University of New England**, wrote an article in August 2024, titled **"Are the latest NAPLAN results really an 'epic fail'?"** [45]. She challenges the interpretation of the data and assumptions drawn, saying, *"we need to be cautious about narratives that Australian students' performances in NAPLAN and other standardised tests are getting worse."* Her research on data between 2008 and 2022 [46], based on data from three international assessments, the Progress in International Reading Literacy Study, the Trends in International Mathematics and Science Study and the PISA, along with the only Australian assessment, the NAPLAN, contradicts and shows no long-term decline in results.

As I conclude, with many of these standardised tests, her report highlighted the following: *"If state and federal governments are serious about resolving the problems in Australian schooling, a first step will be to interpret the evidence about students' literacy and numeracy accurately."* She continued: *"The consensus of the four largest assessment programmes undertaken by Australian students since 1995 thus fails to support the prevailing narrative of a broadscale decline in academic skills attainment,"* which really makes us stop and think about what we are truly trying to measure.

I could go on, delving into more and more countries, highlighting the national need for a report card of some shape or size, alongside adapting various ways to inspect and score the performance of schools, but, that's the reason for the lengthy introduction to this chapter. Are we measuring the right things when we stamp a school as being good (or not) or attempt to rate our broader national system? Numbers, grades, and output from summative assessments are easy to collate and arrange neatly in a league table. Much like a checklist of things we review in a very narrow in-person inspection window; whilst well intentioned, it often leaves the things we hold most dear, the real "secret sauce" of our schools, unseen and unreported.

So, what could we measure?

A 2023 journal article in **Oxford Academic** titled **"What is a Good School, and Can Parents Tell? Evidence on the Multidimensionality of School Output"** [47], asked another key question, namely: Is a school's causal impact on test scores a good measure of its overall impact on students? The research was undertaken using data covering the population of Trinidad and Tobago (*we are certainly stacking up our virtual airmiles in this chapter*), estimating individual schools' causal impacts on high-stakes test scores, low-stakes test scores, dropout, teen motherhood, teen arrests, and labour market participation. Their conclusion stated the following: *"From a policy perspective, our results suggest that school impacts on test scores may not be the best measure of a school's impacts on longer-run outcomes. Accordingly, policymakers should be cautious (and thoughtful) regarding using test score impacts in accountability systems ... and may wish to adopt a more holistic view of school quality."* It, too, much like in my comments responding to NAEP, highlighted that the immediate government and parental perceptions of the best schools based on test scores didn't necessarily align with the child's long-term success. Imagine that ☺.

I'm really mindful that based on perceptions, we also often see somewhat of a self-fulfilling prophecy, in that based on simplistic performance metrics, parents understandably want to send their child to schools that appear to have the best metrics. The 2020 article in the **American Economic Review,** titled **"Do parents value school effectiveness?"** [48], found in their research that *"[p]arents prefer schools that enrol high-achieving peers, and as a result of attracting these students, the schools generate larger improvements in short- and long-run student outcomes. Preferences are unrelated to school effectiveness and academic match quality after controlling for selection based on peer quality."* Conversely, it is difficult for schools that don't carry that matching perception from parents to deliver a similar rate of improvement with their cohort.

Linked to the above, going back to 1955, **Friedman** [49] argued that giving parents freedom to choose schools would improve education. His argument was simple, taking the same view as treating education in the same way as consumers access markets for other goods and services: You pick what you perceive to be the best. More recent reports, however, including **"Is Education Consumption or Investment? Implications for School Competition"** [50] highlighted that *"households often seem to choose schools based on their absolute achievement rather than their value added."*

This disconnect between perceived grade outcomes as "the measure" and the wider human capital value add can be found everywhere. A 2023 article in **Education Week,** titled **"Charter Schools Are Outperforming Traditional Public Schools"** [51], highlighted that a new study shows that charter school students are now outpacing their peers in traditional public schools in maths and reading achievement, cementing a *"long-term trend of positive charter school outcomes."* So, they are doing better than public schools, right? It must be if it is a long-term trend.

How then, do we reconcile that with this 2020 research in Texas from the **Journal of Labour Economics**, **"Charter schools and labour market outcomes"** [52], concluding that *"We find that, at the mean, charter schools have no impact on test scores and a negative impact on earnings."* Once again, look at the broader measure of ultimate outcomes. Look at the longer term, and very different metrics appear compared to the narrow academic snapshots.

In the 2013 book *Achieving Quality Education for All* [53], **Deborah Meier** was cited as saying, *"At the very least, school should be a place where children are not treated as though they are data or numbers in someone else's policy war, or as only 'future' members of society as though their present experience is not important in and of itself."*

The scene has been set

So, after setting the scene alongside the published data and research I could access, and covering how we currently inspect, measure, and grade our school performance, we arrive at this core challenge: What really is a good school and what is a good measure of that?

Is it based on its academic scores, parental perceptions that are often linked to the scores, and associated numerical data? Is it related to what is seen during a short window of an inspection, or is it something much more? We could take a steer from the research above and say we measure over a 10- to15-year window assessing where our children end up as adults, which isn't going to make anyone responsible for short-term oversight very happy! We could say an inspection needs to go much broader and deeper, so let's extend that further to a week or two. We could say schools are best placed to self-assess, and a long-term link with a school improvement partner would provide a more nuanced and credible external validation of what we see (and I lean towards that as a more constructive and supportive method of oversight), but we also need to be clear on what we think is important to measure.

Let me leave this quote with you to ruminate on, before we take a look at a couple of questions I wanted to focus on within this chapter and, in doing so, capture the insights from others across education.

Rather than referring to floor targets and Ofsted grades as the only measure of organisational success, children need us to be talking about how schools develop enterprise, how we can enable them to access opportunities to learn a wide-range of languages and understand and engage with other cultures, how we teach and instil resilience and adaptability, and how we ensure that children are empowered masters of technology. It is time for all trusts, schools and leaders to collectively change the discourse to what really matters.

- Helen Barker, head of Kyra Teaching School Alliance

The joy of metrics

Do test scores and league tables actually define success,
or do they create a culture of anxiety and narrow teaching?

Nope, not in their current format and application, and yes, they do. There, that was a quick section. Don't worry, I think we can go a bit beyond that sentence with a slightly more collegiate view.

Let me paraphrase the sentiment from an excellent article by a good friend of mine, **Nic Ponsford**, the founder of the **Global Equality Collective**, in *Schools week* [54], where she explains that data plays a pivotal role in the day-to-day operations of schools, influencing everything from test score analysis to attendance tracking. However, the manner in which we leverage this data can sometimes have negative consequences for our students' overall wellbeing and development.

She rightly highlights that, too often, we find ourselves dedicating more time to discussing academic performance metrics than focusing on the broader aspects of students' wellbeing. Although we frequently claim that wellbeing is a top priority, our attention and resources allocated to understanding students' sense of belonging and the barriers they face in learning are minimal. This narrow concentration on grades and learning attitudes overlooks the richness of students' experiences and passions—the very reasons behind their learning challenges. Moreover, it reinforces existing inequalities and marginalises our most vulnerable students.

As she says, when we fail to distinguish between students' lived experiences and their academic performance, we place the burden on individual teachers to connect with students about their interests. This approach is far from ideal, especially if these connections aren't systematically captured. Even worse, it reduces the likelihood that schools, as institutions, will effectively address the obstacles students encounter.

She cites that we could learn a lot by new approaches like "**warm data**" [55], which refers to information that focuses on the connections and relationships within larger complex systems. It helps us understand how different parts of a system (and even different systems) are linked together and affect each other. Essentially, warm data looks at the context and the relationships between things, rather than just the individual pieces. That's a complicated way of saying we gain more value from joined up data that is linked, contextually providing a broader sense of the child. Instead of schools working to meet the metrics on dashboards, shouldn't the dashboard data be the one that best supports the needs of our students? Think back to my introduction and the research challenging those big decisions made on questionable and narrow data.

Perspectives from within

Professor Bob Harrison, a former principal, chair of governors, and education advisor, reminded me of the following: "*Test scores are a very narrow definition of success. They measure what can be measured and not necessarily what is of value to learners, employers and community.*" This is a view that is precisely in line with the sentiment shared in this chapter and few seem to disagree.

There is balance and challenge on this topic. school and trust leaders are rightly mindful that right now, they need metrics. They need data to report, as thin or flawed as it might be, it's better than nothing. I wanted to capture the perspectives of many other voices within the system, and they were all helpful on unpicking the conversation further.

Dr. Ian Young, CEO (chief executive officer) of **Peterborough Keys Academies Trust,** noted: "*They are necessary and important and must always be designed to provide meaningful and fair data. There is an inevitability to some anxiety existing around these, but that should be positive if managed appropriately.*" He wanted to highlight that there is a risk of teaching narrowing as a high-stakes assessment approach, but this may be necessary to ensure key skills and knowledge is in place and retained.

Dr. Tim Coulson, CEO of **Unity Schools Partnerships,** shared: *"Test scores and league tables take excuses away from the weak leader with low expectations but are a blunt tool for school leaders that want to shift accountability to others and in turn create anxiety and narrow teaching."* I like that; it's succinct, and whilst I would challenge the narrowness of data assessed, it's important to recognise that part of the conversation has to be doing the best with what we have, how it can help and hinder, whilst also keeping an eye towards change.

Simon Luxford-Moore, the head of e-Learning at the **Erskine Stewart's Melville Schools (ESMS)** in Edinburgh, shared a pragmatic perspective on test scores and league tables: *"They currently do get blamed for a lot of anxiety and negative feelings but, ultimately, it's just data—and a snapshot of a single moment in time—at best."* There is some real consideration here; in essence, he was saying that often the scores and tables don't do any damage, but the interpretation of them does.

Tracy O'Brien has been in education for over 30 years and is currently a headteacher in London. She shared, *"I think value added measures are often a better measure of success. Contextual Value Added was really positive at GCSE and took context into account."* That is a fair point, but alongside that, don't we want to capture what else we have added to a child's toolkit in terms of their personal development, skills, etc? She's not wrong, within the current narrow window of review, but it could be so much better. I have to drop in here, caring is sharing, after all, that Tracy has written two excellent leadership books; both sit on my shelf and may well be of interest: *School Self Review* [56] and *Rethinking School Inspection* [57].

When we are talking about some of those really high-stakes tests, like GCSE's, I was keen to speak to folks like **Tim Smale**, who has been an educator for 20 years, who shared: *"I really do think they narrow teaching and create anxiety for teachers and students alike. All too often we school teaching content designed to fit the parameters of the exam."* He also shared with me his perspective, which I agree with, that a lot of decisions about a child's life are made on the outcome of a few letter grades that reflect, really, as Tim saw it, as the privilege of your upbringing and your ability to recall a lot of unnecessary content under a huge amount of time pressure. Now, a change to our formal qualifications is a whole new topic, but that ripples backwards into how we plan for, and teach to the test, and focus our cross-hairs on the academic indicators, often instead of those other holistic measures mentioned by Nic Ponsford.

I always keep an eye on the insights of **Matt Jessop**, head teacher at Crosthwaite C of E School. He thinks differently than many and is happy to challenge the current frameworks and norms. Like everything we have discussed, this isn't a one-size-fits-all model, and what works for some won't for others. As he articulated with me, *"If a family/pupil chooses a school or setting that can help support them on their pathway to FE/HE because that's what they want then fine—it's their choice: it's a laid pathway for many and relevant to future skills and employment. If a pupil attends a school like this because it is their closest, but is not academically inclined, so their needs aren't fully met and does not do well, then this would* *be an example of where test scores and league tables are harmful and have narrowed the definition of success."*

Often, the pressure is from high above, and that's easy for anyone a few steps removed to critique, but harder when you are directly accountable. As Matt shared, *"It's a brave Head Teacher or SLT that chooses to define success as something that isn't measured by such external accountability systems, and often much harder to measure—quantitative measurements of happiness, satisfaction, interest etc. are possible, but not recognised by the powers that be as being valid."* Amen to that. I's not always a critique of having systems of measure and accountability, it's changing our lens on what we measure so we aren't left being misled (for some students) by the narrow few that exist.

The consensus

We test too much, we judge schools too much on those narrow singular measures, and human nature means that more and more quality time that could benefit the broader educational journey of a child is spent preparing for the test, even when educators themselves don't hold value in the outcome. What do I know, eh? The system knows better.

So, I would argue that while metrics like test scores are seen as necessary for accountability and reporting, they are widely acknowledged to be incomplete measures of a student's success and a school's effectiveness. There is a consensus on the need for more holistic approaches that consider broader educational outcomes. The problem is that implementing significant change remains a big challenge within the current system. We will come on to that in subsequent chapters, but in the meantime, reflect within your school on how you would measure your school being good, which metrics help, and which hinder your assessment.

Defining "goodness" beyond data

What about student well-being, equity and long-term outcomes?

Let's be direct right out of the box. When managing a system at scale, it makes sense and is often the most cost-effective way to deliver a "service," but our unwillingness to flex away, or alongside, a one-size-fits-all education offer is the foundation of many of the issues and inequalities we consistently see in our system. My introduction shared lots of research and perspectives that challenge the mindset that pure academic achievement is the finite measure of a child's long-term success. Increasingly, as you will read in the next chapter, the acquisition of personal and professional skills counts just as much as retained knowledge. It's clear we need a happy blend of both to empower us to be our most able selves in the adult world.

Ironically, around the world, in the most established (old) education systems, we like conformity and standardisation, but then, for some reason, when it comes to the continuity of our curriculum, we have hard breaks where it is almost entirely disconnected. Imagine if it was more fluid and joined up; perhaps then we would have a bit more time in the earlier years of our education to broaden the child's skills and experiences, too.

As a system, perhaps because of the perception that change equals cost, probably because we are all happiest in our comfort zone, we fear innovation, even when we see it being adopted all around us. Certainly that's the case with technology, perhaps because the leaders of our school systems leading change find this a topic they have the least confidence in themselves, or by the nature of it being recent, have the least practical experience of using it themselves in the classroom. I cover plenty of this in my chapter dedicated to AI; it's a biggie.

We are also cursed with a very short-term focused mindset and, sadly, a national mandate. I discuss this topic more when discussing the barriers to the growth of our education system, but in a nutshell, evidence shows time and time again that political leaders want change that is introduced, implemented, and outcomes measured within one political cycle. Decisions are made with an eye on the resulting political capital raised. As a result, we tinker around the edges and avoid the big long-term decisions. Occasionally, national systems are given an opportunity to make that big change. I don't want to detour too far here, but Estonia is an example of a high-performing education system often lauded by PISA and others. They had a catalyst, "independence," in March 1990, which was followed within 18 months by the new legislation for an education system [58] for the population, which was radically different. I am hoping we don't have such a significant point in time, but we need an "education independence" moment.

Feedback from the profession

I'm going to provide just a few of the responses shared with me on that simple question: What is a good school?

"A good school is where every child is successful, where both data and the individual matter and the culture is that everyone is involved in creating the good school."

"Where students and staff are happy to be in school, feel valued and have a sense of belonging. Where students are given opportunities to learn and grow not just in academic subjects but as individuals. Where staff feel supported by their senior leaders and have access to good quality CPD."

"A good school is a happy school where staff and students want to come to every day. Where people are respectful and kind, where everyone wants to learn and is aspirational for themselves."

"A school which understands learning is not just academic and that passion and curiosity need fostered to grow minds."

"A good school prioritises kindness, relationships and collective efficacy. They are fun places to be, where the culture looks to maximise teacher time and teaching and learning are regularly discussed. The staff know about and care about, the students, and there is a determination to encourage teachers to stimulate their intellectual curiosity."

"One that teaches children kindness."

"Where everyone belongs, feels safe and productive. Where intentional inclusion and social capital is strong and embedded."

"A good school is built on a strong foundation of care, empathy, resilience, and creativity, with a leadership team that curates and choreographs this culture inclusively. By valuing diverse perspectives and opinions, the school remains focused on the students and their future, rather than being anchored in the past experiences of the staff."

"Happy achieving learners and compassionate and caring teachers and support staff."

"A good school is firstly one where they feel safe, supported and happy. A strong culture of safeguarding and behaviour management is necessary for this. A good school explicitly recognizes and supports diversity and inclusion. Then, the curriculum they follow should be well designed for and delivered by staff who are well-trained and strongly motivated. A culture of strong staff development and support exists in a good school. Beyond this, a good school will seek to create many meaningful and varied experiences for children beyond the curriculum—through sport, music, drama, clubs, trips and celebrations."

I am really hoping that you, too, will see those common themes reflected. I asked colleagues to share as if they were giving me a summary when we met in a lift; it's the things they are most keen to reflect on about their schools. I don't see these values being amplified or visible in a constructive way on any external inspection report. Elements, yes, but certainly not with the weight and priority our educators hold them in. We want all our learners to thrive, yet we are expecting them to all follow the exact same journey for 14 years through education and think that will work for all. Are we surprised some shine and some diminish?

Would it not be a good foundation to say we want all our learners to be happy? Happy learning, happy memories, and hopefully a future love of learning. That's a combination of culture and ethos within our schools, coupled with the flexibility of a curriculum that can flex and bend to ensure it meets the academic and skills needs of each child, and provides the opportunities and experiences a future child for the workplace in 2040 might need. Pause right now and think back to a positive memory of your educational journey. Was it the classroom or the trips and experiences that resonate? What if they were much more intertwined?

Keeping with the topic, **Tim Coulson** provided me a slightly more formal summary, but it can still align with what I have just said: *"A good school is where it is not defined by its catchment and parents are not dissuaded by a prevailing culture to which they do not subscribe."* I agree, we want parents and children to want to come to our schools, so based on earlier research in the chapter, we also need to shift parental perspectives that the academic league tables are the only goal of a good school that will allow their child to thrive. I really do think there is capital in looking more long term at children's outcomes and shaping that back into our schools' "value" alongside being pragmatic, using the digital tools we have at our disposal to capture a broader sense of the nurture and enablement our schools offer to our students alongside their academic progress.

How about we redefine progress? Let's be honest. Many secondary schools already challenge the progress data with a cautious eye to the child's outgoing primary data as an accurate baseline. It's just another small elephant in the room that rarely gets talked about publicly. We absolutely want to reflect on their learning journey and broaden it to capture knowledge and skills acquisition. Imagine if our critical thinking skills, digital skills, etc., were "emerging or secure," if we could capture resilience, happiness, and creativity in soft measures to provide a broader sense of why a school is good.

Looking beyond

This is sadly one big cycle; our government wants data, data to reassure the electorate, data to reassure businesses and investors of our future workforce skills, and data to compare with every other nation in our desire to highlight who we are better than. Yes, we need a clumsy way of holding schools accountable, and we do need to hold schools accountable, but if we all know we are being held accountable for only half of what we do, isn't it evident that our focus has become a self-fulfilling prophecy with eyes drawn more and more to the tests?

We have a good system in international terms, so we are right to be proud of much of what we provide our children, and we have ridden on the coattails of our "reputation" internationally for a long time, but that isn't going to be the case much longer if we keep claiming a false definition of "good." I know it's an awkward topic and I know it infers criticism of those delivering it, but let's point our fingers a bit higher up the food chain and be clear: Our current system is good for many children but inadequate for others, but even where it is good now, with a huge shift in what we need to equip our children with for a digital workplace, it is rapidly sliding into requires improvement. No tinkering, just empower system leaders to reform it before it's too late.

What does this all add up to?

I've done my best to consolidate the main elements that really define a good school, one where we can celebrate the breadth as well as the heights. I have tried to summarise this into six key elements, and I hope you will agree and see how they would reflect your school:

1. **Well-rounded measures of success**: A good school isn't just about grades or outcomes. It's a place where every child succeeds, in their own way—whether that's academically, creatively, or personally.

2. **Happy people**: At the heart of it, a good school is a happy one. Children and staff should feel valued, safe, and that they belong. It's a space where kindness and respect are at the heart of the daily routine.

3. **Supportive leadership**: We all know that good leadership makes all the difference. Teachers need to feel supported and get opportunities to keep growing professionally. A strong school culture revolves around making the teaching and learning journey a priority.

4. **Inclusion:** A good school ensures everyone feels included. Diversity isn't just acknowledged; it's embraced. The whole community feels like they belong and are collectively contributing to something important and valued.

5. **More than the curriculum:** A good school knows that learning goes beyond a framework. It is about fostering curiosity, creativity, and giving children the chance to explore their passions through the broadest possible provisions and experiences.

6. **Amazing teaching and learning:** At the core, of course we want everything we do in our schools to be done as well as possible. Setting expectations for amazing and inspiring teaching and subsequent outcomes is still really important, we just want to nudge those measures of outcomes to be broader and fairer for all.

7. **Promote a culture of care:** Kindness, empathy, and care aren't just for the checklists—they're the foundation of a good school. Everyone, children, teachers, and support staff, need to feel supported both academically and emotionally. It's a place where people genuinely look out for each other and that counts for a lot when we evaluate our schools.

References

1 "School Inspection Handbook," Ofsted, 2024 [Online]. Available: https://www.gov.uk/government/publications/school-inspection-handbook-eif
2 "Learning About Teaching - Initial Findings From the Measures of Effective Teaching Project," Bill & Melissa Gates Foundation, 2010.
3 R. Coe et al., "What Makes Great Teaching," The Sutton Trust, 2014. [Online]. Available: https://www.suttontrust.com/wp-content/uploads/2014/10/What-Makes-Great-Teaching-REPORT.pdf
4 "Teaching and Learning Toolkit," Education Endowment Foundation, [Online]. Available: https://educationendowmentfoundation.org.uk/education-evidence/teaching-learning-toolkit
5 "Independent Review of Teachers' Professional Development in Schools: Phase 1 Findings," Ofsted, May 2024. [Online]. Available: https://www.gov.uk/government/publications/teachers-professional-development-in-schools/independent-review-of-teachers-professional-development-in-schools-phase-1-findings
6 "Education Reform Act," Department for Education, 1998. [Online]. Available: https://www.gov.uk/government/publications/school-inspection-handbook-eif

7. "English Baccalaureate," Department for Education, [Online]. Available: https://en.wikipedia.org/wiki/English_Baccalaureate
8. "The EBacc 10 Years On: Should It Stay or Should It Go?," National Association of Head Teachers (NAHT), 2019. [Online]. Available: https://www.naht.org.uk/News/Latest-comments/Thought-leadership/ArtMID/590/ArticleID/786/The-EBacc-10-years-on-should-it-stay-or-should-it-go-Case-study-three
9. "ASCL Analysis Shows Collapse in Creative Arts A-Level Entries," Association of School and College Leaders, 13 August 2024. [Online]. Available: https://ascl.org.uk/News/Our-news-and-press-releases/ASCL-analysis-shows-collapse-in-creative-arts-A-le
10. "SEND Review: Right Support, Right Place, Right Time," Department for Education, March 2022. [Online]. Available: https://www.gov.uk/government/consultations/send-review-right-support-right-place-right-time
11. "SMSC in Education: Everything You Need to Know," Votes for Schools, 2024. [Online]. Available: https://www.votesforschools.com/blog/smsc/
12. "Guidance on Promoting British Values in Schools," Department for Education, 2014. [Online]. Available: https://www.gov.uk/government/news/guidance-on-promoting-british-values-in-schools-published
13. "The Vital Role of Extracurricular Activities for SEND Pupils," Huntingdon Research School, March 2024. [Online]. Available: https://researchschool.org.uk/huntington/news/secondary-case-study-the-vital-role-of-extracurricular-activities-for-send-cohorts
14. "Good Career Guidance Report," Gatsby, 2014. [Online]. Available: https://www.gatsby.org.uk/uploads/education/reports/pdf/gatsby-sir-john-holman-good-career-guidance-2014.pdf
15. "Closing the Attainment Gap," The Sutton Trust, 2024. [Online]. Available: https://www.suttontrust.com/our-research/closing-the-attainment-gap/
16. "Review of Best Practice in Parental Engagement," Department for Education, 2011. [Online]. Available: https://www.gov.uk/government/publications/review-of-best-practice-in-parental-engagement
17. "Parental Engagement Toolkit," Education Endowment Foundation, 2021 [Online]. Available: https://educationendowmentfoundation.org.uk/education-evidence/teaching-learning-toolkit/parental-engagement
18. "Do Parental Involvement Interventions Increase Attainment," Nuffield Foundation, 2013. [Online]. Available: https://www.nuffieldfoundation.org/sites/default/files/files/Do_parental_involvement_interventions_increase_attainment1.pdf
19. P. Allen-Kinross, "Schools with Deprived Pupils 'still Less Likely to be Judged Good', Admits Ofsted," SchoolsWeek, 16 December 2019. [Online]. Available: https://schoolsweek.co.uk/schools-with-deprived-pupils-still-less-likely-to-be-judged-good-admits-ofsted/
20. "Beyond Ofsted," 2023. [Online]. Available: https://beyondofsted.org.uk/
21. J. Perryman, A. Bradbury, G. Calvert and K. Kilian, "*Beyond Ofsted - Final Report of the Inquiry*," National Education Union (NEU), 2023.
22. OECD, "Organisation for Economic Co-operation and Development (OECD)," [Online]. Available: https://www.oecd.org/
23. OECD, "Programme for International Student Assessment (PISA)," 2023 [Online]. Available: https://www.oecd.org/en/about/programmes/pisa.html
24. "National Education Association (NEA)," [Online]. Available: https://www.nea.org/
25. C. Long, "What Can We Really Learn From the 2022 PISA Test Results?" neaToday, January 2024. [Online]. Available: https://www.nea.org/nea-today/all-news-articles/pisa-2022
26. "The National Center for Fair and Open Testing," FairTest, [Online]. Available: https://www.fairtest.org

27 "Interpreting PISA Results: It's Poverty, Stupid (With a bit of the iPhone)," FairTest, 2023 [Online]. Available: https://fairtest.org/interpreting-pisa-results-its-poverty-stupid-with-a-bit-of-the-iphone/
28 "OECD and Pisa Tests are Damaging Education Worldwide," The Guardian, 2014 [Online]. Available: https://www.theguardian.com/education/2014/may/06/oecd-pisa-tests-damaging-education-academics
29 "The Foundation for Education Development (FED)," [Online]. Available: https://fed.education/
30 OECD, "PISA High Performing Systems for Tomorrow (HPST)," [Online]. Available: https://www.oecd.org/en/about/projects/pisa-high-performing-systems-for-tomorrow-hpst.html
31 M. Stevenson, "Education for Human Flourishing," OECD, 2023.
32 K. Kristjánsson, "Recent Work on Flourishing as the Aim of Education: A Critical Review," *British Journal of Educational Studies*, vol. 65, pp. 87–107, 2017.
33 H. Gardner, Truth, Beauty, and Goodness Reframed: Educating for the Virtues in the Age of Truthiness and Twitter, Basic Books, 2011.
34 F. Ministry of Education and Culture, "Reflections on Competences for Human Flourishing," December 2023. [Online]. Available: https://www.oecd.org/en/publications/survey-of-adults-skills-2023-country-notes_ab4f6b8c-en/finland_f8ab67af-en.html
35 "Every Student Succeeds Act (ESSA)," U.S. Department of Education, 2015.
36 "No Child Left Behind (NCLB) Act," U.S. Department of Education, 2002.
37 "The National Center on Education and the Economy," NCEE, [Online]. Available: https://ncee.org/
38 "Inspection Systems: How Top-Performing Nations Hold Schools Accountable," National Center on Education and the Economy (NCEE), 30 May 2018. [Online]. Available: https://ncee.org/quick-read/how-top-performing-nations-hold-schools-accountable/
39 N. C. f. Education, "The Nation's Report Card," [Online]. Available: https://www.nationsreportcard.gov/
40 T. Loveless, "The NAEP Proficiency Myth," Brookings Institute, 13 June 2016. [Online]. Available: https://www.brookings.edu/articles/the-naep-proficiency-myth/
41 C. E. Finn Jr, *Assessing the Nation's Report Card: Challenges and Choices for NAEP*, Harvard Press, 2022.
42 A. Kingsley, "Ignore NAEP. Better Yet, Abolish It," Education Week, 06 June 2022. [Online]. Available: https://www.edweek.org/teaching-learning/opinion-ignore-naep-better-yet-abolish-it/2022/06
43 "National Assessment Program - Literacy and Numeracy," Australian Department for Education, 2024 [Online]. Available: https://www.education.gov.au/national-assessment-program/national-assessment-program-literacy-and-numeracy
44 "Everything You Need to Know About SATs," Department for Education, 05 May 2022. [Online]. Available: https://educationhub.blog.gov.uk/2022/05/05/everything-you-need-to-know-about-sats/
45 S. Larsen, "Are the Latest NAPLAN Results Really an 'epic fail'?," The Conversation.com, 14 August 2024. [Online]. Available: https://theconversation.com/are-the-latest-naplan-results-really-an-epic-fail-236782
46 S. A. Larsen, "Are Australian Students' Academic Skills Declining? Interrogating 25 Years of National and International Standardised Assessment Data," *Australian Journal of Social Issues*, pp. 1–32, 2024.
47 D. W. Beuermann, C. K. Jackson, L. Navarro-Sola and F. Pardo, "What is a Good School, and Can Parents Tell? Evidence on the Multidimensionality of School Output," *The Review of Economic Studies*, vol. 90, no. 1, pp. 65–101, 2023.

48 A. Abdulkadiroğlu, P. A. Pathak, J. Schellenberg and C. R. Walters, "Do Parents Value School Effectiveness?" *American Economic Review*, vol. 110, no. 5, pp. 1502–1539, 2020.
49 M. Friedman, "The Role of Government in Education in Economics and the public interest," 1955.
50 W. B. MacLeod and M. Urquiola, "Is Education Consumption or Investment? Implications for School Competition," *Annual Review of Economics*, vol. 11, pp. 563–589, 2019.
51 L. Stanford, "Charter Schools Are Outperforming Traditional Public Schools: 6 Takeaways From a New Study," Education Week, 06 June 2023. [Online]. Available: https://www.edweek.org/policy-politics/charter-schools-are-outperforming-traditional-public-schools-6-takeaways-from-a-new-study/2023/06
52 W. Dobbie and R. G. Fryer, "Charter Schools and Labor Market Outcomes," *Journal of Labor Economics*, vol. 38, no. 4, 2020.
53 P. Hughes, "What is a Good School?" in *Achieving Quality Education for All: Perspectives from the Asia-Pacific Region and Beyond*, Springer, 2013, pp. 21–23. Available: https://link.springer.com/book/10.1007/978-94-007-5294-8
54 N. Ponsford, "Labour Must Rethink Schools' Whole Relationship With Data," 22 August 2024. [Online]. Available: https://schoolsweek.co.uk/labour-must-rethink-schools-whole-relationship-with-data/
55 "Warm Data Labs," The International Bateson Institute, 2018 [Online]. Available: https://batesoninstitute.org/warm-data-labs/
56 T. O'Brien, *School Self-Review – A Sensible Approach: How to Know and Tell the Story of Your School*, John Catt Educational Ltd, 2022.
57 T. O'Brien, *Rethinking School Inspection: Is there a Better Way?* John Catt Educational Limited, 2023.
58 M. Lees, "Estonian Education System 1990–2016 "Reforms and their Impact"," 2016. [Online]. Available: https://4liberty.eu/wp-content/uploads/2016/08/Estonian-Education-System_1990-2016.pdf

The shifting need for skills versus current curriculum offers

I do not expect anyone reading this book to be surprised to see a discussion about the curriculum starting early. From the outset, I want to say that healthy conversations are typically found within the context of evolution rather than revolution. I am also conscious that there are many disparate views on this subject and within reason, there is no singular way of proving who is or isn't right on the topic, but I am going to have a go at trying to unpick the key strands.

As with most discussions, I find it helpful to start with a sense of where we are now, and how we arrived here and then unpick the "why" we need to consider change.

Setting the scene

I have tried to ensure a broad perspective incorporating international systems where I can within the book, but I will kick off by looking at this from an England perspective, as that is where I have most lived experience.

It's a challenge to decide how far to go back to set some context, but I decided that the output from the 1861 **"Newcastle Report"** [1] was a handy line in the sand for the core reforms in England. The government set up a royal commission on the **"State of Popular Education in England,"** which ran from 1858 to 1861 under the chairmanship of the Duke of Newcastle. It made the first recommendation regarding access to education for all (or the working classes as it was described). There were two subsequent commissions, **"The Royal Commission on the Public Schools,"** resulting in the Clarendon Report on private schools, which led to the **Public Schools Act** [2], and the **"Schools Inquiry Commission"** reported in 1868 on the schools for the "middle classes."

This is not my attempt at an extended history lesson, but a point in time when education for all became a parliamentary act. Perhaps more as an aside, it also highlights the mindset of separating what different social classes needed from education.

All three of these commissions fed into the creation of the **Elementary Education Act** [3] of 1870, commonly known as the **Forster's Education Act** and which set the framework for education for all children up to the age of 12. The act stands as the very first piece of legislation to deal specifically with the provision of education in England and Wales. Most importantly, it delivered for the first time a commitment to the provision of education on a national scale. It established a system of 'school boards' to build and manage schools in areas where they were needed. The boards were locally elected bodies that drew their funding from the local rates. A separate act provided something similar in Scotland in 1872 [4]. *Just for fun and in a monetary context, the annual funding allocation for all schools by parliament was just over £800,000 (for the country).*

We won't go too far on our impromptu history lesson, but the somewhat controversial **Balfour Education Act** eventually abolished these school boards [5] of 1902, and replaced them with approximately 300 local education authorities (LEAs) whose remit also included secondary education for the first time. At this point, it started to feel familiar with what we know today.

Naturally, once you have a universal act for the provision of education, you also need to decide what that education looks like. So, this is where I must make a small confession. There have been plenty of occasions when discussing education in England where I have referenced a broader narrative, that of our curriculum being heavily linked to the Industrial Revolution and the British Empire. I can probably paraphrase that as one where we knew that no matter where our future workforce was across the "Empire," we wanted them to acquire those core skills of numeracy and literacy to allow them to become productive citizens wherever they may end up working.

In my first published book, ***My Secret #EdTech Diary: Looking at Educational Technology through a Wider Lens*** [6], in 2021, I was fortunate enough to have Professor Bob Harrison write my foreword, and in that, he reflected that *"the design principles of our education system stem from a bygone era and were predicated on the dominant industries at the turn of the century – steel, coal, textiles, shipbuilding and was strongly influenced by a form of Taylorism* [7].*"* So, the confession is that this is something I have mentioned a few times, but in truth, it isn't something I have ever unpicked in more detail, so this chapter has proven a timely stimulus. I'm hoping you find it interesting, too.

In my effort to signpost just how far we have come, I thought I would share the six "standards of education" outlined in the 1872 **Revised Code of Regulations**, which came from the Elementary Education Act, as the starting point of our curriculum journey (Table 2.1).

Table 2.1 Standards of Education contained in the Revised Code of Regulations, 1872

	Standard I
Reading	One of the narratives next in order after monosyllables in an elementary reading book used in the school.
Writing	Copy in manuscript character a line of print and write from dictation a few common words.
Arithmetic	Simple addition and subtraction of numbers of not more than four figures, and the multiplication table to multiplication by six.
	Standard II
Reading	A short paragraph from an elementary reading book.
Writing	A sentence from the same book, slowly read once and then dictated in single words.
Arithmetic	The multiplication table, and any simple rule as far as short division (inclusive).
	Standard III
Reading	A short paragraph from a more advanced reading book.
Writing	A sentence slowly dictated once by a few words at a time, from the same book.
Arithmetic	Long division and compound rules (money).
	Standard IV
Reading	A few lines of poetry or prose, at the choice of the inspector.
Writing	A sentence slowly dictated once, by a few words at a time, from a reading book, such as is used in the first class of the school.
Arithmetic	Compound rules (common weights and measures).

(Continued)

Table 2.1 *(Continued)*

	Standard V
Reading	A short ordinary paragraph in a newspaper or other modern narrative.
Writing	Another short ordinary paragraph in a newspaper, or other modern narrative, slowly dictated once by a few words at a time.
Arithmetic	Practice and bills of parcels.

	Standard VI
Reading	To read with fluency and expression.
Writing	A short theme or letter, or an easy paraphrase.
Arithmetic	Proportion and fractions (vulgar and decimal).

The above became the standard "litmus test" of proficiency and was linked to requiring compulsory attendance until at least the age of 13 unless the child had managed to meet the required standards.

Don't worry, I am not going to re-create the curriculum offer in detail for every iteration over the last 100 years; it would make for a big book but hardly add any insights at a micro level to this conversation. However, the focus on the core reading, writing, and arithmetic is still very much at the heart of our education provision. I'm also not going to try and argue it shouldn't be; this discussion is much more framed around what else should be in "the pot" for inclusion. I am fully supportive of continuing to develop those core numeracy and literacy skills. We might want to reflect on the relevance and applicability of some of the curricula offered for those stands, mind you.

I am sure many can drill down and decide which elements taught in mathematics are still valid and which other aspects are perhaps missing. Flippantly, I might suggest I've never needed matrices since I left school, but I wish someone had taught me how to calculate the APR (annual percentage rate) before I took out any finance. I am sure you get the gist. Anyway, that is for another day (or chapter), at the very least.

Current curriculum

For now, the broader conversation about our current curriculum offer falls into my "awkward questions" category as often, challenging the current offer is somehow conflated with challenging the professionalism and skills of our educators and implying they are failing in some way. That, of course, is entirely false, and many broaden their teaching to reflect many of the topics and skills employers need today. Perhaps that's despite the curriculum demands rather than as a result of them. Since, for example, the introduction of the new General Certificate of Secondary Education (GCSEs) by the former Education Secretary **Michael Gove** in 2014, changes in the national curriculum have shifted the emphasis towards "knowledge-rich" learning [8].

Those reforms have continued to spark debate over the future direction of our education system. I strongly advocate that knowledge also provides context, but in a new artificial intelligence (AI) world where the answer to most "facts" is a Siri or Alexa shout away, is the balance still correct when the ability to ask the right question is often more powerful than the response?

Perhaps I need to differentiate here, as one set of "skills" we develop is our learning skills, and it's fair to say that there has been plenty of debate about whether schools should aim to teach students generic learning skills or whether they should focus primarily on teaching subject-specific knowledge. **Tricot and Sweller** [9] (2014), for example, argued that teaching generic skills doesn't work since, in order for us to think creatively or critically, we first and more importantly, have to be knowledgeable about the subject. That is my "context" point from above, I guess.

The **Chartered College of Teaching** [10] introduced a **"Learning Skills Curriculum"** as a research intervention within a secondary school between 2010 and 2014 where the students eligible for free school meals were identified by Ofsted as being "well above average." Their first three-year (interim) findings showed significant gains in subject learning among their cohort, compared with a control cohort, with accelerated progress among students from disadvantaged backgrounds. This was initially documented by **Mannion and Mercer** (2016) in **"Learning to Learn: Improving Attainment, Closing the Gap at Key Stage 3"** [11], whereby the end of year 9, there was a statistically significant (10.1%) increase in the proportion of students achieving or exceeding their target grade, compared with the control cohort. The full research is very well documented in Mannion and McAllister's 2020 book *Fear Is The Mind Killer: Why Learning to Learn Deserves Lesson Time – and How to make it work for Your Pupils* [12] and is well worth a read.

Some of the elements they included within their learning skills curriculum will likely feature later in this chapter, and it's also important to remember they were focusing on the marginal gains from each element "stacking up" to have a more significant impact overall. The main elements were self-regulation, metacognition, collaboration, oracy, formative assessment, personal effectiveness, thinking and reasoning skills, transfer, the shared language of learning, and, of course, ongoing Continuous Professional Development (CPD).

I hope we can all accept that the world is changing at a rapid pace, and this directly influences the outcomes we want to achieve from education. We often hear about those 21st-century skills, which in itself can be contentious as a topic. But building on my earlier chronology of our education system's roots in the Industrial Revolution, many argue it is unsuited to the wholly different context of our current society. **Sir Ken Robinson** writes about this in his 2016 book *Creative Schools: The Grassroots Revolution That's Transforming Education* [13], where he argues for *"an end to our outmoded industrial educational system"* and proposes *"a highly personalised, organic approach that draws on today's unprecedented technological and professional resources to engage all students, develop their love of learning, and enable them to face the real challenges of the twenty-first century."*

When I talk to peers, more often than not, it is not a lack of appetite to try and incorporate more skills (learning and life) into the mix; it's the absolute lack of capacity to do so when the school day is already so full and staff capacity is already exceeded. I'm keen also to add that wherever possible, schools are always endeavouring to teach learning skills to their cohort.

Embracing skills

I have a later chapter in the book covering accessibility and equity in our current systems and how that also challenges the balance of our curriculum. There is a growing recognition of the need to shift towards a more skills-focused approach to improve student learning outcomes. Research [14] emphasises the importance of curriculum design in mitigating learning difficulties and subsequent academic failure, especially for students with diverse needs.

The Organisation for Economic Co-operation and Development (**OECD**) has undertaken research as part of their 2015 **"Future of Education and Skills 2030"** [15] project, which aims, over time, to build a common understanding of the knowledge, skills, attitudes, and values students need in the 21st century. No small task. There are two strands of work: one is learning and teaching for 2030 and the other is an international curriculum analysis. As part of their work, a 2019 **OECD Learning Compass** [16] was created, which highlights *"the knowledge, skills, attitudes and values students need not just to weather the changes in our environment and our daily lives, but to help shape the future we want."* It also includes the competencies or skills deemed most important for students to thrive in the future. Alongside three different types of skills, cognitive and metacognitive, social-emotional, and practical and physical, it also signposts the four key types of knowledge acquired: disciplinary, interdisciplinary, epistemic, and procedural. The increasing recognition of skills and their growing relevance in the educational journey emphasises the need for us to challenge some of these "elephants in the room" and those questioning the need for change.

As **Andreas Schleicher**, director of the **OECD Directorate for Education and Skills**, said in 2019 [17]: *"Education is no longer about teaching students something alone; it is more important to be teaching them to develop a reliable compass and the navigation tools to find their own way in a world that is increasingly complex, volatile and uncertain. Our imagination, awareness, knowledge, skills and, most important, our common values, intellectual and moral maturity, and sense of responsibility is what will guide us for the world to become a better place."*

I could have picked a dozen or more topics to cover in this chapter, but I felt three seemed to be most prevalent. The first is asking if a rigid curriculum can realistically keep up with the rapidly changing demands of the future job market. Then, thinking about our ever-growing focus on the value of human skills prompts the following question: Is focusing on teamwork, adaptability, and critical thinking more vital than rote memorisation? Lastly, in an effort to promote and develop soft skills (or power skills as they are increasingly becoming), we have to also ask the last question: How do we further cultivate essential skills like communication, problem-solving, empathy, resilience, and more?

I asked **Professor Bob Harrison**, whom I mentioned earlier, for his perspective and in his usual direct and consolidated style he simply said the following: "*The current national curriculum is not fit for purpose and needs radical reform. There is an over reliance on content, facts and knowledge and insufficient attention paid to skills, collaboration and communication.*" This view is clearly echoed by the renewed OECD focus.

If we roll back a couple of decades from now, in a 1999 report, **The National Advisory Committee on Creative and Cultural Education** (NACCCE) [18] said in the context of the purpose of their report, in relation to helping young people get jobs: "*We live in a fast moving world. While employers continue to demand high academic standards, they also now want more. They want people who can adapt, see connections, innovate, communicate and work with others. This is true in many areas of work. The new knowledge-based economies, in particular, will increasingly depend on these abilities. Many businesses are paying for courses to promote creative abilities, to teach the skills and attitudes that are now essential for economic success but for which our education system is not designed to promote.*"

Now, remember we are two plus decades on, but have we seen any tangible shift in our offer? Have we seen a broadening to support creativity and the arts (those most human aspects), or a further narrowing of our curriculum? Sadly, I see the latter.

So now we have set the scene. Let's dive into the awkward questions I want to unpick.

PREPARING FOR THE UNKNOWN

Can a rigid curriculum keep up with the rapidly changing demands of the future job market?

I think some real-world perspectives might help us bridge the theoretical divide. I spoke to **Sam White**, a former maths teacher with experience in secondary, further education, and alternative education who crossed the divide outside of education into her current role as a learning evangelist for Glean.

Her perspective was: "*As a former teacher, when I entered the technology industry, I was lost. Lost looking for a curriculum plan, a half-termly team meeting in a world of agile sprints. What helped me navigate this period of unease were *communication skills, collaboration skills, critical thinking skills, and so much more. As an adult with decades of work experience in and out of the education system, I struggled to adapt to the current ways of working in industry. If I struggled as an adult what chance do young people have? I visited a school recently and gave a talk to staff on accessibility. I was told headphones are not allowed in their school as when young people arrive in the industry, they won't be allowed headphones. I corrected this teacher. In our office, over 90% of our team wear headphones from calm loops to overhead noise cancelling buds for listening to music while working. It's all allowed. In fact, the individual's needs, which means they want to use headphones, are celebrated. A million miles away from this school's approach to getting students ready for the world of work."*

Others often communicate Sammy's perspectives, albeit this was quite a specific example of our educational perspectives of the workplace being out of step, especially after such a rapid change post-pandemic. Furthermore, yes, I often wear headphones when working. The advent of Teams and Zoom has flipped that perspective a full 180 degrees.

There is a disconnect between the curriculum-defined expectations of suitable skills our learners acquire and those that a rapidly evolving workplace requires. Is it any surprise that with that pace, there will be a lag in education reacting to that? Honestly, no, but at times, that lag is generational, and that is where the problems come to the fore.

Soft or power skills

I need to nail my colours to the mast; I am a strong advocate of skills, those soft skills that are now very much the power skills employers are looking for. I must confess, I did think foolishly that I had coined that phrase of power skills, but I have subsequently seen it used by several writers, and I doubt they were listening to me previously ☺.

In a 2022 **Thomson Reuters** article, **"Why 'power skills' is the new term for soft skills in the hybrid work world,"** Natalie Runyon [19] shared that interpersonal, communicative, and similar "soft" leadership skills are being rebranded as "power skills" in today's remote and hybrid work environments. I shared a similar theme in a 2022 *Forbes* article titled **"Is Knowledge Obsolete?"** [20]. There is one skill we all need, and that is to know how to work together. As humans, we are social by design, so understanding empathy, wellbeing, and how we interact, communicate, and collaborate with people is vital. Take our experiences during the pandemic: For many, the absence of face-to-face contact was detrimental – and the lack of social interaction, in general, has led to an epidemic of mental health issues.

We have always put our trust in the education system to prepare our children for the future. The current model worked well in previous decades, but it feels like it is falling short in today's world. In this fast-moving technological age, we cannot honestly know what the workplace will look like in ten or even five years, other than it will be more digital-heavy and remote, with people working from anywhere and everywhere. The key to operating successfully in that environment will be human skills: dialogue, negotiation, adapting, strategising, and collaborating. This reinforces the question: Shouldn't we now focus more on the skills than the knowledge?

I asked **Pete Read**, CEO of **Persona Education**, a life skills and online learning platform for children, if a rigid curriculum could keep up with the rapidly changing demands of the future job market, and what employers want from their future workforce. He responded: *"In a word, no. Automation and a new division of labour between humans and machines will disrupt 85 million job descriptions globally. (World Economic Forum, Future of Jobs Report). The future workforce therefore needs to be able to do the jobs that machines cannot, so alongside the technical and digital skills required for this future workforce, there is a massive requirement for a range of social-emotional skills, also known as life skills or soft skills. 8 out of 10 employers now say life skills are the most important skills (World Bank) and 92% of employers say life skills are critical in hiring decisions (LinkedIn)."*

He also referenced two rounds of **OECD** research across 16 countries published in 2021 and 2024 show that social-emotional skills fall 30% during teenage years. We know these are key life skills for career success, including open-mindedness, task performance, collaboration, and motivation to achieve. So, it was clear to him (and is to me) that a rigid academic curriculum is no longer the best way to prepare young people for today's job market – schools and colleges need to place much more emphasis on life skills.

In the workplace

Interestingly when we look at the demand side for our future workforce, Pete also referenced recent LinkedIn research among learning and development professionals who identified the top requirements as resilience, adaptability, communication skills (in-person and remote), emotional intelligence, cross-functional collaboration, leadership, change management, stress management, time management and creativity, as well as technology skills and digital fluency. The balance of expectations has firmly moved towards the skills agenda.

I could list a few hundred salient articles here highlighting the importance and relevance of skills for the workplace. There can really be no argument remaining about their need, and to be explicit, expectations from employers. Education, therefore, has the challenge: in a full teaching curriculum, how on earth do we add more to the list? Bear in mind for your younger learning in key stages 1 and 2, the former **Qualifications and Curriculum Authority (QCA)** published a guide for primary schools recommending up to 32% of the teaching week should be spent on teaching English, 21% maths, and 9% science; that's not far off two-thirds of the time allocated on those foundational subjects. This was guidance, not statutory, but I have no doubt many timetables are shaped by this. I have been in some schools where it feels like 110% of the time has been directed to phonics alone, all from external pressures on statutory measures.

This is absolutely a conversation about blending skills into teaching those foundation subjects and removing some of the restrictions on how they are expected to be delivered. Reflecting on that balance, **John Sibbald** a specialist digital leader in education with 30 years of experience teaching, leading, and governing in Manchester secondary schools, shared with me: *"Learners need to know stuff for the next stage in their education or career. The amount and depth of stuff should reflect their strengths and enjoyment of a subject. But learners need to develop their skills alongside their knowledge – skills that enable young people to solve complex problems through collaboration, leadership and teamwork."*

John is someone who walks the walk and helped shape and deliver **Greater Manchester's Baccalaureate MBacc** [21], designed to provide young people at KS3 and KS4 with industry-led opportunities to develop their work, life, and social skills alongside selected digital skills throughout the curriculum. It also aims to help teachers teach their curriculum and provide learners with line of sight to good jobs locally. For a small amount of context, Mayor of Manchester **Andy Burnham** wanted Greater Manchester's digital sector to become 'world-class,' employing 95,000 people by 2026. Creating a baccalaureate to guide technical education locally is central to his plans for developing highly skilled, workplace-ready young people. This might be pretty isolated, but with the will and the right advisors at the table, we can change that recipe of content and skills when we want to.

Skills or agency

At this point, we might also want to consider what we are arguing for. Do we want greater skills acquisition for our students or greater agency? Now, that is quite nuanced, but in essence, it means acquiring fluency in those skills but critically combining them with the ability to apply them appropriately to real-life problems. That's agency; it's not either-or. We need to develop the foundational skills and then the understanding of how to apply them. In many ways, that is why problem-based learning (PBL) can be a real enabler. I really like the way Syliva Chard encapsulated this when she said, *"One of the major advantages of project work is that it makes school more like real life. It's an in-depth investigation of a real-world topic worthy of children's attention and effort."*

For those not familiar, **PBL** is a pedagogical approach that enables students to learn while engaging actively with meaningful problems. Students are given the opportunity to problem-solve in a collaborative setting, create mental models for learning, and form self-directed learning habits through practice and reflection (**Schmidt et al.** [22]; **Hmelo-Silver** [23]). I am likely preaching to the converted on this topic and have no plans to go into more detail as it's absolutely not my area of specialism. I did read a 2007 article on **Edutopia** titled **"Why Is Project-Based Learning Important?"** [24], where **Lee Shulman**, president of the **Carnegie Foundation for the Advancement of**

Teaching, said, "*Teaching has been an activity undertaken behind closed doors between moderately consenting participants.*" He suggested that PBL promotes lifelong learning because PBL and the use of technology together enable students, teachers, and administrators to reach out beyond the school building. Students become engaged builders of a new knowledge base and become active, lifelong learners. They said that this approach teaches children to take control of their learning, which is their first step as lifelong learners.

Given the capacity within the academic week, one of the most likely ways we can create a greater focus on skills is fundamentally about how we include approaches within our existing curriculum offer. Once again, it's evolution, not revolution. **Shemal Rajapakse**, entrepreneur and CEO of the learning app **Wizzie**, said, "*As students progress into secondary education, the curriculum should pivot towards fostering active engagement and problem-solving skills. It's essential that we equip young people not just with static knowledge, but with the ability to think critically and innovate. This approach will better prepare them for the unpredictable dynamics of future workplaces and enable them to meet the diverse needs of future employers.*"

There is nothing wrong with a knowledge-based curriculum, right? One that lends itself to traditional teacher-focused pedagogical practices. After all, that's the basis of the national curriculum in England [25], which ties in with the quote, "*ensuring that every child has a firm grasp of the basics and a good grounding in general knowledge,*" articulated by then–schools minister **Nick Gibb**. At the same time, he also said, "*It is vital that we return our curriculum to its intended purpose – a minimum national entitlement organised around subject disciplines.*" Hmm, reviewing most of Mr Gibbs's quotes, they all seem to have a backwards-facing narrative, and therein lies many of the challenges we face today. I have revised his quote into one that I would prefer we take forward.

It is vital that we move our curriculum to deliver its intended purpose – a broad national entitlement built around equipping our children with the knowledge and skills needed for adulthood and the workplace.

– Al Kingsley

What do you think? I think it's much more reflective of what we need so desperately.

Have we been teaching the wrong things?

We are often quick to step over this conversation, sometimes because, at the heart, it asks the question, have we been teaching the wrong things? (This is quickly taken as an implied critique of our educators.) Or that it would be a lot of work to reframe some of our classes, or we have no capacity to add anything else into the curriculum, or most frequently, there are other far more pressing challenges. If we can get past the false critique of educators and recognise that this is about a lack of flexibility and guidance from the top down nationally, some countries have been more receptive to change, and some have had an economically driven catalyst. I cover some of those contextual drivers at a macro level in the United Kingdom in my book **My School & Multi-Academy Trust Growth Guide** [26], but that is for another day (or book, in this case).

Should I suggest that skills are new and something we have never included before? Absolutely not. A child's learning journey already includes a raft of skills acquired, so this conversation is about how we prioritise more time to encourage the development of key skills we know will be most valuable to the child in adulthood. I was reading the excellent book **Seven Myths about Education** by **Daisy Christodoulou** [27] recently, which I mention in a future chapter; however, one opinion she shared I think is salient here, namely, she challenges whether the 21st century fundamentally changes anything.

Putting those soft skills covered under the umbrella of 21st-century skills, she argues that all those priorities of problem-solving, creative thinking, critical thinking, and communication/relational skills are not new. Using the example of a Mycenaean Greek craftsman (which seemed quite specific) needing to have interpersonal skills to work with others, they needed to adapt and innovate in their work. She argues that it is pretty patronising that, before this century, nobody was required to think critically, solve problems, collaborate, innovate, and so on. She has a point, and I agree. Nevertheless, skills refine, evolve, and shape based on context, and it is very different now.

Indeed, the Mycenaean craftsman did not have to worry about developing digital skills, was not competing for his job with a machine, did not have to watch the lives of craftsmen all over the world on a tablet, and build his self-confidence in his craftsmanship, but absolutely at the core, these skills are not new. They have just evolved and, as a result, primarily because of technology, have been massively amplified in their importance. I would encourage you to read her book. It is excellent, but constructively on this topic, the solution is not just to ensure that everyone gets equitable access to traditional education. We need to move away from our comfort zone and recognise that "traditional" is not enough and many of our learners will not engage without it being relevant and reflective of their lived experience.

We find ourselves in a constant struggle between the arguments for introducing more skills into our curriculum, those that more relevant to the requirements of today's employers and those needed for individuals in a new, digitally connected and social world, with the equally valid argument that we need to retain a knowledge-rich curriculum. It's perhaps no surprise that we end up in a position of stasis rather than constructive reform. What do we tend to do? We fall back on historical research, the evidence we can secure to support our position.

I often see work from 40+ years ago cited as the basis to maintain our current position. A frequent one is the 1988 book **Cultural Literacy: What Every American Needs to Know** by **E. D. Hirsch** [28], cited as *"[a] must-read for parents and teachers; this major bestseller reveals how cultural literacy is the hidden key to effective education and presents 5000 facts that every literate American should know."* He was an influential advocate of a "core knowledge" curriculum, arguing that the network of information that all competent readers possess in the background information stored in their long-term memory is what allows them to pick up a newspaper, read it, grasp the point and the implications, and it alone, gives meaning to what they read. Was he right? At the time, yes, probably, and much of what he shared translates to today. But would he have shared the same in a world of AI bots and voice-activated smartphones?

Cognitive scientist **Daniel Willingham**, whom I will mention in more detail shortly, said, *"Trying to teach students skills such as analysis in the absence or synthesis in the absence of factual knowledge is impossible."* [29] He highlights that factual knowledge must precede skills.

Prioritise

So, with that in mind, back to Hirsch. Do we need to know there was an American civil war? Yes. Do we need to learn why it happened and the outcome? Yes again, but then we get into a grey area. Do we need to remember dates and names and locations? Is it as relevant in a world of "Hey Siri" or "Hey Alexa"? The details are at our fingertips now; doesn't that shift how many of his "5,000 facts" remain still helpful?

The basis of context gained and needed from content knowledge is absolute, and I have no doubt Hirsch and Willingham are far wiser than me, but I still argue we now have a much tougher choice of defining what knowledge is purposeful and what is "facts" for fact's sake. The world has changed seismically in the last five years. The tools we use at work, the advent of AI, hybrid working, and social platforms ... it would be foolish to suggest that none of this needs to influence our thinking. As you will see in my chapter on AI, most human skills are now being amplified. They will carry more value and weight in the future, so we need to reflect that balance within our curriculum ... and quickly.

SKILLS VERSUS CONTENT

Is focusing on teamwork, adaptability, and critical thinking more vital than rote memorisation?

I know this is a contentious topic, as frankly, we need a blend of both, and it's easy to read and assume the critique is that "all" we do currently is provide content for memorisation, and that patently is not the case, but it's certainly a large part. It's still hugely important, given the content we consume ultimately provides the context for us to apply those newly acquired skills. Once again, it is not a choice but a discussion of how much priority we place on both. We are living in an ever-digitised world, with AI rarely out of the headlines (*see my subsequent chapter on this*); the goalposts move in terms of where our human skills are most valuable.

Someone I have huge time and respect for is **Professor Rose Luckin**, who wrote in her book ***Machine Learning and Human Intelligence: The future of education for the 21st century*** [30] that "*AI is brilliant at performing the routine cognitive skills of knowledge acquisition. The information that can be processed and learned by readily available machine-learning systems are way beyond our human capability.*" It naturally poses the question, do we want our education system to focus on teaching our children the things AI is best at, or should we perhaps focus on the bits where we have more purpose and value as human beings?

A different perspective

Writing this book has provided me with a real catalyst to broaden my reading and research; I'm a self-professed lifelong learner, but like everyone, there are times when I feel that my reading "sphere of influence" is too narrow, and I have to consciously stretch my choices. Based on a recommendation, I got a copy of ***CleverLands: The Secrets Behind the Success of the World's Education Superpowers*** by Crehan [31]. Before I knew it, I was reading about the Confucian mindset and a Chinese proverb: **"A clumsy bird that flies first will get to the forest earlier."** Hang in there; I promise I haven't lost the plot.

Crehan expands on work undertaken by **Li** [32] by comparing cultural learning approaches in the East and West. There was a perceived disconnect between students in American classrooms not being engaged in learning in contrast to Chinese schools, where all students worked hard at their studies. I'm paraphrasing, which you can probably guess. According to Li, our approach to learning in the West is based on long-standing intellectual views that began with the ancient Greeks. (*We might bump into Daisy's Mycenaean craftsman shortly.*) The three central ideas are that human curiosity about the world is the inspiration for knowledge, that the individual is the sole entity for discovering and success, and that learning privileges those with superior intellectual ability.

Take that long-standing foundation for Western education, and you can translate it to if you aren't curious about learning, you will not be motivated to learn, that the reason we learn is driven by personal benefit, and whether you are good at learning will depend on your individual attributes (how smart you perceive yourself to be). The same research in China and Japan saw that the primary driver replacing those above was simply "effort." They undertook a survey asking students what percentage of intelligence was due to effort and what was due to talent or innate ability. European Americans saw effort accounting for 36%, Japanese students accounted for 55% [33]. They concluded that Asian cultures still recognise a difference between people's innate abilities but don't see that as important, seeing effort as the biggest driver of performance. So, back to my "**clumsy bird**" proverb—it means having a mindset that even someone who is naturally less intelligent can still perform better than others if they try hard enough.

If we take all of the above on board and recognise the drivers for wanting to learn, curiosity as a driver to engagement, relevance, and the association of personal benefit from what they are learning and a current curriculum that amplifies the narrative that the smartest achieve best, now is the window for broadening our offer. By making it more relevant to learners and valuing all skills equally, but recognising those most human ones first in our increasingly digital world, and with revised pathways that lead to equitable success (not just traditional academia), this has to be the way forward.

The decision has to be student-led. What do they want and need, and is there more on the wish list than the acquisition of knowledge? Like any sector, we often end up in a conversation about supply and demand; the consumer votes with their feet. We have a problem right now that an increasing number of students' "feet" aren't arriving at school at 8:40 each day. It's not the sole driver here, but it doesn't seem a leap to say that if students don't feel that they are learning and acquiring relevant skills that they can see the point of, they will be disengaged and not have the motivation to attend. I mentioned him earlier, so now is a good time to further check out the perspectives of **Daniel Willingham**, a cognitive scientist and his excellent book *Why Don't Students Like School?* [29]. I always like a straightforward title!

In a similarly straightforward way, **Willingham** asked the question, "*How can I teach students the skills they need when standardized tests require only facts?*", acknowledging that since the 2000s, the importance of standardised tests has increased, leaving little opportunity in his opinion to analyse, synthesise, or critique in favour of recall of isolated facts. I know many teachers who feel their time is lost by having to focus on preparation for external tests of one kind or another. His thoughts were that asking children to memorise isolated facts is far from enriching. However, research has shown that those skills teachers want to teach their students to analyse and think critically do require extensive factual knowledge. He simplified it as "in order to think, you need something to think about." So, those critical thinking processes such as reasoning and problem-solving are intertwined with content or factual knowledge stored in our long-term memory. I'll call it context, which helps shape our thinking skills.

Therefore, if we want to develop our human skills so that our students can be successful in adulthood, we can't just introduce them into the curriculum in isolation. We need to interweave them with the curriculum content already available, albeit with perhaps a few modernisations of the aforementioned content. Skills versus content: They are a matching set; neither is particularly impactful without the other.

Shifting the focus

Pete Read responded to this subject, saying, *"The simple answer is that students still need to learn both content and skills. But the focus on skills definitely needs to increase, especially as practically the entirety of human knowledge is now available to anyone with an Internet connection, meaning the 19th/20th Century need to retain specialist knowledge is much less than it once was. However, that's not to say that the majority of learning time should be focused on skills. An integrated approach is best, where social-emotional skills become part of every lesson. Alongside that, significant time should also be set aside in the timetable to focus purely on life skills."* That's curriculum balance, particularly in light of what we have seen as an actual narrowing of curriculum priorities is absolutely the key. Breadth of provision, breadth of course styles, and assessment models allow for skills to be more purposefully offered and acquired in school.

I suspect that the vast majority of readers here *(perhaps I am being optimistic, referring to any readership as vast ☺)* will be familiar with Bloom's 1956 **"Taxonomy of Thinking Skills"** [34], which aims to move students from lower- to higher-order thinking. Knowledge to comprehension, application to analysis, evaluation to synthesis—that's without doubt the starting point from which to build those additional skills. In 2001, a revised taxonomy was published: **"A Taxonomy for Learning, Teaching and Assessing"** [35, 36]. In the revised taxonomy, knowledge is at the basis of these six cognitive processes, but its authors created a separate taxonomy of the types of knowledge used in cognition: factual, conceptual, procedural, and metacognitive. The latter moves us closer to a place to develop the topic at hand.

So, let me answer the first part of the question: Are these skills more important than rote memorisation of facts or content knowledge? No, not more important, but unlike our current position, are they as significant? Yes, I really think so, and as time goes on, that weighting will show even further.

There is plenty of research highlighting that skills like teamwork and adaptability have been linked to better long-term outcomes, as students who engage in collaborative, project-based learning environments are often better prepared for the interdisciplinary demands of modern work and life. The research in **"Conversations on Critical Thinking: Can Critical Thinking Find Its Way Forward as the Skill Set and Mindset of the Century?"**, by **Sellars et al.** [37], says: *"The capacity to successfully, positively engage with the cognitive capacities of critical thinking has become the benchmark of employability for many diverse industries across the globe and is considered critical for the development of informed, decisive global citizenship. Despite this, education systems in several countries have developed policies and practices that limit the opportunities for students to authentically participate in the discussions, debates, and evaluative thinking that serve to develop the skill set and mindset of critical thinkers."*

In their research, Sellars et al. highlighted four significant trends that emerged as essential issues to be considered in any attempt to effectively incorporate critical thinking skills into education systems. These were identified as (a) cultural, social, religious, and political sensitivities; (b) the purposes for which critical thinking may be incorporated into classroom discourse; (c) the lack of clarity on what is meant by critical thinking; and lastly, (d) the need for clarity around the pedagogical perspectives and strategies, which have the potential to engage students in the cognitive "capacities" of critical thinking.

Let's get critical

The phrase *critical thinking* does tend to be used in different ways, so I am not entirely surprised that at times, ambiguity limits progress in curriculum adoption. Let me introduce what I think is a nice encapsulation by Facione [38] when he said, "*We understand critical thinking to be purposeful, self-regulatory judgment that results in interpretation, analysis, evaluation, and inference, as well as explanation of the evidential, conceptual, methodological, criteriological, or contextual considerations upon which that judgment is based.*"

That really works for me, and I'd encourage you to read Falcone's paper **"Critical Thinking: What It Is and Why It Counts"** [38]. It walks you through the considerations in arriving at a definition and its relevance. Those core critical thinking skills are a combination of cognitive skills and dispositions. I am really mindful of not turning this discussion into a lecture, given my intended audience will likely already be well informed, so I am going to try my very best to keep at a high level to support the question at hand. So, experts [39] summarise cognitive skills at the core of critical thinking as interpretation, analysis, evaluation, inference, explanation, and self-regulation.

In the context of disposition, the research experts used a metaphorical phrase, **critical spirit** (in a positive way). They meant this to highlight "*a probing inquisitiveness, a keenness of mind, a zealous dedication to reason, and a hunger or eagerness for reliable information.*" I promise you that the last definition will align strongly with many employers' wish list of future employee traits.

Perhaps at this point you might feel I am labouring this point, but when I started my research and writing my views on the importance of critical thinking, it was very much aligned with skills I knew employers looked for in their workforce. However, wearing my education hat, I am just as keen on how this filters through to the broader life skills of our children. The approaches to life and living, which characterise critical thinking from their research, include:

- Inquisitiveness with regard to a wide range of issues
- Concern to become and remain well informed
- Alertness to opportunities to use critical thinking
- Trust in the processes of reasoned inquiry
- Self-confidence in one's own abilities to reason

- Open-mindedness regarding divergent worldviews
- Flexibility in considering alternatives and opinions
- Understanding of the opinions of other people
- Fair-mindedness in appraising reasoning
- Honesty in facing one's own biases, prejudices, stereotypes, or egocentric tendencies
- Prudence in suspending, making, or altering judgements
- Willingness to reconsider and revise views where honest reflection suggests that change is warranted

The relevance of so many of these elements in our AI-driven, technology-laden, social media–rich, fake news–driven, and anxiety-heightened world seem fundamental to where we need to shift our focus. Falcone shared a perspective from a much wider lens, saying: *"History shows that assaults on learning, whether by book burning, exile of intellectuals, or regulations aimed at suppressing research and frustrating the fair-minded, evidence-based, and unfettered pursuit of knowledge, can happen wherever and whenever people are not vigilant defenders of open, objective, and independent inquiry. Does this mean that society should place a very high value on critical thinking? Absolutely!"* We could take another reflection on the shifting political landscape around the world right now, and perhaps, if our eyes are sufficiently wide open, we would see why this is so, so important today.

Finding balance

To avoid any imbalance, we absolutely do not want to forget creative or innovative thinking, the type that leads to new insights and perspectives, or that library full of creative output from poetry, dance, literature, inventions, and so much more.

So, in conclusion, let's not dismiss the discussion on the value of teaching more skills simply because the research says content knowledge is key. That is a convenient redirect; both are important. Time and capacity in the timetable may be a limiting factor. However, the reality is that the revised approach will have to be how we can further weave skills acquisition into our pre-existing curriculum offer and empower teachers with the flexibility to adapt their approach and methodologies to meet this need. We don't have a choice; we can't leave our children informed but without the skills to prosper in adult life.

EMBRACING "SOFT SKILLS"

How do we cultivate essential skills like communication, problem-solving, empathy, grit, and more?

I think we have covered much of the rationale for this question already in the chapter, but let's go a bit further with those fluffy "soft skills." Where does it come from? The term *soft skills* was first introduced in U.S. Army training courses in the early 1970s to refer to interpersonal skills rather than those needed for operating machinery or using weapons [40]. We can probably concur that soft skills were seen as the less important, more invisible skills.

How times have changed, and now more than ever, these attributes sit at the front of the queue when it comes to our most valuable personal assets. A whole series of books is available focusing on our soft skills, including the highly popular **Leader Series** [41, 42], covering how to use soft skills to get hard results. Sadly, they do not have one on writing, or rest assured, I would be busy digesting, but topics such as managing people, presenting, impact, resilience, and wellbeing are all featured across publications.

In my mind, soft skills include communication, organisation, teamwork, empathy, problem-solving, emotional intelligence, and influencing abilities. I increasingly refer to them as power skills. In the workplace, they are not ancillary but foundational to an employee's technical expertise. They transform knowledge into action and action into results.

Empowering Teams: Knowledge Is Power, but Collaboration Is a Superpower

I came across a quote in my research, which I am not able to source the origin of, but in essence, it said, in a world increasingly characterised by constant change, having the skills to adapt and thrive is paramount. It doesn't matter if you're a seasoned professional or an enthusiastic learner; **"soft skills are the wings that will elevate you to new heights."**

I'll just throw in a "digital" reminder from **John Sibbald:** "*Work, life and social skills need to developed in conjunction with digital skills. Digital skills are the rocket fuel for work, life and social skills and should not be delivered in isolation; otherwise, they will not be honed and provide agency.*"

Matt Jessop, head teacher at Crosthwaite CE Primary School, shared his (by no means exhaustive), summary of some of the areas we should consider: -

- Recognising that technology isn't an add-on, but a core skill set, embedded from a young age with cybersecurity and misinformation taught properly, and AI used where beneficial.

- Promoting outdoor learning commitments and sessions that foster resilience, independence, and a connection to nature, with environmental stewardship, entrepreneurship, and even some data science.

- Making sure soft skills like communication, critical thinking, and teamwork are prioritised – with time to talk, discussion of current affairs and their impact on us all, learning from history, and looking at how we can avoid making the same mistakes.

- Ensuring mental health is nurtured, not overlooked – a core commitment, with individual and whole-school work and support networks.

- Support for each individual's needs – clear recognition that we are all neurodiverse and we have systems in place to support all.

- Introduce micro-credentials that children can earn that offer flexible pathways to success – our existing assessment and accountability systems that are imposed on us fail too many.

- Support an increase in our thematic approach to teaching and learning, holistic approaches that educate, shape, and support each individual.

OK, I suspect I am pushing against an open door on the topic of the need and value of soft skills; if you are not with me on that, then I apologise, and perhaps a refund is the best next step for you.

The question at hand is how do we foster and develop these soft skills within our classrooms? I read an interesting article from **EtonX**, an online subsidiary founded by **Eton College** in 2015, titled **"Classroom tips to help integrate soft skills"** [43]. The essence of the article was identifying that many educators know that high exam scores don't always equate to being fully prepared for life beyond the classroom. Of course, some students can flawlessly recite lines from Shakespeare, spell complex words, or recall historical dates with ease. However, those abilities don't necessarily translate into the skills needed to lead a team, manage emotions when receiving feedback, or influence others effectively.

They identified that while traditional academic skills like memorisation have their place (see previous topic), they fall short in preparing students for the rapidly evolving workplace. In a world where information becomes outdated quickly, success increasingly depends on the ability to build strong relationships, think creatively, solve problems in real time, and communicate with clarity. They, too, conclude that these are the skills that will equip students for future challenges.

So, how do we incorporate the development of these key soft skills into our classroom? I am going to say none of these suggestions are new or particularly innovative, but it's the application with purpose that's really key. These are the seven areas highlighted.

1. **Build Confidence** – Confidence is the bedrock for developing any soft skills. It's what allows students to overcome fears, take on new challenges, and bounce back after setbacks. As educators, we can help build confidence by giving students real responsibilities and recognising their efforts, not just their results. This can be done through roles in the classroom, public speaking opportunities, or specific praise for how they've tackled a task.

2. **Encourage Independent Learning** – If we constantly spoon-feed students information, they become too dependent on us. Encouraging them to think

critically and find answers for themselves is far more effective. By guiding students through autonomous learning, we help them grow in confidence and develop important problem-solving skills. Rather than giving all the answers, pose questions that spark curiosity and encourage them to explore.

3. **Collaboration and Teamwork** – Group work is invaluable for developing interpersonal skills that are vital in the real world. By working together, students learn how to manage goals, communicate effectively, and support one another. Whether in pairs or larger groups, giving students a chance to collaborate mirrors real-life project work, fostering skills like negotiation, empathy, and teamwork.

4. **Promote Problem-Solving** – Challenges will arise in the classroom, but instead of solving them for the students, let them figure things out. Teach them to identify the problem, evaluate options, and think creatively about solutions. This way, they learn how to tackle obstacles head-on and develop resilience in the process.

5. **Embrace Mistakes and Failure** – Mistakes are an inevitable part of learning. How students handle them can either limit or enhance their development. Encourage a growth mindset, reminding students that mistakes are learning opportunities. By framing failure as a stepping stone rather than a roadblock, we can help them embrace the power of "yet" – as in, "You can't do this YET, but with effort, you will."

6. **Use Hypotheticals and Role-Play** – Role-playing and hypothetical scenarios can be great tools for helping students see things from different perspectives. These activities not only make lessons more engaging but also build empathy and communication skills. A really important point is that because they're slightly detached from reality, they give students a safe space to explore without the pressure of personal investment.

7. **Foster Reflection and Self-Awareness** – Helping students reflect on their actions, thoughts, and emotions is key to developing soft skills. Encourage self-reflection by incorporating reflective questions into regular activities, helping students become more self-aware and better equipped to navigate their development.

I do want to stress that this is as much of a reminder and a refocus as anything else. I am really keen to clarify this is already well established in teaching practice for most, but always, it's about marginal gains with greater awareness and prioritisation.

It's good to be self-reflective, and I think I am good at it, but you do have to make time to really reflect. For me, my driving motivator is curiosity. Calling myself a lifelong learner is just a more formal way of saying I'm naturally curious. As we all know, curiosity serves as the catalyst for collaboration in the classroom, too. When students are curious, they tend to ask more questions, seek answers, and engage in meaningful discussions with their classmates and in a classroom that fosters curiosity, students are more likely to extend themselves beyond their comfort zone to form interest groups and collaborate with their peers in a more meaningful way to uncover answers to their own questions.

Let's be curious

Curiosity and critical thinking go hand in hand. Curiosity sparks a desire in students to question the world around them, explore different viewpoints, dig deeper into topics, and seek answers to their own questions. When students engage in curiosity-driven tasks, they naturally enhance their critical thinking skills by tackling real-world problems and thinking analytically. Encouraging this type of learning creates an environment where students become active participants in their education, constantly questioning, analysing, and problem-solving. I am mindful that some of this can dovetail nicely with the earlier points around project-based learning, too.

Talking about steps for embedding better communication and problem-solving skills in the classroom seems a much clearer pathway; it is perhaps more challenging when we reflect on children's awareness, empathy, and resilience. There are some great resources for supporting teachers, such as the **"Cultivating Awareness and Resilience in Education"** (CARE) [44] for teachers program, which is a professional development program designed to provide teachers with the skills they need to manage the social and emotional demands of teaching.

Our students all arrive at our schools with different experiences and at various points on their personal development journey. Many of the foundational approaches are common, however. Reading **"The Trauma-Sensitive Classroom"** by **Jennings** [45], the foundations beyond, of course, understanding trauma and anxiety, are a focus on building supportive relationships, creating those safe spaces and supporting prosocial behaviour. We have to identify the strengths of each child in order to find the pathways we can build along.

In a journal article, **"An adaptation-based approach to resilience,"** Ellis et al., [46] propose: *"To improve intervention outcomes in stress-adapted children and youth, we need to uncover a high-resolution map of specific cognitive abilities that are enhanced as a result of growing up under high adversity conditions. That would enable the design of interventions that work with, instead of against, these abilities."* I think this is a really relevant point as often, due to time and capacity constraints, we often see a less nuanced and more one-size-fits-all approach when looking at adapting within our classroom. I do, however, fully recognise that under the Special Educational Needs and Disabilities Coordinator (SENDCO) and their team, every effort is provided to adapt a highly personalised support plan for each child.

Providing those early, child-centric assessments and interventions is key, but once we take a more class-centric perspective, those soft skills of empathy really cover a wide range of skills. You might have a few in mind, but having researched **"The Formative Five: Fostering Grit, Empathy, and Other Success Skills Every Student Needs"** by **Hoerr** [47], I was immediately overwhelmed by a full alphabet of suitable terms, which probably just highlight that nuance I referred to earlier:

- Acceptance
- Bravery
- Creativity
- Diplomacy
- Engagement
- Friendliness
- Generosity
- Helpfulness
- Insight
- Judiciousness
- Kindness
- Loving
- Magnanimity
- Nurturing
- Optimism
- Persistence
- Questioning
- Responsibility
- Sincerity
- Truthfulness
- Understanding
- Vigorousness
- Warmth
- Xenial (I had to Google this one; it means "being hospitable.")
- Youthfulness
- Zest

He condensed this down in his **"Formative Five": Empathy, Self-Control, Integrity, Embracing Diversity and Grit."** I also liked his acknowledgement that identifying an absolute set of attributes is much akin to determining *"how many angels can dance on the head of a pin."* It's not possible. However, he does identify that his core skills are all **"habits of mind"** [48] in that they reflect a child's sense of self and their relationship with others.

Grit is sometimes used to describe a child's resilience, determination, and perseverance when faced with challenging tasks. Thinking back to my comments earlier on the East versus West research, grit is not determined by intelligence or talent, but rather a willingness to persevere in the face of failure or struggle. Earlier research cited shows that the impact of grit on student performance can be more important than a student's intelligence.

Given the growing challenge with social, emotional, and mental health (SEMH) and the associated anxieties of many learners, a focus on ways to develop grit in the classroom has to be something that gains greater visibility in our child development priority list (and yes, I know it's already a very long list). When **Angela Duckworth** gave a **TED Talk** on grit [49], she identified it as one of the most important predictors of success in 2013. Perhaps not surprisingly, her associated 2016 book ***Grit: Why passion and resilience are the secrets to success*** [50] was a bestseller and encapsulated the simple concept of "sticking with things over a very long term until you master them." As children, that definition of long term may be shorter, but the core message is absolutely consistent.

Some of the strategies we see to support developing grit in the classroom include telling students that they expect them to succeed but letting them know help is there, sharing stories of notable people who have shown grit to accomplish a goal, and encouraging students to track their own accomplishments.

There is no doubt that the perceived rigidity of our curriculum, which is absolutely not fit for purpose in 2024, leaves little time for significant variability. However, the conversation surrounding skills often is presented as being an extra subject to add to the timetable, and a reason why we can't fit it in, rather than recognising, as many of these examples share, that a significant amount can be woven into our existing curriculum and is heavily focused on how we teach and the opportunities we provide for our learners to develop their broader skill set. Let's not use the packed curriculum as a reason to mitigate skills acquisition; instead, use it as a catalyst of opportunities to feed our innovative educators.

We all want to see an improved curriculum that equips children for the future, with life skills, digital skills, and other soft skills all taught to prepare them for the huge range of challenges and opportunities that lie ahead – and which our existing national curriculum and assessment systems currently fail to do.

> *"Give a man a fish and he eats for a day. Teach him to fish and he eats for a lifetime."* Lao Tzu

Moving forwards

We have covered quite a lot of perspectives and research here, so how might we consolidate that down into some key areas of focus and hopefully, priority. I've done my best to encapsulate those below.

1. **Shift from "soft" to "power" skills**: We need to stop treating communication, empathy, problem-solving, critical thinking, and other skills as afterthoughts. These skills are in demand like never before and are key to workplace success, not just nice value adds.

2. **Get digital skills started early**: Digital literacy is a must, but it can't be taught in a vacuum. Blend it with real-life skills for context so that children are better prepared for their digital futures.

3. **Outdoor and holistic learning**: Give children at all stages opportunities to build resilience and independence through outdoor learning, while also mixing in real-world skills like entrepreneurship, environmental care, data science, and more.

4. **Personalise support for every child**: Every student's different, and we need to recognise that. The more we can create flexible pathways for success, whether that's through micro-credentials or just better support systems that cater to their individual needs, the better. Capacity is the limiting factor but the aspiration has to push the change.

5. **Develop grit and resilience**: Teaching children how to push through setbacks is key. Share stories of resilience, let them track their progress, and encourage them to see failure as part of the journey, not the end of it. I like my "failures are stepping stones to success" as all-encompassing this.

6. **Mental health and inclusion first**: A good school should actively support mental health and inclusion. From safeguarding to solid support networks, this needs to be central. In most cases it already is, but the system and supporting services limit the pace and scope of support that can be offered.

References

1 *The State of Popular Education in England*, Vol.1, H.M. Stationary Office, 1861.
2 "Public Schools Act," UK Parliament, 1868. [Online]. Available: https://en.wikipedia.org/wiki/Public_Schools_Act_1868
3 "The Education Act," UK Parliament, 1870. [Online]. Available: https://www.parliament.uk/about/living-heritage/transformingsociety/livinglearning/school/overview/1870educationact/
4 *Education (Scotland) Act*, UK Parliament, 1872.
5 *The Education Act (Balfour Act)*, UK Parliament, 1902.

6. A. Kingsley, *My Secret# EdTech Diary: Looking at Educational Technology through a Wider Lens*, Hachette UK, 2021.
7. F. W. Taylor, "Taylorism," Wikipedia, 2022 [Online]. Available: https://en.wikipedia.org/wiki/Frederick_Winslow_Taylor
8. S. Giraud-Reeves, *The Facts of the Matter: England is Shifting to a 'Knowledge-Rich Curriculum'*, Social Market Foundation, 26 July 2021. [Online]. https://www.smf.co.uk/commentary_podcasts/the-facts-of-the-matter-england-is-shifting-to-a-knowledge-rich-curriculum/
9. A. Tricot and J. Sweller, "Domain-Specific Knowledge and Why Teaching Generic Skills Does Not Work," *Educational Psychology Review*, vol. 26, no. 2, 2013.
10. "Chartered College of Teaching," [Online]. Available: https://chartered.college/
11. J. Mannion and N. Mercer, "Learning to learn: Improving Attainment, closing the Gap at Key Stage 3," *The Curriculum Journal*, vol. 27, pp. 1–26, 2016.
12. J. Mannion and K. McAllister, Fear Is the Mind Killer: Why Learning to Learn Deserves Lesson Time - and How to make it work for Your Pupils, John Catt, 2020.
13. K. Robinson and L. Aronica, *Creative Schools: The Grassroots Revolution That's Transforming Education*, Penguin Books, 2016.
14. D. C. Simmons and E. J. Kameenui, "A Focus on Curriculum Design: When Children Fail," *Focus on Exception Children*, vol. 28, no. 7, pp. 1–16, 1996.
15. "Future of Education and Skills 2030," OECD, 2015 [Online]. Available: https://www.oecd.org/en/about/projects/future-of-education-and-skills-2030.html
16. OECD, "Learning Compass 2030," 2019. [Online]. Available: https://www.oecd.org/content/dam/oecd/en/about/projects/edu/education-2040/1-1-learning-compass/OECD_Learning_Compass_2030_Concept_Note_Series.pdf
17. OECD, "Future of Education and Skills 2030," 2019.
18. "All Our Futures: Creativity, Culture and Education," National Advisory Committee on Creative and Cultural Education, 1999.
19. N. Runyon, "Why "Power Skills" is the New Term for Soft Skills in the Hybrid Work World," Thomson Reuters, 18 February 2022. [Online]. Available: https://www.thomsonreuters.com/en-us/posts/legal/power-skills-rebranding/
20. A. Kingsley, "Is Knowledge Obsolete?," Forbes Technology Council, 07 March 2022. [Online]. Available: https://www.forbes.com/councils/forbestechcouncil/2022/03/04/is-knowledge-obsolete/
21. J. Sibbald, "Greater Manchester's MBacc: What Digital Skills Education Could Look Like," AQi, 12 October 2023. [Online]. Available: https://www.aqi.org.uk/blogs/greater-manchesters-mbacc-what-digital-skills-education-could-look-like/
22. H. G. Schmidt and J. H. Moust, *Factors Affecting Small-Group Tutorial Learning: A Review of Research*, Routledge, 2000, pp. 19–51.
23. C. E. Hmelo-Silver, "Problem-Based Learning: What and How Do Students Learn?," *Educational Psychology Review*, vol. 16, pp. 235–266, 2004.
24. "Why Is Project-Based Learning Important? The Many Merits of Using Project-Based Learning in the Classroom," Edutopia, 19 October 2007. [Online]. Available: https://www.edutopia.org/project-based-learning-guide-importance
25. "National Curriculum," Department for Education, 2014. [Online]. Available: https://www.gov.uk/government/collections/national-curriculum
26. A. Kingsley, *My School & Multi Academy Trust Growth Guide*, John Catt Education, 2023.
27. D. Christodoulou, *Seven Myths about Education*, Routledge, 2014.
28. E. D. Hirsch, Jr, *Cultural Literacy: What Every American Needs to Know*, Random House USA Inc, 1988.

29. D. T. Willingham, *Why Don't Students Like School?: A Cognitive Scientist Answers Questions About How the Mind Works and What It Means for the Classroom*, Jossey-Bass, 2021.
30. R. Luckin, *Machine Learning and Human Intelligence: The future of education for the 21st century*, UCL IOE Press, 2018.
31. L. Crehan, *Cleverlands: The Secrets Behind the Success of the World's Education Superpowers*, Unbound, 2018.
32. L. Jin, *Cultural Foiundations of Learning: East and West*, Cambridge University Press, 2012.
33. D. Stipek, *Motivation to Learn: Integrating Theory and Practice*, Allyn and Bacon, 2002.
34. P. Armstrong, "Blooms Taxonomy," Vanderbilt University Center for Teaching, 2010.
35. L. Anderson, D. Krathwohl, P. Airasian, K. Cruikshank, P. Pintrich, R. Mayer, J. Raths and M. Wittrock, *Taxonomy for Learning, Teaching, and Assessing, A: A Revision of Bloom's Taxonomy of Educational Objectives*, Pearson, 2001.
36. M. Forehand, "Blooms Taxonomy - From Emerging Perspectives on Learning, Teaching and Technology," 2011. [Online]. Available: https://cft.vanderbilt.edu/wp-content/uploads/sites/59/BloomsTaxonomy-mary-forehand.pdf
37. M. Sellars, R. Fakirmohammad, L. Bui, J. Fishetti, S. Niyozov, R. Reynolds and N. Thapliyal, "Conversations on Critical Thinking: Can Critical Thinking Find Its Way Forward as the Skill Set and Mindset of the Century?" *Education Sciences*, vol. 8, no. 4, 2018.
38. P. A. Facione, *Critical Thinking: What It Is and Why It Counts*, Measured Reasons and The California Academic Press, 1992.
39. P. E. Facione, "Critical Thinking: A Statement of Expert Consensus for Purposes of Educational Assessment and Instruction," The California Academic Press, 1990.
40. B. Donovan, "Soft Skills - definition," 2024 [Online]. Available: https://www.britannica.com/money/soft-skills
41. A. Tang, *The Leader's Guide to Resilience: How to Use Soft Skills to Get Hard Results*, FT Publishing International, 2021.
42. M. Brent, *The Leader's Guide to Managing People: How to Use Soft Skills to Get Hard Result*, FT Publishing International, 2013.
43. C. S. Chong, "Classroom tips to Help Integrate Soft Skills," EtonX, 1 04 2019. [Online]. Available: https://etonx.com/classroom-tips-to-help-integrate-soft-skills/
44. P. A. Jennings, A. A. DeMauro and P. Misschenko, *Handbook of Mindfulness-Based Programmes*, Routledge, 2019.
45. P. E. Jennings, *The Trauma–Sensitive Classroom – Building Resilience with Compassionate Teaching*, W.W. Norton & Company, 2018.
46. B. J. Ellis, J. Bianchi, V. Griskevicius and W. E. Frankenhuis, "Beyond Risk and Protective Factors: An Adaptation-Based Approach to Resilience," *Perspectives on Psychological Science*, vol. 12, no. 4, p. 561–587, 2017.
47. T. R. Hoerr, *The Formative Five: Fostering Grit, Empathy, and Other Success Skills Every Student Needs*, ASCD, 2016.
48. A. L. Costa and B. Kallick, *Learning and Leading with Habits of Mind: 16 Essential Characteristics for Success*, ASCD, 2008.
49. A. L. Duckworth, "Grit: The Power of Passion and Perseverance," TED Talks, 09 May 2013. [Online]. Available: www.youtube.com/watch?v=H14bBuluwB8
50. A. Duckworth, "Grit: Why Passion and Resilience are the Secrets to Success," Vermilion, 2017.

When it comes to system growth, is leadership always putting the children first?

I've included this question in my book as I feel that it is one of the biggest "elephants" in the room. That said, I am keen to delve deeper as I write this and see if the perceptions genuinely match the truth. We probably need to start with what I am referring to in terms of system growth, and I should add the caveat that it is framed largely based on my experiences and roles in the English education system. As always, there is quite a bit of scene setting before we get to the questions.

HOW THE EDUCATION LANDSCAPE IS CHANGING

As you will likely know, England has been transitioning from a broad base of local authority schools with a gradual move to schools gaining academy status. They were introduced by former Prime Minister **Tony Blair** in the early 2000s, but the vast majority have become academies since a change of government in May 2010, when legislation, the **2010 Academies Act** [1], significantly expanded the programme's remit.

Prior to the act, only secondary schools could become academies, and they were required to secure a sponsor to convert. Since 2010, primary schools have also been permitted to become academies, free schools [2] have been introduced, and a sponsor is no longer required for conversion.

There was significant appeal in the early stages, and there were financial incentives in funding terms when initially moving from local authority control, which I might add is certainly no longer the case, but more broadly, it was attractive given the amount of local autonomy an academy had under its new status. Supporting that view, in the **OECD**'s [3] **Programme for International Student Assessment** (PISA) [4] data, this resulted in England becoming the highest-ranked country in "school autonomy" over resource allocation in the 2012 PISA rankings. Albeit their focus was on curriculum and assessment, not broader operational autonomy, in the context of impact on outcomes, they stated: *"PISA shows that school systems that grant more autonomy to schools to define and elaborate their curricula and assessments tend to perform better than systems that don't grant such autonomy, even after accounting for countries' national income"* [5].

State of the nation

According to the **2024 Academies Benchmark report** [6], as of March 2024, there were 10,746 academy schools in England, with a further 851 in the pipeline to convert. All of these are part of a multi-academy trust "MAT" (or single-academy trust, "SAT") cohort of more than 1,300 trusts in England. In the **FFT Education Data** report in July 2024 titled **"The current state of play for MATs"** [7], they reported that the vast majority of academies are part of a MAT: 89%, with the remaining 11% operating as SATs. They also noted, *"There are currently fewer MATs than there were in 2020, but there's been a marked increase in the number of larger MATs over the last few years, although smaller MATs of fewer than ten schools still make up 75% of all MATs"* (Table 3.1).

In my book *My School and Multi-Academy Trust Growth Guide* [8] (2023), John Catt Education, I provide a much more detailed "state of the nation" in terms of the MAT landscape and also highlight the gradual shift from smaller to medium and larger-scale MATs, as reflected in the table above. The Fischer Family

Table 3.1 MAT Sizes 2020–24

	2019	2020	2021	2022	2023
Average MAT Size	6.25	6.67	7.1	7.54	8.1
Largest MAT Size	72	74	75	79	89
MATs of 2–9 Schools	1,014	977	949	921	881
MATs of 10–19 Schools	144	163	185	198	219
MATs of 20+ Schools	48	54	63	69	78
Total No. of MATs	1,206	1,194	1,197	1,188	1,178

Source: FFT education datalab.

Foundation (FFT) data groups 2–9 school MATs into one group, but as that's where much of the activity is, I wanted to shine a slightly more narrow spotlight on that cohort as well.

As you can see from the graph, using data from **The Education Company** [9] in 2023, between 2018 and 2022, the number of small 2 and 3 school MATs had reduced, the 4 and 5 school MATs had remained relatively stable on the chart, but the larger 6+ school MAT numbers had grown significantly. This certainly aligns with both government ambitions and an underlying need to utilise economies of scale within the current and very challenging funding landscape (Figure 3.1).

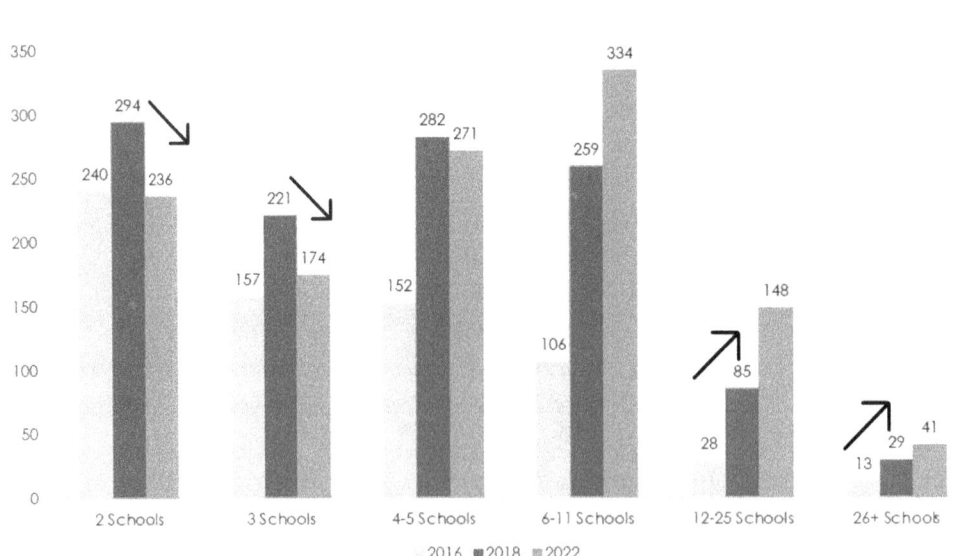

Figure 3.1 Size of Multi Academy Trusts, by number of schools 2016-2022. (From FFT Datalab.)

For more regional nuance, the July 2024 *TES Magazine* article "**MAT Tracker: mapping the country's multi-academy trusts**" [10], they highlighted the following: "*Analysis of official data also shows that the average MAT oversees eight schools, and academies in the South West tend to belong to the biggest MATs, with 13.4 schools on average.*" It is worth noting that there are still over 1,000 single academy trusts in England, despite a sustained move towards bigger groups of schools, which aligns with an objective of "Strong and Sustainable MATs."

In my role as a MAT chair, the discussions around growth are high on the agenda and have been for some years; initially, it's probably fair to say that it was driven by looking at leveraging those economies of scale, building a broader base of excellence at both primary and secondary, and sustainability. However, for most schools, it was also brought to the fore by the Department for Education's 2022 **"Opportunity for All: Strong Schools with Great Teachers for Your Child"** [11] white paper, accelerating the aspirations for all schools to become academies and each academy trust to be on a path to a sustainable size by 2023. This then shaped the Draft Schools Bill.

Growth at the forefront

So, growth and consolidation of the MAT landscape is not a surprise, albeit we might acknowledge that the draft Schools Bill in its present form was withdrawn by **Gillian Keegan** in December of 2022 and did not become policy. Much of its intent has continued to drive activities, however, and for many smaller MATs, the concept of 7,500 students or at least 10 schools have become very familiar numbers and a catalyst for reviewing our strategic growth plans with a fresh pair of eyes. For some, it's to aim for that level, and for other larger MATs, it has been to look at how they might respond to opportunities that come their way, consolidate, and review capacity.

So, while the white paper isn't a direct factor anymore, I also hope we all acknowledge the sentiment and strategic expectation Nadhim Zahawi covered within the paper is still very much the ambition of the department when he stated, "*all schools will either be in strong trusts this decade or have "plans to join or form one.*" The tipping point has been passed, the majority of our mainstream school's landscape is now under the academy umbrella, and the government (as of 2024) sees sufficient scale and capacity of MATs as a key measure.

To further remind us of this underlying expectation and driver, Rt Hon Minister Nick Gibb (Minister of State for Education) responded to a written question on the 2030 ambition for all schools to be part of a strong trust as set out in the aforementioned whitepaper in parliament on 9th February 2023. Mr. Gibb renewed the government's aim to see "the vast majority of schools in trusts before 2030" [12]. More specifically he said:

The Department is focused on continuing to improve standards in schools, providing the best education for children, including for those from disadvantaged backgrounds and with special educational needs. The best way for this to happen is for all schools to be in strong families of schools, benefitting from the support of the best in the group, and the resilience that comes from being part of a larger group of schools. That is why, over time, the Department would like all schools to be in a strong multi-academy trust, because we see the positive impact it can have on children's lives. If we get this right, then we will see the vast majority of schools in trusts before 2030. The Department is exploring how to further support the growth of strong multi-academy trusts through the Regulation and Commissioning Review.

It's fair to say this sparked discussion and debate, not least as we have been on a bit of a "journey" from the narrative that big MATs are best, to wanting to protect diversity and locally focused MATs and now back to what feels full circle towards larger MATs, with sufficient capacity and scale to deliver both change and stability being the new preference. **Harris Federation** CEO, **Sir David Moynihan,** said in a 2022 article in **Schools Week** titled **"White paper: What academy shakeup means for trusts, councils and schools"** [13] that *"overall the reforms created a coherent blueprint"* and the **Confederation of School Trusts (CST)** welcomed the all-MAT drive.

It's certainly not unreasonable to conclude that, given the continued funding and financial challenges for schools and MATs, the economies of scale and financial reserves of larger MATs compared to small local entities present them as a more secure long-term option. Or you could just fund all schools better; just saying!

As I said in my introduction, I wear quite a few hats, one of which is on the Regional Schools Director's Advisory Board for the East of England. I'm serving my third term on the board and can see first hand the acceleration in both conversions and consolidations over the last few years. I will share this view again, with the caveat that no one size fits all, the general concept of MATs growing to a critical mass (will be a different measure for each) to have stability, capacity for continuous improvement, financial economies of scale, better retention through progression options, etc. I maintain it is a really sound one and I support it. I understand where the broader government message of having strong MATs was intended, so I think, as a rule, growth is definitely good, but nuance is key here, and it's about the timing, pace, alignment of values, and direction that are the real keys to successful decision-making.

I most definitely don't think this is a universal view, and because no one size fits all, in some cases there will be perfectly sound reasons not to grow your MAT; for example, we have no desire to spread to schools beyond our "sphere of influence," which is defined by us internally as a maximum of a 30-minute drive. To evidence further the national mindset data captured by the **Education Company** and the

British Educational Suppliers Association [14] (BESA) in November 2022 [15], it was highlighted that:

- 70% of trusts are planning to grow through the acquisition of other academies.
- 63% of trusts expect academies to ask them to join.
- 56% of trusts expect to have to encourage academies to join their trust.
- 10% of trusts expect to be encouraged to merge with another trust.

You might be thinking, I certainly am, that it's all well and good having a national focus on growing our academy system and ensuring all schools end up academised, but why do we want to grow, and do we know if it actually is a beneficial thing to do?

Why do we want to grow?

This has been at the heart of discussions for strategic planning within our trust and, to be honest, it's the reason that I have been approached and invited to visit so many other trusts across the country over the last few years. It's fair to say that in any organisation we need to have a constant appraisal of our current structures and organisational state of play, our areas of strength, and, of course, our own areas for development. We will likely all find areas for development, and if we don't, then it's fair to say we probably aren't looking hard enough or simply not asking the right questions. With that in mind, how does our core focus on school improvement find itself directly linked to a broader conversation about growth?

There are quite a few areas that fall within this, so perhaps we could jump to our risk register and start running down those key rows that we reflect on a termly basis, so if our challenge, for example, is staff retention, then perhaps it's because we can't provide sufficient opportunities within a single or small cluster of schools for staff progression. Perhaps we don't have the capacity either centrally or within our schools to effectively support curriculum improvement, and a growth strategy could unlock that by bringing in other schools with suitable specialist experience. I always pause at this point and think of Sir David Carter's book *Leading Academy Trusts: Why some fail and most don't* [16] and his view that our aim should always be that every school should be a "**net capacity giver**" within your MAT.

These are just two examples, so let's consider a few of the most common drivers I have encountered while visiting other trusts. I should also declare quite a few of these apply to my own MAT considerations as well. This is an ever-changing list, but I think it's a good starter, and as with any summary, I share this in no particular order.

Drivers for growth

2022 white paper's aspirations for growth by 2030

I had to put this one first because we've just been chatting about it a few pages back. Seriously though, whether we like it or not, this has been a massive talking point for MAT leaders and LA school governing bodies. While the intentions laid out in the white paper haven't quite transformed into concrete policy, they've certainly set the stage for future growth ambitions. We're all aware that it's still a national focus to build system capacity and push forward with the academisation process.

Concerns about isolation

One thing we can't ignore is the concern of being left on our own. As we plan for the future, it's only natural to wonder about the decisions other schools and MATs are making. While our primary focus should be on our own schools and trusts, it's wise to consider the broader landscape and strategic plans of nearby schools. For instance, if we aim to establish a centre of excellence in our area, knowing which schools excel in certain aspects can help us form valuable partnerships. It's worth asking ourselves, *"What happens if we wait and all local schools have already joined other trusts?"* Without taking action, we risk being caught off guard and unable to grow as we wish. Therefore, it's essential to identify schools in our vicinity that share our values and could benefit from closer collaboration. This ensures we're proactive rather than reactive when planning for our school's future.

Diminished local authority support and capacity

This one's a bit tricky and definitely varies by region, but here's the gist: as more schools transition to academies, fewer remain under the direct support of local authorities. In some areas, this shift has reduced the LA's capacity due to decreased funding. While some regions have handled this transition well, others have seen a decline in support, prompting schools to consider joining established MATs. Schools may feel frustrated by limited access to services and support, especially as the LA's resources dwindle. Despite the challenges, local authorities still play a crucial role, especially in supporting vulnerable children, providing governance support, and handling admissions. It's important to assess whether staying with the LA offers the best support or if joining a MAT could provide more benefits.

Financial factors

Finance is always a big factor, isn't it? Changing from an LA school to an academy doesn't magically unlock new funding anymore, like it might have back in 2010. So why does finance remain a key driver? The concept of "economies of scale" becomes essential. By pooling resources, schools can reduce costs, such as sharing staff or negotiating better deals for services. For example, a group of ten schools purchasing services together can negotiate discounts compared to buying individually. Sharing staff across schools can also help reduce salary costs. While you don't need to be part of a MAT to benefit from shared resources, developing informal relationships with other schools can lead to cost savings and potential collaborations.

Leadership changes

It's true – leadership changes often trigger schools to consider their options and potentially change their status. Whenever there's a shift in leadership, it's natural to pause and reflect on what's next for the school. We'll delve deeper into this topic later, but for now, it's enough to say that leadership transitions provide an opportunity to reassess and plan for the future.

New schools planned in your area

When new schools are planned nearby, it often raises questions for trustees or governors. Should we bid to operate it if we're already a MAT? Even if it's a presumptive process managed by the LA or a free school bid, the opening of a new school in your area presents an opportunity to consider. Could we add value, or could the new school add value to us? After weighing these questions, it often boils down to our capacity to manage a successful bid and project, and whether we know how to proceed. My experience with free school bids taught me that no matter how logical the next step seems, there are no guarantees, which is why our growth strategy should explore all opportunities.

I've been involved in three free school bids. We were successful in opening a brand-new secondary school, then successful again bidding to open a feeder primary for the secondary. We got a constructive grilling at interviews for both, but a fair chance to share our vision and values. To keep an air of positivity here, I won't mention our third bid, where we lost out to a faith school, which was interviewed under a different process. I may have just mentioned it.

Concerns about standards

It's no secret that improving standards often requires adequate resources, staff, and specialists. The mainstream media may simplify this as a good versus bad teacher issue, but it's more complex than that. Schools sometimes struggle due to a lack of time, tools, and staff capacity. If a nearby MAT is excelling in these areas, it makes sense to consider partnering with them to learn and improve. When struggling to find a clear plan for intervention or the right people to support change, looking outside for assistance can be a smart move.

Ofsted or regional schools director intervention

Occasionally, a tough Ofsted inspection or concerns raised by the regional schools director can drive change. If a school remains "requires improvement" over multiple inspections or significant concerns are highlighted, intervention might be necessary. This can involve moving a school or even an entire MAT to ensure it receives the support needed. Being involved with the Regional Schools Advisory Board has given me insight into the challenges faced by academies and trusts, and sometimes intervention is vital for the benefit of students. While planning for growth, don't forget to keep a close eye on existing schools to avoid unexpected drivers of change.

Recruitment and retention

Who isn't concerned about this in the education sector? The conversation goes beyond pay and workload to why someone would want to join our school or trust and how we can retain their skills. We might be proud of our schools, but it's crucial to assess what makes us attractive and how we can improve. Larger trusts can offer more progression opportunities and central support, while smaller trusts might have a strong community ethos. Finding the right balance between scale and individuality is essential to attract and retain talent.

Approaches from other multi-academy trusts

It's inevitable – sometimes, all your internal planning is disrupted when another MAT approaches you. If you lead a successful school, academy, or MAT, you've likely experienced this. The key is whether you dismiss these offers or share them with your trust chair and trustees. This serves as a reality check on how others perceive your schools and trust. It might reflect your trust's engagement within the local area, marketing efforts, recent results, or other factors.

Specialisms

I am keen not to miss the unique specialisms that some schools and trusts have, especially around Special Educational Needs (SEN) or alternative provisions. As I have discovered on my physical travels, some also have a unique focus on climate and sustainability, the arts as well as plenty more. This could be a driver to consolidate with other like-minded schools or an opportunity to expand a specialism offer or consolidate that expertise across a broader regional or national base.

You'll likely align with a number of these, and equally, some won't apply. That, of course, is why the decision to go is not black and white and can only be decided upon once you have considered all of the factors specific to your schools and trust. This summary from **Caroline Derbyshire** is a good example:

> *Saffron Academy Trust in Essex has grown surely but steadily from 4 to 9 schools since 2019 and in addition we have formed a Teaching School Hub. Our emphasis is on school improvement rather than growth for growth's sake.*
>
> *We aspire to provide non-selective state education of exceptional quality, with great teachers in every classroom, so we are careful not to take on too many projects too quickly. Remaining human in scale is important to us because our approach to school improvement is bespoke and applied and involves changing cultures in schools not just performance outcomes. We do it through supporting schools with the resources, expertise and the systems they need, and we are careful to make sure that these add value to the school's own improvement plans. As such we are keen to remain a medium-sized MAT of perhaps 5 secondaries and 10 primaries at most.*
>
> ***Remaining human in scale (I line-manage, visit schools, and meet headteachers every week) is crucial to our approach.*** *We try to do things "with" and not "to" our schools. Our Headteachers form an Executive Group. They are the senior, not middle leaders in the Trust.*
>
> *- **Caroline Derbyshire, CEO, Saffron Academy Trust***

Within the strategic plan that I drafted for my trust, we subsequently refined our main questions for discussion down into this pseudo-checklist:

- **Student Outcomes** – Could this change positively affect student performance and achievement?
- **Financial Benefit** – Does it enhance the potential spending per student on educational resources?
- **Staff Recruitment and Retention** – Will it help in both attracting and retaining staff?
- **What's Right for the Community** – How does this change fit with our commitment to being a community-focused school that offers equal opportunities for everyone?
- **Target Audience** – What age group are we focusing on for growth and developing key stage excellence?

- **Capacity and Pace** – Does the trust have the capacity right now to expand, and how quickly is that realistically achievable?
- **Department for Education's (DfE) Broader Aspirations** – Does this align with our wider plans to grow and become an even stronger and more sustainable MAT?

Central to the consideration of any growth opportunity, is the question of whether we believe we can genuinely add value. As a trust, we consider we have honed expertise in certain areas and, therefore, there are some opportunities where we believe our involvement would bring about a better outcome for all stakeholders.

This connects to our sense of moral purpose. It should not be a case of always moving with a particular policy paradigm: core values need to be kept in mind in the strategic decision-making process.

– Dr. Helen Price, CEO, Hampton Academies Trust

Is growth good?

This is something I have wrestled with for quite some time, and I suspect most if not all, system leaders have too. It's not explicitly a "big is better" conversation because there isn't a linear scale that says, for every school you add to your MAT you get x% better (as if), but we might also conclude this is an arc rather than a straight line, and just to make things complicated it really depends on what you are measuring. I'm probably going to need to keep this relatively simple for fear of it ending up becoming a book in itself, so let's have two categories: "curriculum and outcomes" and "operational efficiency." They are pretty broad and possibly even clumsy categories, but I reckon they help differentiate for our measuring criteria. From the 11 topics or drivers for growth, you'll see not all are explicitly about delivering a shift in grades in the traditional sense, and are much more about long-term sustainability.

We probably also need to flag at this point that there are some amazing MATs and some amazing LA schools and some less than great in both categories. While we need to group for the purpose of discussion, I really don't want to miss the point that every school is unique, and ultimately, the "status" badge over the door doesn't define it.

Outcomes

Let's go straight to this one, as I am well aware you can always find a statistic to suit your argument in both directions, but at the heart of this is to ask, do MATs have better outcomes than LA schools, and do larger MATs perform better than smaller ones?

This is a really subjective thing to measure, partially because, particularly under the academy sponsor status, MATs will be adding schools requiring support and improvement to their families on a regular basis, so when you measure outcomes, many of those schools that are not where they need to be will be recent additions to MATs. And for balance, there are plenty of academies that are not performing to the highest academic levels or are coasting, so again, the badge doesn't always define the outcome.

Let's have a look at some of the surveys and research that have been undertaken. **The Local Government Association** [17] undertook research in 2023 and their study found that, as of 31 January 2023, 93% of council-maintained schools were rated outstanding or good, compared to 87% of academies that were graded since they converted [18]. You might reflect on why it's not surprising that, in their capacity, they were keen to highlight this outcome, but **Dr. Mary Bousted**, joint general secretary of the **National Education Union (NEU)**, said the findings *"highlight the inherent harm of the Government's push to full academisation within multi-academy trusts."*

Perhaps unsurprisingly, this announcement was followed by an article in *SchoolsWeek*: "Fact check: Do council schools really outperform academies?" [19], which reported *"there are some big flaws in the main findings picked out by the Local Government Association (LGA), which have been seized on to call for a return of new council schools and to criticise the government's academy reforms."*

The article picked up on my earlier point explaining that there were only two routes to becoming an academy; schools with higher Ofsted ratings can choose to convert, but schools deemed to be struggling after being rated "inadequate" are taken away from council control. Those sponsored academies are forced to join a trust, which is tasked with improving them. **Steve Rollett**, deputy chief executive of the **CST** [20], pointed out that the report *"fails to recognise that over time the trust sector has taken on most of the schools that were long term challenges."* He also summarised that *"the LA sector has been left "with an unrepresentative and incomparable body of schools" – as all of its failing schools have been taken away and turned into academies."*

On a more focused assessment for those sponsored schools that were required to academise, in the same article, **Professor Daniel Muijs**, a former head of research at Ofsted, is quoted as saying *"the 'test' for sponsored academies was whether they are improving. And data in the actual report suggests they are indeed the fastest improving group."*

Are we any better informed from that? I don't think so, and as I said, we can craft data to suit our position most of the time. You have hopefully picked up from my first chapter, but I am also not of the view that an Ofsted grade is not something we should hold too much stock in, but it's all we have had for a while.

In a 2017 report from the **Education Policy Institute** [21], **"School Performance in Academy Chains and Local Authorities"** [22], their key findings follow: *"Overall, we find little difference in the performance of schools in academy chains and local authorities. The type of school – academy or local authority – is, therefore, less important than being in a high-performing school group."* This may seem unhelpful given the parity reflected, but I think the closing part about being in a high-performing school group is a very salient one and aligns with a number of the 11 "reasons" I shared earlier. In perfect alignment with my earlier comment of recognising there are good and not-so-good schools under every banner, they also stated, *"Indeed, we* *find that both academy chains and local authorities feature at the very top of our performance tables, and at the very bottom."*

I could go on with articles from the **NEU** and others arguing against the academy process and others from the **CST** with strong positive perspectives, but I am not sure any really help. The variability is so great that actually you are always going to be looking at the specific MAT you might want to join, undertaking the right due diligence and how it aligns, adds value and benefits your cohort of children. It's such a case-by-case process; the best guidance is to highlight what to consider rather than provide a fictional yes/no recommendation for you.

However, just when we might feel at an impasse in evidencing the impact on outcomes, we need to make sure we don't forget the second category: operational efficiency. In practice, this is where there are genuinely far more tangible and evidenced gains across the system ... but not exclusively. I'd start by recommending a few questions you might want to consider:

- Will our trust be stronger by growing further or will our school benefit from joining this trust?
- What are our key measures of being "strong"?
- Will both parties be a positive capacity giver to the trust?
- Will there be more opportunities for greater staff retention and progression?
- Will there be a positive impact for learners?
- Will our broader capacity and experience be enhanced?
- Will we be financially stronger/more resilient as a result?
- What is our board appetite for risk?
- Will there be an opportunity to broaden our collective offer?
- Will we be able to attract additional funding?
- Will we be able to attract or retain staff more easily?
- Do any of the skills from the incoming school or MAT align with our current development priorities?

When we start thinking of tackling recruitment and retention, scaling our systems, competitive purchasing, economies of scale, and funding a stronger central service stream, the arguments make a lot more sense. The **British Educational Suppliers Association** [14], for example, shared in their 2023 **MAT Financial Insights survey** the growing number of MATs that have implemented central purchasing models. Twenty percent of trusts are now looking at GAG (general annual grant) pooling (including for reserves), of which I am not a fan, but if I take just the example of centralised purchasing, in their survey, 21% of schools delivered substantial savings from a centralised purchasing model, 76% delivered some savings, and only 3% saw negligible savings. When the topic switched to centralised human resources procurement, those numbers were 19% substantial, 66% some, and only 19% negligible and were very similar for the procurement of utilities and estate management services.

A separate report, **"New report shows practical strategies for MAT growth"** [23], published in *Education Business* magazine in February 2023 showed one noticeably upwards trend was towards GAG pooling alongside greater centralisation of resources. Perhaps unsurprisingly in the current funding climate was an article in *FE News,* titled **"More MATs pooling GAG and reserves to look after 'financially weaker schools' or 'target additional resource'"** [24], which was from the findings of a survey among 155 trusts exploring how they were evolving their approaches to needs-based budgeting. The 2024 **"Academies Benchmark Report"** by **Kreston** [25], indicated that 61% of trusts are now fully centralised. If your approach is to utilise a top slice (we do), then an interesting item in the report was that for small MATs, the average top slice was 7.4%; for medium, it was 6.3%; and for large, it was 5.4%. The variation in average rates between small, medium, and large MATs is noticeable, suggesting synergies and savings are being achieved as trusts grow.

Hopefully we have set a fairly broad scene for this topic and there are a few awkward questions I wanted to put on your radar for consideration.

THE POWER OF PERCEPTION

Do leaders delay growth, such as joining MATs for the sake of autonomy and independence rather than the real needs of students and school?

Goodness, this one really is an awkward question. It is on my list as much as because I think I have experienced it myself. "Think" is a key word in that sentence, as often it is about perceptions. However, I see regions where there has been growth in MATs, some primary, some secondary led, some a nice mix, and within that, there are primary schools who are adamant it is not for them and they are happy as a "stand-alone" LA school, only to then reach out as soon as there is a change of leadership at the school.

That might be a coincidence; it might be a justifiable lack of perceived "value added" when moving into an established MAT, or it might be a desire to retain the autonomy of their schools for as long as they can.

It's a touchy subject, as I have never heard a head say that is the primary driver, but it's hard not to feel that way. This probably feels like a topic where I am singling out "selfish" heads of schools, but I'm really not. Joining a MAT is by no means a golden ticket to success; there has to be the right fit and benefit to both parties. Perhaps, of course, under a sponsorship status, that will be a little more one sided.

I asked **Tim Coulson**, chief executive of **Unity Schools Partnership** [26], who has spent over 40 years in schools, local government, and the Department for Education for his initial response to my question and it was fairly succinct "yes." Some school leaders do delay growth, to retain autonomy and independence. Tim sits with me on the current **Department for Education Advisory board** for the East of England [27], a role I have done for just over five years, so it is fair to say we get to see a lot of the activities, discussions, and movement across the region.

I also spoke to **Dr. Ian Young**, CEO of **Peterborough Keys Academies Trust** [28], who shared a slightly different perspective. He commented: "*In my experience, such delays can arise from the governing body rather than the headteacher. This can be down to a perception that the school will be diminished or swallowed up somehow by a larger organisation. The headteacher may see more clearly benefits that it could bring.*" That's an interesting balancing point. We naturally assign the ultimate decision to the head teacher, but as I am sure you will appreciate, the decision is made by the governing body, not the head, albeit I hope they are allowed to inform the discussions heavily. Perhaps this also reflects the variability of governance "strength" and accountability.

Using the **"Scheme of Delegation"** within an academy, that decision-making falls to the board of trustees. Just as an aside, while most CEOs do currently, since 2024, best practice is that trust senior leadership team (SLT) members do not sit on the board of trustees.

Different voices

Perhaps there are other voices feeding into this conversation. There is no secret that most LAs would rather maintain control over their local schools and will often be quite vocal in dismissing the pathway for schools to join more formally. In fact, it is somewhat of a self-fulfilling prophecy: the fewer schools remaining under the LA remit, the smaller the central funding pot they are able to retain, the smaller the team and services they can offer their schools and, over time, potentially, that encourage schools to look elsewhere for support. As a rule, the union voice has been one that is largely against academisation, with the **NEU** [29], for example, setting out their "**case against academisation**" [30] in 2022, claiming that academisation is driving down staff pay, terms, and conditions; alienating communities; and has caused the fragmentation of the education system. That's pretty direct.

As chair of a community MAT in my city, I do not recognise that at all; we stick to the "Burgundy Book" for all our staff pay and conditions (STPC); we are wholly community-focused and have created a close-knit cluster of schools that remain outward looking. It's OK. Before you think it, I will also acknowledge that no two trusts are the same, and some likely have different perspectives or priorities.

The NEU shared plenty of research, including a 2018 report by **University College London's Institute for Education** [31], which found "*there was no positive impact on the attainment and progress scores of pupils in MATs when compared to equivalent non-MAT schools. Pupils in larger MATs (those with 16-plus schools) did worse, particularly in secondary schools.*" An **Education Policy Institute (EPI)** report [32], published in 2018, stated, "*It revealed that academy chains are* *"disproportionately represented" among the worst performing groups of primary schools, with 12 making it into the bottom 20."*

To be honest, there were dozens of similar articles I could have included here, but, and this won't be a shock, there are just as many highlighting the benefits, too. On the point of data flagged above by the EPI, the 2023 **House of Lords** report **"Improving schools' performance: Are multi-academy trusts the answer?"** [33] explained that many schools joined MATs because they were underperforming; therefore, they started from a lower base. The government highlighted that more than seven out of 10 sponsored academies were now rated good or outstanding compared to about one in 10 of the local authority-maintained schools they replaced. One thing that is acknowledged is variability; figures in the same report did acknowledge that MATs had a greater variation in performance. The higher-performing MATs performed better than the better-performing maintained schools, and the lower-performing MATs performed worse than the worst-performing maintained schools.

Ofsted, those lovely folks we all like, undertook research [34] in 2019 based on interviews with people who work in MATs, where they identified plenty of advantages and disadvantages. These are summarized in the following list.

Advantages included:

- improved back-office support enabling leaders to spend more time on "instructional leadership" rather than finance, administration, and HR
- economies of scale in contracts such as cleaning and catering
- challenges and support offered by the MAT, leading directly to school improvement
- sharing data with other schools and moderating it together
- support from peers and MAT central staff
- opportunities for collaboration, such as shared planning and examples of good practice
- workforce improvements such as training, opportunities for progression, recruitment, and leadership support

Drawbacks identified by the staff interviewed included:

- a proportion of the school's budget being paid to the MAT, with the school not being confident of receiving commensurate benefits
- centralisation and loss of decision-making power
- slower decision-making
- perceived pressure on MATs to expand and concern about how this could impact individual schools
- difficulties sharing good practice because of schools not being located close together or having different characteristics

The autonomy fear

It's an encapsulation of real feedback, so who am I to challenge? However, I do have to highlight that nobody is comfortable saying, "I will lose some autonomy." It's a natural "elephant in the room" and an entirely understandable one. Sometimes that journey also includes some of the team losing their roles altogether, so who wouldn't be defensive of that journey? I'm also really concerned by the departure rates of heads and senior leaders from education altogether. That is a far more pressing challenge, which I tackle in another chapter.

It seems fair to say that with so many pressures on our schools, perhaps the mental and time capacity needed to consider joining or becoming a MAT is not practical. This quote is taken from a section 8 inspection report of a primary school in Birmingham. I won't mention the name for obvious reasons: *"The process of converting to an academy has placed a high demand on the energies of governors, the head teacher and other senior leaders and it has distracted them from focusing on improving the quality of teaching and learning."* I suspect we can empathise with that.

Now, I acknowledge I am a supporter of the academy system. There, I have said it; my opinion is shaped by having had roles in multiple academy trusts and supporting schools that transition into a trust to gain the needed support for their school improvement journey. When done right, I have seen the positive impacts. The potential for capacity in a trust system, holding specialist support centrally to support our schools, can be hugely purposeful, albeit as **Sir David Carter** said in his book **Leading Academy Trusts** [35], the sweet spot is when every school is a "net capacity giver." Let's also keep balance; not every MAT is fab, and for some schools, they really might not be the right fit ... but over time, that choice will diminish, and we won't grow stood in splendid isolation.

So, do we sometimes see leaders choosing not to academise their school in order to protect their own role? Well, it appears that way to me sometimes, but in practice, it may well be that they don't see the "win" that will benefit everyone. I couldn't find any published work that backed up this perception, perhaps because it never happens, or perhaps the elephant is just too big to talk about when it refers to peers. I get it, but someone has to ask the question, even if to be hopefully reassured by the outcome.

In terms of timings and schools changing status after a new incoming head, well, they may well see things differently, and I have never met a head who is not intentionally thinking of their children as their absolute priority. Let's be open. Ask any employee what they value most in their job, and they will likely feel valued and respected and have a degree of autonomy over their job. These are all very human and consistent values, and we should highlight that when we have discussions around growth, then those emotions cannot trump the long-term future of a school.

Take the lead

Given who the ultimate decision-makers are, I would challenge our trustees or governing bodies to take accountability, undertake an assessment of the pros and cons for growth on a regular basis, and signpost their decision-making in their minutes. Transparency avoids less informed assumptions. MATs should have a strategic growth plan, something that is refined and revisited every year, a document to ensure all stakeholders are on message and aligned. That won't likely exist in a LA school, but it doesn't mean an annual review of their status couldn't be included in the governing body calendar.

Just as a closing take a way, if you are a trust already, perhaps a SAT, and thinking about growth, then your trust board should be reflecting on these questions whenever an opportunity arises that has the potential for you to engage (Table 3.2).

For the next step, I would encourage you to make sure you get a tick in the box for these criteria before moving forwards. Remember, this is something the board and your chair should be leading.

1. Check that they are located within your school or trust's sphere of interest.
2. Check the school's ethos and fit to that of our existing schools.
3. Check that the new school has financial stability and transparency.
4. Check how the addition of the school would impact your schools.
5. Check there is clear and current capacity within your team to engage.

Table 3.2 Trust Board Questions

Student Outcomes	Does this have the potential for positive impact on student outcomes?
Financial Benefit	Does it increase the potential spending per student on resources?
Staff Recruitment and Retention	Will it help us recruit or retain good staff?
What's Right for the Community	How does any change align with our commitment to being a community school and providing opportunities for all?
Target Audience	What is our age range target for growth and building key stage excellence?
Capacity and Pace	Does the trust have the capacity to grow and at what pace is that possible?
DfE Broader Aspirations	Does this support our broader plans to grow and scale to be a strong and sustainable MAT in the national context?

BUREAUCRACY VERSUS BENEFIT

When systems become large, do they lose the flexibility and individuality to truly serve children's needs?

Well, I guess it's on me for choosing these questions; they are all heavily shaped by perceptions as much as the benefit of statistical backing. Does a MAT with 50 schools lose anything over one with 5 local schools, or is it all about the benefits of scale and capacity? Our MAT is on a journey of growth, largely driven by wanting to afford more central capacity so that we can provide more tailored support to our schools. That said, we do not want to become a large MAT; we do not want to extend our sphere of influence too far from our community, keeping all schools visitable by staff within a single lesson's duration. We want to know everyone's name and retain a sense of collective community and collaboration. It is, of course, entirely fair to argue you can do that with a large MAT plus much more, and we do not know how.

On that point of knowing everyone and retaining that community sense, I noted a 2024 **EPI** report, **"The Features of Effective School Groups"** [36, 37], highlighting, amongst many things, that larger MATs have the highest teacher turnover. That could be a bad thing and indicative of more concerning traits, but dig deeper into their data, and they share that at both primary and secondary, their measure of efficiency had a positive association with overall attainment and an even stronger association with the attainment and progress of disadvantaged pupils. That then follows, which, for me, is an important piece of context, noting that higher levels of efficiency are also associated with higher rates of classroom teacher turnover. This highlights that teacher turnover isn't necessarily a bad outcome; if, for example, schools are adept at identifying and retaining only high-quality teachers, this could potentially help drive efficiencies.

Of course, context is king. So while they noted that larger MATs (with ten or more schools in a phase) have, on average, higher rates of persistent absence, suspension, and unexplained exits than smaller MATs and local authorities, for example, they also noted that these larger MATs admit greater rates of disadvantaged pupils and have higher attainment outcomes for low prior attaining and disadvantaged pupils. I fear, as always, we can find a statistic to suit an argument either way.

Financial drivers

I can certainly identify that there are financial economies of scale to achieve in a larger entity, and while the jury is out on whether we distribute core funding to each school directly or "pool" those funds, there are undoubtedly savings at scale. The aforementioned EPI report indicated that *"90 per cent of MATs in our survey used top-slicing (taking a fixed proportion of funding from all schools) rather than pooling funding across all schools. On average, they top-sliced around 6 per cent of school budgets."* They also noted, when considering the cohort of schools "least academised" that at primary, MATs are around twice as likely to have positive in-year balances compared to other group types. Relative balances were, on average, smaller at secondary, but the ratio is larger, with MATs almost three times as likely to have positive in-year balances than other school groups (I need their phone numbers 😉).

Financial sustainability might well be why the Department for Education is so keen to see MATs sustainable, built around ten or more schools or 7,500 students. Finances are high on everyone's radar right now, but much as it's a good media headline, money does not trump the focus on students and their opportunities. **Martyn Oliver**, chief executive of the **Outwood Grange Academies Trust**, articulated in a 2018 *Schools Week* article **"It's not true that academies care more about money than pupils"** [38], I think we can agree that all schools care about money right now, but only in the context of being able to provide all the resources they want for their students.

Is bigger better?

Ian Young, CEO at **PKAT**, shared: *"Having worked in a very large MAT (through its fast growth journey) and a small MAT, my sense is that there is a sweet spot for size in this regard. Large MATs have enormous benefits in terms of the central services they can provide, whether that be on curriculum, systems, technology, subject support or HR. However, geographical proximity is also relevant and relationships and meaningful school to school partnerships benefit from being close to each other. The cluster model can achieve both, but when the Trust exec team start not to know all the Heads well, there can be a risk of individual schools (and the children) not getting the attention they need from the centre. My view is that around 50 schools is where that risk starts to develop."*

That definitely resonates in terms of finding that balance between capacity and community, I would not have picked 50, I would be nearer 15, but the point about regional clusters is important as you can retain that local collegiate working in your cluster while having the support of a national organisation.

Tim Coulson shared that there wasn't always a correlation between bigger and less individuality and flexibility. He rightly highlighted the role leadership plays in shaping this, saying, *"They are, as in all large organisations, dependent on leadership throughout the organisation, but crucially the extent to which the senior leadership empower leadership at all levels,"* so with strong devolved leadership at the trust level, it can result in flexibility and greater autonomy at school level to focus on the distinct needs of their cohort.

There is no immediate detail that I could identify that showed direct evidence that as organisations scale, they cannot continue to operate with flexibility and local nuance. As Tim indicated, it's often about leadership structures and confidence with delegation. No one size fits all here. **Sarah Baker**, CEO of **Team Education Trust**, wrote in a 2023 *Schools Week* article, **"In praise of small MATs: Why bigger doesn't always mean better"** [39] that she felt *"[s]mall multi-academy trusts offer an agility the system needs and a family feel many schools and communities desire."*

In a smaller team, talent has no hiding place.

Perhaps on the scale conversation, the point Sarah made in her article that hadn't immediately jumped into my mind was her thought that when schools are working well, their trusts can often give them more autonomy, while conversely expecting high standards of the trust's team. This virtuous circle, as she describes it, is a defining characteristic of a winning partnership. Her really interesting point raised, however, was that smaller trusts do this on a bigger, more personal scale, meaning their schools are more likely to have a significant role and voice in the direction the trust takes, and in return, smaller trusts can offer a greater depth of understanding and more bespoke support. All really valid points, but with the right systems, a large MAT should be able to do that too, and still ensure all schools have a voice and say in the trust.

I think all of these perspectives highlight that it is not the finite number of schools in a MAT that really matters; it is how they are organised or clustered, how effectively leadership communicates downwards but also facilitates it upwards, and how much autonomy is delegated to individual leaders to ensure personalised and timely decision-making.

Honestly, no, big trusts aren't less flexible or agile; poorly run organisations are, and that is fundamentally not linked to scale, **it's linked to structures and leadership**. But I still like the idea of a smaller trust, but that's just me. More importantly, I think we can distil down my thoughts on this question into the five following points:

1. **Balance between scale and community**: While larger MATs can offer greater resources and support, they risk losing the close-knit community feel. Clustering schools geographically helps maintain relationships and personalised support.

2. **Leadership is key**: The flexibility and individuality of schools within a larger system depends on the leadership structure. Strong, devolved leadership can empower local school leaders to address the unique needs of their students.

3. **Efficiency versus turnover:** Larger MATs often achieve higher efficiency and outcomes, particularly for disadvantaged students, but this can come with higher teacher turnover. This isn't always negative if the focus remains on retaining high-quality staff.

4. **Financial benefits of scale**: Larger systems can achieve economies of scale, which support financial sustainability. However, finances should always remain secondary to the focus on student outcomes and opportunities.

5. **Small isn't always better**: Smaller MATs can offer more personalised support and a stronger sense of community, but with the right leadership and structure, larger trusts can also provide flexibility and ensure schools have a voice in decision-making.

WHO MAKES THE DECISIONS?

To what extent are teachers and students meaningfully involved in the big decisions that affect their schools?

This is a bit of a footnote to this chapter, but it can still be an awkward question, generally, as it can heavily depend on the hat you are wearing. Clearly, we already have a framework that ensures final decision-making in LA schools is made/ratified by the local governing body, with consultation with the LA; then in our trusts, that scheme of delegation maps all decision-making from individual schools through to trust wide topics. Big strategic decisions fall to the board of trustees, hopefully with healthy consultation with the trust members, but in practical terms, and rightly, 99% of operational decision-making falls into the hands of those employed by the trust to lead the organisation. For day-to-day feedback, that might depend on communication flow and receptiveness for capturing a broader voice from other stakeholders.

Keen to get a different perspective, I reached out to **Nic Ponsford**; after 20 years as a teacher, school leader, and coach, Nic wanted to find an accessible means to make ordinary classrooms extraordinarily inclusive. She is the founder of the GEC **(Global Equality Collective)** [40], addressing one of the most significant issues in education: diversity and inclusion. She encapsulated this question perfectly when she highlighted that "*Differing stakeholders are looking for different measures of 'success'. Parents and carers want their children to be safe and to be themselves, learn what they need for their futures and for schools to support home values. Educators measure in terms of their roles, so this can be for assessing and examining key subjects or skills - for individuals or across groups.*"

Matt Jessop, head teacher at **Crosthwaite C of E Primary**, was quite pragmatic with his views: "*Everyone is involved, and pupil voice is a huge part of what happens – in many cases if the school council, tech leaders or ethos team didn't arrange it then it wouldn't happen – staff are very busy! The staff team shapes and guides everything – The HT has final say, but he knows they will ignore him and do what's best anyway if he's stubborn about something!*"

Tim Coulson shared his perspective: "*Teachers are much better when responsible for their learning environments but good schools provide the tools and wider environment for teachers to be successful.*" This reflects very much a layered approach to delegating relevant autonomy.

Clearly, an organisation cannot operate where every decision needs everyone consulted. However, as we reflect on the most significant decisions, particularly around growth, then we should be aware that when it comes to introducing change, we either bring people along on the journey because they feel informed and understand the bigger picture, or we drag them along kicking and screaming. Nobody wants that, but it's surprising how often that happens when trying to move at pace.

Bigger decisions

For the biggest questions, just as we have discussed here, in perhaps joining a MAT or changing your school's status, there will be guidance on consultations with staff, parents, and community to undertake, but that won't mitigate the more nuanced discussions that can happen with the workforce.

If we take some of the best MAT examples, which have really strong and established governance and oversight, a central leadership team who makes considered and valued strategic decisions, who creates an environment that maximises the funds they have available, and then the confidence to empower individual school leaders and staff to be flexible in their approaches, this for me is the sweet spot. Of course, it only works if this is built around good communication. This means listening to staff, students, and parents; making appropriate changes based on that feedback; and embracing consistent communication to all stakeholders, not just on what and when they do things, but clearly explaining the why.

This book is not all about answers; it's intended to elevate the important questions, so they are back on the SLT or trust board discussion list, and maybe, if I am ambitious, help inform and challenge system leaders when considering future policy. Scale and growth in our systems is healthy, but being mindful that the scale can come at a price in terms of stakeholder voice, hopefully, shapes initiatives and processes to proactively mitigate against that ... before it happens. Let's summarise this into a few key takeaways:

1. **Decision-making structures**: While there are established frameworks for governance, such as local governing bodies and trust-level decision-making, most operational decisions are handled by leadership teams, with minimal direct input from teachers and students in strategic decisions.

2. **Varying stakeholder expectations**: Different stakeholders, be that parents, teachers, and students, have different measures of success, highlighting the challenge of attempting to align diverse needs and targets when making schoolwide decisions.

3. **Autonomy and flexibility**: Delegating decision-making at the appropriate levels, such as empowering teachers to manage their classrooms or student councils to drive initiatives, is important for fostering a sense of ownership and engagement.

4. **Consultation and communication**: For significant changes, like joining a MAT, there is typically a formal consultation with staff, parents, and the community, but nuanced discussions with staff are often overlooked. Ensuring regular, transparent communication helps build trust and brings stakeholders along on the journey.

5. **Balancing growth and stakeholder voice**: As schools and MATs grow, maintaining a sense of stakeholder involvement can become more challenging. The best outcomes occur when leadership balances strategic decisions with listening to and acting on the feedback from teachers, students, and parents, ensuring that communication explains the "why," not just the "what" they plan to do.

Further reading

My School and Multi Academy Trust Growth Guide, 2023, Al Kingsley [8]
My School Governance Handbook, 2022, Al Kingsley [41]
The A-Z of School Improvement, 2024, Tim Coulson [42]
Building Culture: A Handbook to harnessing human nature to create strong school teams, 2023, Lekha Sharma [43]

References

1. "Academies Act," 29 July 2010. [Online]. Available: https://bills.parliament.uk/bills/642/publications
2. "Free Schools - Types of Schools," Gov.uk, 2024. [Online]. Available: https://www.gov.uk/types-of-school/free-schools
3. OECD, "Organisation for Economic Co-operation and Development (OECD)," [Online]. Available: https://www.oecd.org/
4. OECD, "Programme for International Student Assessment (PISA)," [Online]. Available: https://www.oecd.org/en/about/programmes/pisa.html
5. "PISA 2012 Results: What Makes Schools Successful? - Volume IV," OECD, 2013.
6. "2024 Academies Benchmark Report.," UHY Hacker Young, 2024.
7. N. Plaister, "The Current State of Play for MATs," FFT Education Data lab, 10 July 2024. [Online]. Available: https://ffteducationdatalab.org.uk/2024/07/the-current-state-of-play-for-mats/
8. A. Kingsley, My School & Multi-Academy Trust Growth Guide, Hodder Education, 2023.
9. "The Education Company," [Online]. Available: http://www.educationcompany.co.uk/
10. "MAT Tracker: Mapping the Country's Multi-Academy Trusts," TES Magazine, 1 July 2024. [Online]. Available: https://www.tes.com/magazine/leadership/data/mat-tracker-multi-academy-trusts-map
11. D. f. Education, "Opportunity for All: Strong Schools with Great Teachers for Your Child," 03 2022. [Online]. Available: https://assets.publishing.service.gov.uk/media/62416cb5d3bf7f32add7819f/Opportunity_for_all_strong_schools_with_great_teachers_for_your_child__print_version_.pdf
12. U. Parliament, "Nick Gibb Response to Question for the Department for Education," 9 February 2023. [Online]. Available: https://questions-statements.parliament.uk/written-questions/detail/2023-01-11/121149
13. Schoolsweek, "White Paper: What Academy Shakeup Means for Trusts, Councils and Schools," 28 March 2022. [Online]. Available: https://schoolsweek.co.uk/white-paper-what-academy-shakeup-means-for-trusts-councils-and-schools/
14. "British Educational Suppliers Association (BESA)," [Online]. Available: https://www.besa.org.uk/

15 "Key UK Education Statistics," British Educational Suppliers Association, 11 2022. [Online]. Available: https://www.besa.org.uk/key-uk-education-statistics/
16 S. D. Carter and L. McInerney, Leading Academy Trusts: Why some fail, but most don't, John Catt, 2020.
17 "Local Government Association," [Online]. Available: https://www.local.gov.uk/
18 LGA, "Better Performance for Council-Maintained Schools than Academies, Says Study," Prospect, 08 2023. [Online].
19 F. Whittaker, "Fact Check: Do Council Schools Really Outperform Academies?," Schoolsweek, 03 August 2023. [Online]. Available: https://schoolsweek.co.uk/fact-check-do-council-schools-really-outperform-academies/
20 "Confederation of School Trusts (CST)," [Online]. Available: https://cstuk.org.uk/
21 "Education Policy Institute," [Online]. Available: https://epi.org.uk/
22 "School Performance in Academy Chains and Local Authorities–2017," Education Policy Institute, 19 June 2018. [Online]. Available: https://epi.org.uk/publications-and-research/performance-academy-local-authorities-2017/
23 "New report shows practical strategies for MAT growth," Education Business, 07 February 2023. [Online]. Available: https://www.educationbusinessuk.net/news/07022023/new-report-shows-practical-strategies-mat-growth
24 "More MATs Pooling GAG and Reserves to Look after "Financially Weaker Schools"," FE News, 05 March 2024. [Online]. Available: https://www.fenews.co.uk/education/more-mats-pooling-gag-and-reserves-to-look-after-financially-weaker-schools-or-target-additional-resource/
25 "Academies Benchmark Report," Kreston UK, 2024. [Online]. Available: https://www.bishopfleming.co.uk/sites/default/files/2024-02/kreston_uk_academies_benchmark_report_2024.pdf
26 "Unity Schools Partnership," [Online]. Available: www.unitysp.co.uk
27 "East of England Advisory Board," Department for Education, [Online]. Available: https://www.gov.uk/government/publications/east-of-england-advisory-board
28 "Peterborough Keys Academy Trust," [Online]. Available: www.pkat.co.uk
29 "National Education Union (NEU)," [Online]. Available: neu.org.uk
30 "The NEU Case against Academisation," National Education Union, 12 August 2022. [Online]. Available: neu.org.uk/advice/your-rights-work/academisation/neu-case-against-academisation
31 "Chaotic Government Reforms are Failing to Tackle Education Inequality," UCL Institute for Education, 07 2018. [Online]. Available: www.ucl.ac.uk/ioe/news/2018/jul/chaotic-government-reforms-are-failing-tackle-education-inequality
32 J. Andrews, "School Performance in Academy Chains and Local Authorities–2017," Education Policy Institute, 19 June 2018. [Online]. Available: epi.org.uk/publications-and-research/performance-academy-local-authorities-2017
33 E. Haves, "Improving Schools' Performance: Are Multi-Academy Trusts the Answer?," House of Lords Library, 11 September 2023. [Online]. Available: lordslibrary.parliament.uk/improving-schools-performance-are-multi-academy-trusts-the-answer/
34 "Multi-Academy Trusts: Benefits, Challenges and Functions," Ofsted, 07 2019. [Online]. Available: https://assets.publishing.service.gov.uk/government/uploads/system/uploads/attachment_data/file/936251/Multi_academy_trusts_benefits_challenges_and_functions.pdf
35 S. D. Carter and L. McInnery, Leading Academy Trusts: Why Some Fail, but Most Don't, John Catt Educational Ltd, 2020.
36 "The Features of Effective School Groups," Education Policy Institute, 16 April 2024. Online]. Available: https://epi.org.uk/publications-and-research/the-features-of-effective-school-groups/

37 L. Hodge, R. Cruikshanks, J. Andrews and O. Gavriloiu, "The Features of Effective School Groups report," Education Policy Institute, 2024.
38 M. Oliver, "It's not True that Academies Care More about Money than Pupils," Schools Week, 05 July 2018. [Online]. Available: https://schoolsweek.co.uk/its-not-true-that-academies-care-more-about-money-than-pupils/
39 S. Baker, "In Praise of Small MATs: Why Bigger Doesn't Always Mean Better," Schools Week, 29 April 2023. [Online]. Available: https://schoolsweek.co.uk/in-praise-of-small-mats-why-bigger-doesnt-always-mean-better/
40 "Global Equality Collective (GEC)," [Online]. Available: www.thegec.education/
41 A. Kingsley, *My School Governance Handbook: Keeping it simple, a Step by Step Guide and Checklist for All School Governors*, John Catt Educational, 2022.
42 T. Coulson, *The A-Z of School Improvement*, John Catt, 2024.
43 L. Sharma, *Building Culture: A Handbook to Harnessing Human Nature to Create Strong School Teams*, John Catt Education, 2023.

Does AI change the role of the teacher?

I really hope you aren't surprised to see the topic of AI (artificial intelligence) appear as one of the chapters in my book. It's been around in various iterations for decades, but since the public launch of **ChatGPT** [1] by **OpenAI** in November 2023 [2], the discussions have simply gotten louder and more frequent. In the broadest sense, the discussions around AI have been sector- and society-wide, and absolutely not one focused solely on its impact on education, but we certainly have had our fair share of conversations and concerns.

Are we scared of it changing or replacing our jobs? Is it dismissed easily because it isn't in the comfort zone of leadership? Is it all smoke and mirrors? Can we trust it ... the list of awkward questions goes on and on and on.

I could be easily persuaded to deviate from the core topic of this chapter and write a guide on the use of AI in education in a much broader sense, but there are already some excellent books on the subject, and given the pace of change, they all have relatively short life spans when discussing specific tools. If I were to draw a Venn diagram right now, you would find that AI permutates across many of the areas we are talking about within education. Technology, particularly AI tools, change the priority of the skills employers want their workforce to arrive with; this becomes a catalyst for curriculum discussions.

Workload feeds into staff recruitment and retention concerns, so naturally, where tools promise (not always accurately) to help reduce staff workload, they come to the fore. When we see information generated by AI tools or social media platforms where we know there may be bias or fake content, it prioritises our need to develop further digital citizenship skills and the ability to challenge and evidence the information we see. When our trusts are looking to support improvement, and AI tools present the potential to proactively analyse vast amounts of student data to help inform decisions, we naturally feel motivated to take a look.

Rightly, we also question the accuracy of the information generated by AI tools, those often highlighted "hallucinations" (*a response generated by AI which contains false or misleading information presented as fact*) [3], we challenge where our data is being shared, we challenge if it removes our need to "think" as humans, how it might allow children to "cheat" and bypass our traditional assessment methods ... the list goes on. At this point, it's not a surprise that the easiest path to take is to do nothing; just wait and see. That's fine, but what you might be missing, even if in an intentional holding pattern, is that it's important to still ensure we are all best informed on the topic for when future decisions may be taken.

International perspectives

I'm fortunate to have an amazing professional learning network covering all corners of the globe, and I spoke with many to seek their firsthand insights for my book. So when asking the question, "**Does AI change the role of the teacher?**", Phillip Alcock, the founder of **AIxPBL**, said, "*Yes, AI is transforming the role of a teacher. It's deconstructing the traditional definition by creating distinct roles within the profession. For instance, during planning, teachers act as AI-enhanced instructional designers, while in the classroom, they take on new responsibilities such as observing, crafting, coaching, and redirecting.*"

He shared a view that for many, they now have the helper they always wanted, they just haven't quite figured out how to communicate with it yet, reminding me that the learning environment is rapidly evolving due to AI enhancements.

As universities adapt, the teacher's role is undergoing a complete metamorphosis from director to coach.

Heading across the globe from the United States, I arrived in Australia with a similar question for **Leon Furze**, a former secondary educator with over 15 years of experience in school leadership, and who is currently studying for his Ph.D. in generative AI and education. said: *"AI is set to significantly impact teaching, but it's unlikely to fully replace human educators. While AI can handle routine tasks and deliver content efficiently, expert teachers bring unique qualities that machines struggle to replicate. We have the ability to form genuine social and cognitive connections with students, improvise and adapt instruction on the fly, and draw upon personal learning experiences."*

Leon articulated to me that educators can also model thinking processes and create a sense of mutual respect that leads to more engagement. We both agree that educators may need to evolve their roles, focusing more on these human elements while leveraging AI for administrative tasks and differentiation. The challenge for teachers will be to articulate and demonstrate their irreplaceable value in an increasingly technology-driven educational environment.

Another view with a slightly different but overlapping perspective was from **Phillip Murdoch**, a specialist design and technology teacher at **Rivermount College**, also in Australia, who said, *"AI does not change the role of the teacher, however it will change the way a teacher does their job. It may change the role of some in education."* I don't disagree. Much of this discussion frames the adaptions of practice, not the replacement of it.

I also reached out to **Carla Aerts**, an independent **AI in Education** consultant, she highlighted: *"In an AI world, in which 'everything becomes learning', dealing with copilots and agents and the exponential change AI is likely to bring, teachers have to become as much of a learner as the learners they teach. We move into an era of co-learning, just like we co-create and co-design. Teachers won't just be a co-learner, they will be a mentor and a coach."*

From all my research on this subject, I know it's critical to ensure a balanced representation of voices is included in the conversation, and I'm fortunate to know and respect a very diverse group of educators. One such person whom I have known for some years and had the pleasure of visiting his amazing school in the Lake District is **Matt Jessop**, the head teacher of Crosthwaite C.E. Primary School. His answer to the question "Does AI change the role of the Teacher?" was initially a rather unhelpful "yes and no."

Fortunately, he expanded from that, saying, *"AI provides us with the beginnings, and we are at the very early stages of AI – it's important to recognise that what is available and what is actually useful is very, very different at the moment (any new 'fad' is enthusiastically adopted, but medium to long term developments will leave us knowing what truly useful technology is) with a wealth of tools that can support teaching and learning, further personalise learning and save time and energy for the teacher. The role of the teacher will still be important, but I believe they will become, increasingly, a facilitator and coach in some ways."* From talking to Matt and others it's clear that this will be very different across the different phases of education and subjects or areas of learning.

So, I hope we can all agree that the consistent position is yes, AI does evolve the role of the teacher (the amount, of course, we can debate later), much like the concept of moving from being the "sage on the stage" to the "guide on the side." This topic is more framed around teacher adaptation and not outright replacement.

So, before we dive into the three key questions I have selected for the topic of AI, it probably makes sense for a bit of groundwork first on what we mean by AI. We can unpick what it currently offers and where we stand right now with the technology. Oh, and no, this isn't the point when I ask a **"bot"** for the answers. This book is strictly AI-free, albeit it helped with some of the research for sure. The next few sections are not detailed guides but more of a spotlight on some of the key topics we (you) should be reflecting on and discussing in your schools. That sounds quite strict, so perhaps I'll revise "should" to "could"; it's very much your call.

What is AI (artificial intelligence)?

I've seen so many different variations of a simple definition for AI, but this one is paraphrased from Google, which defines it as a field of science concerned with building computers and machines that can reason, learn, and act in such a way that would typically require human intelligence or that involves data whose scale exceeds what humans can analyse. On an operational level, AI is a set of technologies based primarily on machine learning and deep learning, used for data analytics, predictions and forecasting, object categorisation, natural language processing, recommendations, intelligent data retrieval, and plenty more.

In a 2024 article by **McKinsey & Company** titled **"What is AI (artificial intelligence)?"** [4], AI is described as *"a machine's ability to perform the cognitive functions we associate with human minds, such as perceiving, reasoning, learning, interacting with the environment, problem-solving, and even exercising creativity,"* which is an excellent condensed summary that I really like. There will be many who have a more complete, more detailed, and more nuanced definition, but as you might have gathered, this book is aimed first and foremost at being accessible, so there is no value in getting into the technical details.

Before we get too far into the definitions, let's review a few of the most common terms with my attempt at a simplified summary.

AI terms (user-friendly version)

AI Term	Description
AI (Artificial Intelligence)	Systems that can learn and adapt, making decisions or predictions without being explicitly programmed for each little thing.
Generative AI	These are AI tools, like ChatGPT, that can create new text, images, or even code based on prompts you give them. It's like having a super-creative digital assistant.
Non-Generative AI	These AI systems focus on analysing existing data and making predictions without creating any new content.
Large Language Model (LLM)	These are super-smart AI systems trained on loads of data to understand and generate human-like language. They're the brains behind chatbots like ChatGPT.
Machine Learning	This is the brainy part of AI where computers use data to get better at tasks over time.
Deep Learning	This is a subset of machine learning with layers of algorithms (like a digital onion!) designed to mimic the human brain, helping with tasks like image and speech recognition.
Natural Language Processing (NLP)	This is the technology that helps computers understand and even talk back in human language. Think of chatbots that actually know what you're saying and can converse with you realistically, in text or audible format.
Personalised Learning	With AI, lessons can be tailored to fit each student's pace and stage.
AI-Driven Analytics	AI can be used to sift through loads of data to spot trends and patterns that can spot gaps in progress or learning.
AI in Assessment	AI tools can help design and mark assessments, potentially spotting patterns in student performance that a human might miss.
Digital Divide	The gap between those with access to digital technology and those without can be fundamental when talking about AI in schools.
Data Privacy	This is all about making sure that any personal info (especially from students) stays safe and sound when using AI tools.
AI Ethics in Education	This involves discussions around how to use AI responsibly in schools, ensuring it enhances learning without replacing human interaction or equity.

Prompt Engineering	The art of crafting questions or prompts to get the best responses from AI models. Think about the best way to ask a genie for a wish.
Algorithmic Bias	This happens when AI systems unintentionally favour certain groups over others because of biased data or flawed algorithms. It's like teaching a robot some bad habits.
Hallucination	This is when AI generates information that seems plausible but is actually incorrect or nonsensical.

There are plenty more I could include, but I suspect the longer the list, the less accessible it becomes, and this book is for anyone in education, not the AI specialists.

Generative and non-generative AI

I've shared some simple definitions and will endeavour to keep the KISS (keep it simple stupid) approach as we continue. Non-generative AI (not generating) doesn't make anything new, it "just" analyses existing data and forms output and predictions based on the task in hand. You will have encountered this traditional AI when using voice assistants like **Siri** [5] and **Alexa** [6] or when **Netflix** [7] provides recommendations for your next viewing based on your previous activity and preferences.

It's also not "new" to us either. Alexa, for example, is based on a Polish speech synthesizer named "Ivona," which Amazon purchased back in 2013, and likewise, SIRI was a spin-off of a project by SRI International [8] and Nuance, which was acquired by Apple in 2010.

Generative AI generates something completely new based on the prompt or instructions you provide. It's easy to identify with recent trends of generating images based on prompts, but it can do far more, from the creation of images to music to computer code to videos. Following is a simple summary of the most common generative tasks (Figure 4.1).

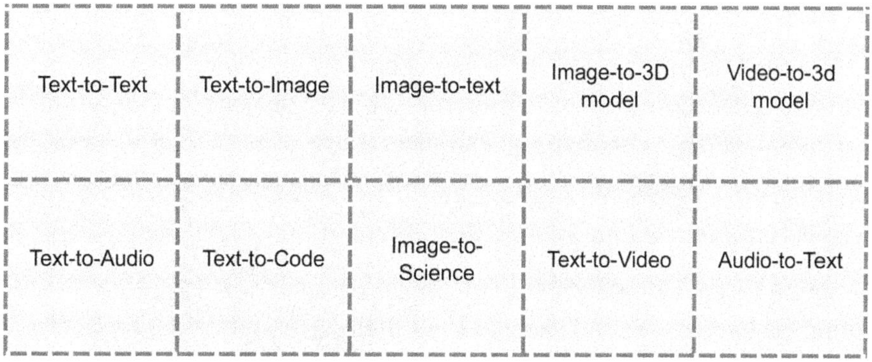

Text-to-Text	Text-to-Image	Image-to-text	Image-to-3D model	Video-to-3d model
Text-to-Audio	Text-to-Code	Image-to-Science	Text-to-Video	Audio-to-Text

Figure 4.1 Most Common Generative Tasks.

Of course, I could list all of my favourite apps here, but in the context of AI, I know there will be better suggestions within the few months my manuscript goes to the publishers and finally hits the shelves. Besides, there are far better companion guides for using AI in education, so I do not intend to replicate them. I'll list a few at the end of this chapter just for good measure.

If you want to take a deeper dive at a policy level, then **UNESCO** (The United Nations Educational, Scientific and Cultural Organization) released an updated **"Guidance for Generative AI in Education and Research"** [9] publication in June 2024, which *"aims to support countries to implement immediate actions, plan long-term policies and develop human capacity to ensure a human-centred vision of these new technologies."* This, of course, is a rapidly moving landscape in which we tend to react rather than pre-empt.

Current discussions in education

You might have noticed if you read any of the education newsgroups, blogs, or posts that there are many parallel conversations happening right now (and likely to for some time to come), but the prominent ones that I think are worth signposting are included below before we dive into my "big three" questions. I do want to stress that these are intended just to highlight the current conversations and themes; I share things you might want to consider but most definitely do not provide outright solutions (I'm not sure they exist just yet).

Opportunities and benefits

Reducing Teacher Workload: How can AI streamline administrative tasks like assessment and lesson planning, allowing teachers more time for student interaction and personalised instruction?

The UK government shared a research briefing in January 2024 titled **"Use of Artificial Intelligence in Education Delivery and Assessment"** [10], which covers many of the core discussion points around the use of AI in schools at a high level, but given we are still in the early stages, it only highlighted there is still a lack of evidence of impact: *"Artificial intelligence (AI) tools have the potential to provide different ways of learning and to help educators with lesson planning, marking and other tasks."* I think, in truth, this is more visible if you start looking a bit harder.

Back in May 2023, then–Secretary of State for Education **Gillian Keegan** claimed that, *"AI could 'radically reduce the amount of time teachers spend marking' and 'take much of the heavy lifting out of compiling lesson plans.'"* I don't disagree with that, but as always, the devil is in the detail and that remains thin at a national level. It's worth noting that marking is the biggest "sap" on teacher time, as highlighted by the **Education Endowment Foundation** (EEF) in their 2016 report **"A Marked Improvement"** [11], where marking was the single biggest contributor to unsustainable workload in the Department for Education's **2014 Workload Challenge** [12] – a consultation that gathered more than 44,000 responses from teachers, support staff, and others.

I am going to be direct and say that, overall, I have seen most of the government's communications around AI being significantly "off the pace" and reactive to what's happening rather than defining a proactive strategic plan.

On a more helpful level, an August 2024 article in **Schools Week** titled **"How we've used AI to reduce teacher workloads"** by Charlotte Bleakley [13], digital lead at Roding Valley High School, said that rather than fear the potential impact of AI on students, they are embracing the technology to help them and their teaching staff. She explained, *"The key is to galvanise early adopters. By creating digital champions and giving them a platform to air their concerns and celebrate their wins, we were able to make significant progress, not just in overcoming scepticism but in honing our implementation strategy."*

I think it's essential to recognise that you need to proactively build awareness of the potential applications of AI across your staff cohort if you want to deliver a coordinated way to help reduce teacher workload. Rather than wait for staff to figure out what might help them individually, many multi-academy trusts (MATs) have crafted strategies for the specific use of AI and, in particular, with a focus on how to reduce teacher workload. Here is a high-level example of how that might look based on an excellent strategy from **Exceed Academies Trust** [14].

- Ensure representation on your AI working group includes school and trust leaders, teachers, support staff, and IT experts.
- Develop and share guidance to help raise the visibility of approved AI tools and to support staff take their initial steps using AI.
- Provide training on the effective and ethical use of AI, including awareness of misinformation, bias, stereotypes, and hallucinations.
- Share prompt crafting examples and guidance to support staff in using AI effectively to reduce workload.
- Scope and evaluate AI tools and resources that could positively impact staff's workload, including lesson planning and assessment.
- Scope and evaluate AI tools and resources that may positively impact teaching and learning.
- Capture and disseminate emerging and best practices from our school teams.
- Share regular information as AI evolves and new tools and resources become available.

I do need to stress this book is not intended to be a how-to guide on any subject, and to do so in the AI context would be a massive rabbit hole I could jump down, but I do want to signpost "prompt crafting" from the above list. Much like the adage with computer programming of "garbage in, garbage out," reflecting bad computer coding makes bad software, in the same way, if you ask bad questions,

Table 4.1 Bad Prompt Versus Good Prompt in AI

Bad Prompt	Good Prompt
"Write me a lesson plan for a year 4 science class that is learning about the water cycle."	"You are an expert science teacher skilled at designing effective lessons for students. Write an engaging lesson plan for a year 4 science class that is learning about the water cycle. The lesson plan should be 50 minutes long and should include a list of key vocabulary words. The lesson plan should also have a learning objective, a list of necessary materials, a brief introduction, an engaging activity, a conclusion, and an activity to assess the learning. Include a risk assessment. It should cover this objective from the English National Curriculum for Science. Identify the part played by evaporation and condensation in the water cycle and associate the rate of evaporation with temperature."

you can't be surprised if you receive less-than-satisfactory answers from an AI tool. I'll share a very simple example of a bad prompt versus a good prompt so that you know what I mean. It's a skill, but it translates well into effective communication skills, too (Table 4.1).

Several educators share the most essential parts of a good prompt in different "frameworks." I particularly like the work of **Dan Fitzpatrick**, "**The AI Educator**," [15] who crafted the initial P-R-E-P framework, which you can apply with this basic understanding:

Prompt – This is the first step when framing your request. By providing the prompt, you are setting the scene and creating a foundation for the rest of the instructions. Provide a clear and concise command. Avoid using vague or ambiguous language.

Role – When you assign an AI role, you help build context so that it has a better chance to accomplish what you want it to. It helps it know how to approach the question and provide an accurate and relevant response. You are essentially telling the AI tool what hat to wear for the task at hand.

Explicit – Be clear and specific about what you want it to do or what information you're looking for. Never assume that it knows what you're thinking or the specifics of what you need. By giving explicit instructions, you ensure it is on the same page as you. Signpost any pedagogical approach or subject specifics you want it to include.

Parameters – Set clear parameters and define the scope and boundaries of the answer, which helps it understand what you're looking for and enables it to provide a more accurate response.

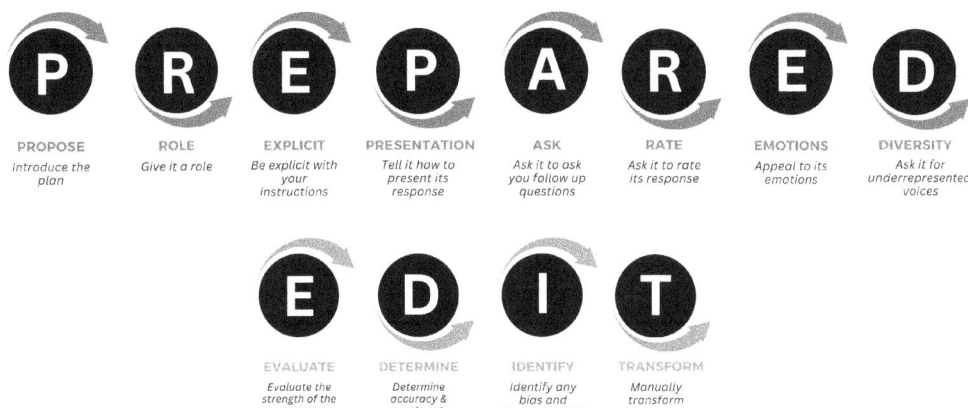

Figure 4.2 Prompting.

Figure Prompting Framework © Dan Fitzpatrick – The AI Educator

I've included this image below from Dan, which makes it easy to understand. For those who want to go a step further, PREP becomes the PREPARED framework, with an additional EDIT step, so try to develop your own understanding through trial and error. I would also encourage you to look at what I consider one of the foundational books for educators using AI, Dan's 2023 book: ***The AI Classroom: The Ultimate Guide to Artificial Intelligence in Education*** [16]. For additional prompting examples and guidance across most subjects, then ***The Little Book of Generative AI Prompts for Teachers*** [17] by **Mark Anderson** [18] is also well worth a look (Figure 4.2).

Well, we got a little off-track there with some specifics that can help on using AI to "potentially reduce workload," but I do also want to signpost comments made by **Leon Furze**, author of ***Practical AI Strategies: Engaging with Generative AI in Education*** [19], who said in a March 2024 article [20]: "*Using generative AI to reduce teacher workload requires thinking beyond the low-hanging fruit. We don't need generative artificial intelligence to write lesson plans or create off-the-shelf for us. That's what we're trained for, that's what we're experts in, and in my experience, that's what teachers want to do.*"

As always, there are times when it can help, times when it can add value, and times when the human is just better suited to the task. We are going to test this further in the chapter.

I asked **Bonnie Nieves**, the founder of **Educate on Purpose** [21], if AI tools will change the role of the teacher in the classroom. Her view: "*Yes, because it facilitates more personalized instruction at an individual level. The role of a teacher now more than ever can be to spend time getting to know students' interests, history, culture, and abilities. Using these, the teacher can differentiate to the level of individual students. Before AI became ubiquitous in classrooms, teachers were able to do this, but with a huge time investment. Now, with AI, the time spent researching and planning individualized instruction can be spent building community and getting to know students.*"

Closer to home for me and a colleague on the Department for Education's regional advisory board, **Clare Flintoff** is the CEO of **ASSET Education**, a MAT in Suffolk, UK. She shared: "*I believe that AI has the potential to transform the role of the teacher and we should welcome it with open arms. Teaching is hard, the hours are long, much of the work is laborious and administrative and too little time is spent developing relationships, listening, observing children learn and having time to consider, reflect and spend quality time with individuals. Over my career in education this situation has got worse rather than better.*" An important thread from Clare's thoughts was to remind us that time is our most precious commodity, and AI has the potential to provide much more of it.

We both recognise that this has the potential to give us choice and opportunity, and hopefully be the impetus to rethink how we organise our schools and revisit the role of the educator to solve those entrenched educational issues like inequality and disadvantage.

I'm trying to ensure a nice balance of international perspectives as we set up this conversation, so I asked the same question to **John Mikton**, the learning coordinator at the **International School of Geneva–La Châtaigneraie**. He answered: "*Yes, AI is definitely changing the role of teachers, highlighting the need for a constructivist approach to education. Teachers must recognize that students bring their own knowledge and experiences, shaped by their social and cultural backgrounds and that learning involves students 'constructing' knowledge from these experiences. Now, teachers create spaces and opportunities to guide and mentor students, helping them develop adaptability, resilience, creativity, and the ability to embrace change. They guide, coach, and encourage students to think beyond the norm, leverage their own innovative problem-solving methods, and view resilience and learning from failure as an asset.*"

I would concur that we aren't replacing the teacher, or we certainly shouldn't; we are seeing technology shape and reframe the pedagogy and the relationship-building approaches. It's helpful that there seems to be growing consensus on this, too.

Personalised Learning: Schools should reflect on the ways AI tools adapt to individual student needs and learning styles to help support diverse learners, including those with special educational needs. Of course, not all are as effective as they might suggest. I cover equity in more detail in my final chapter.

There is a well-established ecosystem of personalised learning platforms and tools that have been used in schools for many years, certainly well before ChatGPT appeared on the scene, and many focus on non-generative AI, in essence, analysing real data from students and making decisions on what topics and questions the system might ask the child next. So, for the more able, that might look like some "stretch and challenge" with further topics and questions, or it might identify a child struggling with a topic and step them back to rebuild their foundational knowledge.

Tools like **CENTURY** [22] which is an online learning tool for students that combines AI with the latest research in learning science and neuroscience, are in this space. **Sir Mark Grundy**, CEO of **Shireland Collegiate Academy**, said, "*The *difference with CENTURY is that it's much more individually directed; it's much more bespoke. We are seeing many more hours of usage, and we put it towards the progress eight increase.*" In tools like **SPARX** [23] maths and science, for example, AI large language models (LLMs) automatically mark free-form written answers to provide immediate feedback to students and can award marks even when the student has phrased their answers differently, including other irrelevant information or have made spelling mistakes.

We appreciate that when talking about education, we are covering all ages and stages, and this 2023 article in *FE Week* titled **"How AI is enhancing assessment, reducing workload and improving FE outcomes"** [24] by the excellent **Aftab Hussain** at **Bolton College**, shared how their "FirstPass" platform, developed by themselves in collaboration with **NCFE** [25] (formerly the Northern Council for Further Education), is using natural language processing (NLP) to support students and teachers in their college. Aftab explains: "*It's an online platform that utilises AI to provide real-time feedback to students as they compose their responses to open-ended questions. The basic premise behind the platform is a simple one: that real-time effective feedback enables learners to develop positive meta-cognition skills as they identify areas for improvement and adjust their work before submitting it to their teachers for commentary and feedback.*" In their report findings, they highlight the positive benefits of providing real-time feedback that allowed learners the opportunity to assess their first drafts and make changes before submitting, and teachers reported that the platform led to improved submissions from learners. As a result, staff spent less time providing remedial feedback.

These are just a few select examples but suffice it to say there are hundreds of tools utilising AI to support personalised learning in our schools. Of course, that does not change the first pedagogical consideration: Why are we proposing to use this tool, how do we intend to use it, and how do we plan to measure impact?

The **World Economic Forum**'s 2024 publication, **"AI and education: Kids need AI guidance in school. But who guides the schools?"** [26], provided a very useful leveller, which sets out seven principles to consider when creating guidance to ensure AI's responsible and effective use in education. These principles are as follows:

1. Purpose: Explicitly connect the use of AI to educational goals.
2. Compliance: Affirm adherence to existing policies.
3. Knowledge: Promote AI literacy.
4. Balance: Identify the benefits of AI and address the risks.
5. Integrity: Advance academic integrity.
6. Agency: Maintain human decision-making.
7. Evaluation: Continuously assess the impact of AI.

These can help shape the AI policy or strategy that you apply within your schools. It feels to me that the key consideration is balance. It's more than easy to be swept along by the tide of enthusiasm, but the need to recognise that AI is not the panacea to all challenges is more important now than ever.

A 2024 article in **Educause** titled **"Will Our Educational System Keep Pace with AI? A Student's Perspective on AI and Learning"** [27] started with a quote by poet and Nobel Laureate William Butler Yeats, who said, *"Education is not the filling of a pail, but the lighting of a fire."*

He further said, *"A timeless goal is to light a fire within the hearts and minds of learners. Today, a groundbreaking invention stands ready to fuel the fire and revolutionise the educational landscape forever: AI."*

For me, that feels a little too presumptuous, not least, as we always seek to utilise evidence-informed tools within our schools. In this case, the jury is still largely out and, in many cases, has not even sat yet. But it is fair to say the potential is absolutely there, and this might be the start of the revolution. I think evolution would be a much more sensible path, mind you.

In the context of personalised learning, the same article said: *"Students, regardless of their backgrounds, possess abundant creativity and originality within their individual passions. AI has the potential to uplift ingenious ideas and showcase brilliant minds that may have been overlooked in the past."*

I think that is something we can all reflect on and agree with; AI most definitely provides an outlet and stimulus for creativity while also creating a long-term risk around the value of what is created if it's all too easy. Art would be a great example of how we embrace the human imagination and artistic capabilities, yet we can also create a digital masterpiece in minutes with a suitably crafted prompt.

Challenges and concerns

Data Privacy and Security: Reflecting on the measures schools should take to ensure compliance with data protection laws and safeguard student information from unauthorised access when using AI platforms.

I think it's imperative that with the advent of AI, while it does add an extra dimension, it fundamentally requires us to sharpen up or practice and challenge existing data protection and privacy procedures in our schools. All of the natural concerns about an AI platform in terms of how it uses, consumes, shares, and stores our data are just as valid for many other non-AI products. In the case of AI, we simply add an additional layer of consideration about the validity and credibility of what is also returned to us.

A report by the **Center for Democracy and Technology (CDT)** in 2023 titled **"Off Task: EdTech Threats to Student Privacy and Equity in the Age of AI"** [28] highlighted that 81% of parents say that guidance on how their child can responsibly and safely use generative AI for schoolwork and within school rules would be helpful. And 72% of students agree that this same guidance would be helpful for themselves.

I shared some recommendations in a 2023 article of **School News Australia** titled **"Don't fear AI: how to harness its power for good"** [29], where I highlighted the following: *"[T]o ensure that students' privacy is maintained, schools must adhere to rigorous technology and data management practices. Many schools have a dedicated data protection officer with thorough knowledge of the legal and regulatory obligations and who is responsible for enforcing them. This officer can take a leading role in ensuring EdTech vendors are completely transparent about what data they collect, where it is stored, who can access it, and for how long."*

We can, of course, start with the foundational considerations we apply to all forms of data in our schools, be that as the school or as the vendor. It starts with accountability, including AI design, as well as subsequent decision-making and risk management by schools. Then we require transparency and openness about how we use data and technology. Thirdly is necessity and proportionality in how we use data, including for AI and asking the right questions (i.e., Does it need to be personally identifiable, rather than anonymised or aggregated data?). Lastly, we must consider security a key topic when engaging with third-party providers.

Reaching out to **Professor Sonia Livingstone OBE**, director of **Digital Futures for Children** [30], she told me: *"While global discussions are underway regarding AI and ethics, these rarely consider children's rights or the specific needs of schools. Indeed, the problems that schools, parents and children already face with Educational Technology – unclear benefits, insufficient transparency, difficulties in obtaining remedy – are magnified as AI-powered EdTech services are rolled out in advance of protections for children's privacy or the quality of their education. There may be much to gain with AI, but children's best interests must not be sacrificed in the rush to profit."*

I do want to signpost here the excellent work of the **Digital Futures Commission** [31] and their work **"Education Data Futures: Critical Regulatory and Practical Reflections"** [32]. They have been hugely proactive in waving the flag for caution with the ever-growing use of student data. As they introduced their work under the umbrella of **"the problem and potential of children's education data,"** they shared: *"The data collected from children at or through their participation in school are exponentially increasing in variety and volume. This is partly mandated by the government, partly determined by schools, and partly driven by the commercial desires of educational technology companies of all kinds, large and small, national and global, user-facing and business-to-business. Increasingly, children's education data seem indispensable to public policy, planning and practice in education, health and welfare, and in schools, teaching, learning and assessment, safeguarding and administration."*

I've shared below the excellent "**11 Child Rights Principles**," which should be at the heart of future policymaking (Figure 4.3).

This isn't an explicit conversation about AI; in fact, this consideration should apply to all technology that requires the use of personalised data. AI perhaps has provided another catalyst, due to the apparent implications of data sharing, to

DIGITAL FUTURES
11 CHILD RIGHTS PRINCIPLES
Research at LSE and 5Rights Foundation

	Principle	Articles
	1. EQUITY AND DIVERSITY Be inclusive, treat everyone fairly and provide for diverse needs and circumstances	Articles 2, 9, 10, 18, 20–23, 25, 30, 37–38, 40 UNCRC
	2. BEST INTERESTS Embed children's best interests in product development, design and policy	Article 3(1) UNCRC
	3. CONSULTATION Engage and listen to the views of children in product development, design and policy	Article 12 UNCRC
	4. AGE APPROPRIATE Develop policies and products that are age appropriate by design and consider using age assurance	Articles 5, 18 UNCRC
	5. RESPONSIBLE Comply with legal frameworks, provide remedies as needed and conduct a Child Rights Impact Assessment	Articles 4, 18, 41–42 UNCRC
	6. PARTICIPATION Enable children's participation, expression and access to information	Articles 7, 8, 13–15, 17 UNCRC
	7. PRIVACY Embed privacy-by-design and data protection in policies and product development and use	Article 16 UNCRC
	8. SAFETY Embed safety-by-design in policies and product development and use	Articles 11, 19, 34, 35, 37, 38, 39, 40 UNCRC
	9. WELLBEING Enhance and do not harm the health and wellbeing of all children	Articles 6, 7, 9, 10, 20, 21, 22, 23, 24, 25, 26, 27, 33, 39 UNCRC
	10. DEVELOPMENT Enable children's learning, free play, sociability and belonging, and their fullest development	Articles 6, 28, 29, 30, 31 UNCRC
	11. AGENCY Support child users' decision making and reduce exploitative features and business models that harm their agency	Articles 32, 33, 34, 35, 36 UNCRC

Figure 4.3 Digital Futures: 11 Child Rights Principles.

bring this to the fore again. Reading an excellent 2024 article from the **NORRAG Global Education Centre** [33], titled **"AI and Children's Rights"** [34], Sonia Livingstone and Gazal Shekhawat call for a global public debate that includes children's ideas about how to develop AI in ways informed by children's rights. The three takeaways were, firstly, to make some headway on immediate practices and processes, policymakers should deploy established child rights approaches. Secondly, to keep a *"holistic and grounded vision, and to incorporate Child Rights by Design in the commissioning, development and use of AI,"* and finally, a slightly broader request to capture in detail how all of this can specifically apply to AI; then, review is needed for the available child rights guidance and application of child rights impact assessments.

I've gone a bit deeper here than intended, but without knowing who might read my book, I don't want to miss the opportunity just to flag the work we still have to do at a national level.

After a quick segway back to the **Education Data Futures** report I mentioned earlier, in which **Heather Toomey** shared, in her article in the report titled **"Turning data into insight and why data sharing is as vital as it is concerning,"** the following: *"While overflowing filing cabinets historically led to a natural need to purge data for practical reasons, the ever-expanding storage presented by large hard drives and cloud servers has led to data lakes, or more often, unmanaged swamps, with the ability to store ever-increasing electronic and intangible personal data without an easy way to evaluate or control it."* For clarity, when we take lots of data we create a pool of data, make it much larger and we arrive at a data lake.

This isn't the place or format to head off into a detailed discussion on data privacy and security, but suffice it to say, whenever there is a conversation about the inclusion of new technology in any shape or form, this needs to be part of the discussion alongside the more standard **Data Protection Impact Assessment (DPIA)** [35] and perhaps now a child rights impact assessment, too. There is a strong argument that we have too much data (I agree) and that, in parallel, we don't use what we have effectively to help inform relevant decision-making either. Please also note "inform," not "direct"; that's important, too.

As an aside, if you or your organisation's data protection officer want to dive a bit deeper, then you should check out **Convention 108+** [36] **and the "Convention for the Protection of Individuals with Regard to the Processing of Personal Data,"** which sets out specific guidelines for data protection in educational settings.

Dave Leonard, the strategic director of IT (information technology) at **Watergrove Trust**, shared in my 2021 book, *My Secret #EdTech Diary*: *"There is a constant battle between security, usability and costs. It's imperative to manage these three elements whilst delivering a safe environment for teaching and learning and making progress towards the goals identified in your organisation's digital strategy."* Often, usability and costs drive the direction of travel, and sometimes we need to ensure *"more speed but less haste,"* especially when it comes to reviewing our data and privacy obligations.

Table 4.2 Potential Benefits of AI in Education

\multicolumn{5}{c}{**Potential Benefits of AI in Education**}				
Content development and differentiation	Assessment design and timely, effective feedback	Tutoring and personalised learning assistance	Aiding creativity, collaboration, and skills development	Operational and administrative efficiency
Plagiarism and academic dishonesty	Reduced student and teacher agency and accountability	Compromised student privacy and unauthorised use of data	Over-reliance and loss of critical thinking skills	Perpetuating societal basis
Potential Risks				

Impact on Skills Development: Could greater reliance on AI tools impact the development of essential skills like critical thinking and problem-solving, and how can educators maintain a balance between AI use and traditional learning methods?

There is a natural balance to be struck here, and as with most things in education, often it is the nuance of the method of application that shapes a positive or negative impact.

A convenient summary highlighting the potential benefits and risks of AI in education was shared by **TeachAI** in **"AI Guidance For Schools Toolkit"** [37], where **Pat Yongpradit**, chief academic officer of **Code.org** and lead of TeachAI, said, *"My sincere hope is that teachers feel guided and supported by their leaders as we all adapt to the changes AI brings to education."* I have summarised this in Table 4.2.

Not only is this a handy encapsulation of the discussion, but as you can see, in the case of skills, they feature as both benefiting from and being at risk from the adoption of AI tools in school. The real discussion point in our schools needs to be the how, as I have discussed earlier, how we plan to use, how we plan to measure impact, and, of course, not forgetting the why. Why are we doing this, and very specifically, does this application actually add value?

The most successful future citizens will possess a core body of knowledge – cultural capital – coupled with the digital, creative and social skills to make use of the technological opportunities that present themselves. We need to design and deliver curricula in all our schools to equip these future leaders. Sir Hamid Patel, CEO Star Academies Trust

A 2024 article in ***eSchoolNews*** titled **"What is the Impact of Artificial Intelligence on Students?"** [38] stated: *"Overall, the positive impact of AI on students includes personalized instruction, enhanced critical thinking skills, and better* *preparation for the evolving demands of the digital age, contributing to a more dynamic and adaptive educational experience. However, responsible implementation and addressing ethical considerations are crucial to maximize the benefits of AI and mitigate potential drawbacks, ensuring a positive and equitable impact on students' overall learning and development."*

To further highlight the yin and yang of considerations regarding skills, 2024 research posted on the **Social Science Research Network (SSRN)** [39], titled **"The Impact of Artificial Intelligence on Students' Learning Experience"** [40] concluded that AI-powered tools can promote active participation, critical thinking, and problem-solving skills, creating learning environments that closely mirror real-world scenarios. However, it also highlighted *"there is a potential risk of over-reliance on AI technologies, leading to a passive learning experience for students. Balancing the use of AI with human instruction and guidance is crucial to maintain meaningful interactions and promote deeper understanding."*

Similar 2024 research shared in ***Cogent Education***, titled **"Critical thinking in the AI era: An exploration of EFL students' perceptions, benefits, and limitations"** [41] highlighted the following: *"The study concluded that AI can be an asset in the development of critical thinking skills, but with caveats that require careful management. A balanced approach that capitalizes on AI's strengths while being aware of its limitations is necessary for cultivating robust critical thinking abilities among EFL students."*

Equity and Access: How can schools ensure equitable access to AI tools and resources to prevent the widening of the digital divide among students?

The digital divide has been a topic that has been discussed and signposted for many years, but perhaps the 2020 pandemic amplified that more than ever the need for all children to have access to a device and connectivity to continue their learning journey. Of course, it isn't just access to a device, but often, it's about the right device and how long they have access to it. We saw households with multiple children of different ages needing to share resources and connectivity, and that potentially disadvantaged their access to the online resources they needed compared to peers.

It's worth reminding ourselves on a global level, according to **UNESCO** [42], approximately half of the world's population (3.6 billion people) still lack an internet connection. Over 450 million, or nearly one-third of students globally, cannot access remote learning or resources.

According to a **Nuffield Foundation**–funded study by the **Institute of Fiscal Studies** in 2022 [43], using data from UK schools, less than 50% of students from low-income backgrounds (measured by whether a student qualified for free school meals) had reached expected levels of achievement at the end of primary school versus 70% of students from better-off families. It doesn't take much of a leap to see that as our curriculum and learning pathways become more digital, this gap risks widening further.

The digital divide isn't just a "home" conversation; it can apply just as easily in our schools, either in comparison to other schools that have more resources or a clearer focus on digital use. Sometimes it is singularly with a school where the digital resources are not suitable for some learners with additional needs. In essence, we might choose the most powerful and complete tool, but in doing so, we create a digital divide between learners.

What is clear to me is that as more sophisticated tools and platforms become available, the digital divide conversation will be as much about digital skills and competency as it will be about physical access to a tablet or laptop with connectivity.

I really liked this simple "evolution of the digital divide" shared in a 2023 article by the **Brookings Institute** titled **"AI and the next digital divide in education"** [44]. **Michael Tucano** summarised it while asking whether access to AI might represent a new (third) digital divide in education – or, to put bluntly, where the rich have access to technology powered by AI and to teachers who can help them use it as part of their learning, while the poor just have access to the technology.

> **The following is the evolution of the "digital divide":**
>
> **The first digital divide:** The rich have technology, while the poor do not.
> **The second digital divide:** The rich have technology and the skills to use it effectively, while the poor have technology but lack skills to use it effectively.
> **The third digital divide:** The rich have access to both technology and people to help them use it, while the poor have access to technology only.

If we choose to embrace and integrate AI tools, chatbots, and more into our curriculum, then we also need to be mindful of ensuring that all learners have equal access to the resources. I often start discussions on "how to evaluate digital tools" with a base set of must-haves, and one is that it is platform and device agnostic, ensuring whatever technology children have at home, they will at least have some level of equity and access.

Sir Hamid Patel, CEO of Star Academies Trust, wrote in a February 2024 article for *SchoolsWeek* titled **"Five policies to make AI-enabled learning safe and equitable"** [45] that AI's potential to transform education must be matched by ambitious policies to ensure its benefits are shared (and its risks are mitigated). He said: *"By the end of this decade, every child should have an AI tutor from the age of five. Making such tools available free-of-charge to families across the country could help eradicate educational inequality far more effectively than several decades of policy and funding."* It is worth noting he was clear that he was not advocating that AI supersedes human interaction.

Around the globe, one of the considerations for access to new (and appropriate) AI tools is affordability. A study conducted in 2023 by the Brookings Institute found that AI-driven tutoring systems are more likely to be used at private schools, while public schools are more likely to adopt traditional teaching methods.

I have to just add to the bottom of this that for some years I have been an ambassador for the amazing folks at the **Digital Poverty Alliance** [46], who have a very simple vision: *"To live in a world which enables everyone to access the life-changing benefits that digital brings."* I would encourage you to check out their work and find ways to support them.

Ethical Use of AI: What guidelines and policies should schools develop to ensure the safe and ethical use of AI? How do we address concerns about academic integrity and ensure that AI tools enhance rather than replace human interaction and judgement?

We are going to cover some of this in more detail in the subsequent topics, but for many, this starts with having a clear adoption plan for the use of AI, which ensures all of those key questions and concerns are discussed and, where appropriate, mitigated early on.

I also shared a perspective for a 2024 article I wrote for **Forbes** magazine titled **"6 Considerations for A School District's AI Strategy"** [47], where I recommend focusing on these six key strands. Firstly, you must define your vision, or, as the **World Economic Forum** [47] shared: *"AI should be employed purposefully to support and enrich the learning experience, promoting student and staff well-being, and enhancing administrative functions. The focus should be on using AI to help all students achieve educational goals while considering equity, inclusivity, and reducing the digital divide."* After that, consider the ethics, being mindful of what information we choose to share with the tool. They learn from what we feed into them, and it's for that reason that we should not use personal data with an unknown source. Then, we should ensure that we think about inclusion and how our technology can improve accessibility and access for all. After that, there is transparency and engagement with parents, lots of good quality training, and finally, looking at different and relevant ways to measure impact.

This has been quite an introduction, but I really feel that all of those key strands needed to be flagged for context. I also want to ensure you have some clear next steps, alongside those I have shared above, so I am signposting the excellent 2024 research and report from the excellent team at **EducateVentures** [48] titled **"Shape of the Future: How Education System Leaders Can Respond to the Provocations of Artificial Intelligence,"** which is a set of insights and recommendations from 23 groups of schools.

8 Strands for you to be mindful of as part of your broader AI strategy

1. Strategic Approach: Advising that MATs should develop clear AI strategies aligned with their own educational vision, governance, safeguarding, and ethical considerations.

2. AI Literacy: They highlighted that there is a pressing need for comprehensive AI awareness and literacy training for all stakeholders within the school ecosystem.

3. Curriculum and Assessment: They identified that the integration of AI will require a review of curriculum content and, as I discussed earlier, assessment methods, with a targeted focus on developing critical thinking and AI literacy skills. (See chapter 2.)

4. Equity and Access: They recommend that MATs should address potential digital divides (as I discuss in chapter 5) and that you should aim to ensure equitable access to AI technologies across all school cohorts.

5. Staff Development: This is no surprise; they highlighted that ongoing professional development is crucial to equipping education stakeholders with the skills to effectively address the opportunities and risks associated with AI.

6. Ethical Considerations: They identified that robust frameworks are needed to address data privacy, bias in AI systems, and the ethical use of AI in education, topics we cover later in this chapter.

7. Research and Evaluation: They recommend that MATs should participate in ongoing research to evaluate the impact of AI on learning outcomes and teaching practices.

8. Collaboration: They recommend, and again, I fully support that enhanced cooperation between MATs, educational bodies, and technology providers is needed to share best practices and look to standardise approaches to AI implementation.

Lots for you to reflect on from this chapter so far, but now I have set the scene; these are the key questions I want to discuss further.

Right now we are AI aware in the broadest sense (hopefully). Let's dive into a few choice questions that seem to be on the rise.

AI AS COLLABORATOR

Could AI become the base for assessment, lesson planning, and basic instruction, freeing teachers to be mentors and facilitators?

I have hopefully sowed the seeds of this question in the introduction to this chapter, sharing examples and approaches for generating lesson plans and effective resources for teachers, as well as draft resources. To be totally honest, many of the school leaders I talk to have a view, but often it's anecdotal and not from personal insights or practical experiences. AI is already embedded in many tools we use in our schools to help accelerate tasks. There is little left to debate on the topic of lesson planning; it's already being done regularly by many, and the limitations are more likely to be prompt crafting skills or the definitions provided. That's not to imply the output will be perfect; it will need human nuance and frequent tweaking, but the basic legwork will be done for you. Can you automatically craft lesson plans without any human revision? I haven't seen the evidence to suggest any platforms have a level of accuracy that wouldn't warrant some level of human oversight.

On this particular topic, **Phillip Alcock** shared: *"Undoubtedly, AI will take on mundane and challenging roles that are easily systematized. With advancements like memory in chatbots and versatile 'personalised bots' capable of multiple tasks, teachers' roles will shift as AI generates lessons. This allows teachers to tailor aspects like discussion, metacognitive strategies, and social-emotional interventions. Daily lessons can be adapted to recent events, and teachers will need to listen and participate in workshops and events actively."* I agree with him, but in plenty of cases, we aren't quite there yet to have full confidence.

Thinking about the speed of advancements in AI, and curating resources to support teaching, **Leon Furze** commented: *"Multimodal generative AI is already on a path to becoming the next major production medium for digital technologies. If we consider how word processors and slide show software impacted digital text, then it's easy to see how GenAI might be the next 'platform' for media production."*

Leon and I absolutely agree that teachers have a role that extends beyond mere facilitators though; to me, that role is as a designer, not just a producer. I think the debate is over on the topic of AI's potential to support lesson planning. It's arrived, and many are refining and using it with purpose. When I think back to the topic of the pressures on teacher retention, workload, and wellbeing, time-saving tools fall high on the priority list for system leaders ... or should!

As **Clare Flintoff** shared, *"Imagine having expert personalised guidance, tailored to your preferred way of learning, with just the right amount of challenge that helps you to see your progress and keeps you motivated to learn more. From the perspective of the learner, this sounds great."* We can all reflect on this and consider if teachers were able to work with AI, creating personalised learning opportunities for every student in their class, this could be a good thing and certainly an improvement on the current system of much more generic planning, grouping, and intervention.

One word of caution: Time-saving curation of lesson plans and resources does NOT remove the role of the educator in this process. As **Carla Aerts** shared, *"this will need to be carefully scaffolded, curated and supported. This would need to happen in co-creative, collaborative and critical environments that are never led by the technology, but by the human who knows how to be in the driving seat. AI should not be seen as THE panacea for workload, but as an augmenter and enabler to free up time for teaching (and learning)."* If we remember nothing else other than AI and any other tool is never going to see the panacea to workload, or teaching or learning, then we won't go too far wrong.

So, AI has the potential to become a core tool for tasks like lesson planning and basic instruction, hopefully freeing teachers to concentrate on mentoring and guiding students. However, the core message is that it's essential that teachers maintain their role as experts, using their experience and intuition to ensure AI responses are accurate and reliable. It's also important for teachers to address issues like bias in AI prompts. With a balanced understanding of AI's strengths and its limits, then we can enhance creativity and provide more personalised support while using technology to help streamline some of those administrative tasks.

AI and assessment

Hmm, now the tricky one I have been procrastinating on for quite a bit. It's probably a topic I should be writing about in another year's time: **AI tools for assessment**. The jury seems to be a "yes, but" verdict. Yes, AI tools do provide assessment features, naturally depending on the type of assessment. Quickly constructed formative assessments, multiple-choice quizzes, and so on can be used to accelerate automated feedback and signpost areas to improve, linked to rubrics, etc. As we move into the analysis of essay writing, for example, the evidence gets much thinner. The guiding light seems to be that we need to consider our current assessment approaches more critically. Does the assessment design really measure what we want it to measure? And always asking how else we might ascertain students' learning.

I asked **Matthew Wemyss**, the assistant school director at the **Cambridge School of Bucharest**, in Romania, if AI could become the base tools for assessment, lesson planning, and basic instruction, and his response was emphatic: *"Absolutely. It can become a foundational tool for tasks like assessment, lesson planning, and even basic instruction, giving teachers more space to focus on being mentors and facilitators. I've actually started a programme where students engage with a chatbot to map out a customised learning pathway through their units. They begin with a self-assessment, then work with the bot to create a bespoke plan and even design their own rubric. Over the course of a four-week project, the AI helps students pace their progress, direct them to resources, and interact with them to keep them on track."*

Whilst there is a clear yes to this topic, the "but" still really rings loud for me. To date, the pedagogical implications of integrating generative AI into educational assessments remain fairly invisible in the mainstream academic literature, albeit that may reflect my research skills. That said, some research, including **Smolansky et al.** [49], highlights that, within a higher education context, there may be gaps between students' and teachers' perspectives on how to achieve the best assessment approach, highlighting from their surveys that teachers preferred adapted assessments that assume AI will be used by the students and encourage critical thinking. The students' reaction was mixed, largely due to concerns about a loss of creativity.

A similar piece of work at the higher education level was undertaken and shared in a research paper, **"Perceived Impact of Generative AI on Assessments: Comparing Educator and Student Perspectives in Australia, Cyprus, and the United States"** by **Kizilcec et al.** [50], highlighting that the growing use of generative AI tools built on LLMs questions the sustainability of traditional assessment practices and identifies essay and coding assessments as being most impacted.

Mark Anderson, often known as "the ICT evangelist" is a former school leader with more than 20 years of experience in the classroom, said: *"This is the wrong approach, AI should be seen more as a co-intelligence that needs guidance, think Padawan and Jedi. AI is amazing but it needs the right ingredients in order for it to be used to its best. Think of baking. You might have the best oven in the world, but if you use old eggs and flour, you'll unlikely yield good results. It's those expert teachers who will make the most of AI to inform improvements and productivity gains in the areas mentioned above which isn't something which would hold true for all teachers."*

I think it's fair to say that there also seems to be much more research in the context of higher education, perhaps reflecting an earlier adoption and the nature of assessment for older students. As always, if you look hard enough, though, there are still some early shoots of evidence to identify. The research paper **"Challenges and opportunities for classroom-based formative assessment and AI: a perspective article"** by **Hopfenbeck et al.** [51] discusses the opportunities that AI brings to help address long-standing challenges in formative assessment and also reviews the new challenges that are introduced by AI within formative assessment approaches.

They highlighted that to carry out a formative assessment, teachers need to understand each student's progress and how to help them reach their learning goals. In a traditional classroom, this can be tricky since it involves keeping track of the whole class and giving individual feedback. Teachers might do this through self-assessment, peer assessment, or group work, but finding ways to tailor feedback for everyone is challenging. They also shared that research has shown that these practices are difficult to implement at scale and in approaches that are sustainable over time [52].

Much of the foundation of their research showed that capacity and workload limited the level and detail of formative assessment that can be undertaken, and with that in mind, AI provides an opportunity to help mitigate some of that. They highlighted: *"[A]nother significant opportunity that AI offers for formative assessment is the improvement of feedback both in quantity and quality. The main goals of formative assessment are to provide constructive feedback based on students' responses and to help teachers design differentiated instructional strategies and sustain students in self-regulating their learning. AI can delve into the data to identify the patterns on which dynamic, customized, individualized, and visualized feedback can be automatically generated."* This referenced research by **Gardner et al.** [53] on automated essay scoring systems and computerized adaptive tests. This felt like a bit of a rabbit hole to dive down into, but with the paper titled **"Artificial intelligence in educational assessment: 'Breakthrough? Or buncombe and ballyhoo?",** how could I resist including some ballyhoo to the discussion?

The conclusion drawn from the research undertaken by **Hopfenbeck et al.** was presented as a set of suggestions on how to integrate AI successfully into formative assessments. I attempt to summarise these as follows:

- Use AI to help with feedback, especially in large classes where it's tough for teachers to give everyone timely responses.

- Encourage students to take more responsibility for their learning by setting goals, tracking progress, and adjusting their strategies based on automated AI feedback.

- Make sure students understand the importance of using AI ethically, particularly in assessments.

- Guide students in using AI, helping them interpret feedback and set realistic learning goals.

- Support collaboration between teachers and researchers to study how AI affects learning and engagement.

- Acknowledge that the role of teachers is evolving with AI-enhanced learning (we aren't there yet, and it's moving at pace).

That feels like a pretty good baseline to include in your planning as AI becomes more relevant and appropriate for your school.

It feels to me that assessment design is also key to utilising AI tools effectively. For example, if we flip it 180 degrees and are trying to mitigate students using AI to produce their answers (or, as some might define, "cheat"), then research by **Rudolph et al.** [54] recommends the following: *"To ensure that it is your students who are completing assessments and demonstrating their learning, assignments and assessments should be constructed in such a way that they are challenging to complete using AI tools or by copying from external sources."* That is not a revelation, to be honest, and I suspect most will already be reflecting on this, but thinking about the design can help build confidence in the quality of the resulting assessment.

An assessment scale

Just on that point concerning students using AI to produce their work (perhaps more typically in the context of higher and further education), and I apologise as this is a small detour, we need to build into our policies an approach to ensure students are made aware of the potential consequences of misusing AI academically. The **"AI Assessment Scale"** (AIAS) by Perkins **et al.** [55] allows for the integration of generative AI tools into any educational assessment by outlining the different levels of AI usage allowed in assessments. It is intended to provide clarity and transparency for both students and teachers and potentially offers an approach to assessment that recognises the opportunities of AI (rather than banning) while still signposting that there are situations where AI tools may not be pedagogically appropriate or allowed.

It's certainly a topic that requires teachers to refine their approaches. A research article from the **Chartered College** titled **"AI and assessment: Rethinking assessment strategies and supporting students in appropriate use of AI"** [56] highlighted that traditional assessment methods often fall short in capturing students' true abilities and fostering authentic learning experiences, and the introduction of AI tools could further complicate accurately assessing student learning.

Asking the right questions

I had the pleasure of being invited to the **Association of Head Teachers in Essex** summer conference this year, and as an extra bonus, I was speaking alongside **Daisy Christodoulou**, someone I have respected for many years. I would also encourage you to check out her latest book, ***Seven Myths about Education*** [57]. I wanted to just insert this into the discussion as she was speaking about assessment approaches and happened to signpost the variability in the simple process of students undertaking multiple-choice tests. Quick formative assessment with our students and we get confidence in where they are with their learning. So, let me ask you a quick multiple-choice question: What is the capital of the country Namibia in Africa?

Is it (a) Windhoek, (b) Rehoboth, (c) Walvis Bay, or (d) Oshakati? Any ideas? How about if I had asked someone else to draft the same question to their readers, but they chose to give them these options: (a) London, (B) Sydney, (c) Windhoek, or (d) New York? Does that feel a bit easier? So, can we now compare the pass rate between my multiple-choice test and those from the easier one, given they were both about the same subject and just set by two different people? You can hopefully see where I am going with this. Any assessment needs to have some human cross-referencing if we want to have confidence in comparing and contrasting data, and that's just as relevant with AI tools. There is, of course, the potential to remove that variability of human questioning across class groups with an appropriate AI tool, too.

I'm going to drop that old computer programming adage in for a second time, "garbage in, garbage out," which refers to bad code equalling a resulting bad program. But the same can apply to assessments at all levels: bad questions, or inconsistent questions = bad assessment data. AI applications can generate and undertake assessments for you, but confidence comes from the human review, refinement, and nuance of how they are presented.

In the context of AI use for basic instruction, we might differ on the definition, but I would argue there are plenty of well-established personalised learning platforms; some that I mentioned earlier provide a good level of instruction and guidance on a curriculum pathway.

I reached out to **Dr. Rachelle Dené Poth**, who is a Spanish and STEAM (Science, technology, engineering, and mathematics) teacher at **Riverview School District** in Pittsburgh, USA, who shared, *"AI can be leveraged as an assistant for teachers to enable teachers to have more time with students and colleagues. The teacher still needs to have the human connection and build relationships with students, which is something that AI cannot do."* In the context of providing guidance, she also shared that *"AI may be able to provide guidance, as some chatbots have been created and are in place to provide emotional support. However, this cannot be a replacement for a teacher because of the uniquely human characteristics that we possess. An emotional connection exists and grows over time between a teacher and a student, a mentorship that AI cannot replicate."* Amen to that.

Kat Cauchi, a former UK primary teacher and community engagement manager at **NetSupport** [59], said: *"Staff need the time to evaluate AI tools and learn to best utilise them for them to have the intended outcomes, however, if this can be done and with the right tools selected I think there is potential here to save teachers time and cut down on bureaucracy so teachers can do the part of their job that they love – teaching!"* So as Kat and Rachelle share, it's a foundation of the right tools, confidence in their use, and recognition that they are part of the recipe and don't replace the key human and emotional ingredients.

You could do a lot worse than looking at the guidance shared in the 2023 paper by **Arran Hamilton**, **Dylan Wiliam**, and **John Hattie** titled **"The Future of AI in Education: 13 things we can do to minimize the damage"** [60]. They proposed regulations to slow down the rate of AI advancement, *"so that we can collectively think and agree which of the four scenarios (or other destinations) suits humanity best. Otherwise, the decision will be taken for us, through happenstance and it may be almost impossible to reverse."* They shared a perspective that there is a grave risk that we then become de-educated and de-coupled from the driving seat to the future. Highlighting that with all the hype about AI, we need to properly assess these risks to collectively decide whether the AI upsides are worth it and whether we should "stick or twist." Their paper aimed to consolidate the debate and reduce the probability that we, as they reference *"sleepwalk to a destination that we don't want and can't reverse back out of."*

Allowing for the knowledge that the time it takes this manuscript to arrive as a book on your desk (and thank you for purchasing), it's clear that the use of AI in assessment is not a maybe topic any more; it's happening, and there are some excellent tools and frameworks and following closely behind, guidance to try and maximise the benefits it can offer. It is not without risks, it is far from perfect, and the more we adopt, the more we need to empower and be mindful of human oversight.

This is not a race, however; as evidence grows, we will be better able to refine where it can add the most value. For now, here are the key considerations to ensure you have firmly on your radar:

1. **A time-saving tool**: AI has already demonstrated its ability to assist with tasks like drafting lesson planning and assessment, but it won't replace teachers. Teachers still need bring their expertise and human oversight to ensure AI-generated content is accurate, relevant, and aligned with their individual students' needs.

2. **Personalised learning**: AI can certainly enhance personalised learning by creating customised lesson plans and assessments, allowing teachers to focus more on mentoring and guiding students. However, teachers should always aim to co-create and fine-tune (check) AI-generated output to ensure it fits the purpose.

3. **AI and assessment limitations:** While AI can help streamline certain types of assessments (like quizzes or basic tests), its role is more nuanced, and with complex assessments, such as essay writing, it is much more limited. Teachers need to design assessments thoughtfully to ensure AI supports, rather than undermines, authentic learning ... and assessment.

4. **The ethical use of AI**: We all need to be aware of ethical concerns with AI, such as bias in prompts, data privacy, or simple misuse. Schools need clear policies and guidance to help students and teachers use AI responsibly, ensuring it enhances rather than detracts from the learning process.

5. **The human connection:** AI can never replace the emotional and relational aspects of teaching. Teachers play a crucial role in building relationships, fostering emotional growth, and providing the mentorship that AI cannot replicate. The focus should remain on empowering teachers to use AI simply as one of a number of tools, to enable them to have more time to do the important aspects of teaching.

THE ESSENTIAL HUMAN TOUCH

Can AI ever replace emotional connection, personal guidance, and the inspiration of a great teacher?

I love this quote by **William Arthur Ward**, referenced in the 2010 article **"The True Teacher"** by Fred Herbert [61], who said, *"It's been observed that, "The mediocre teacher tells. The good teacher explains. The superior teacher demonstrates. The great teacher inspires."*

he says that proponents of increased use of AI education also claim that AI will soon be able to perform the first three duties. But what about the fourth? Education is, after all, a fundamentally human endeavour.

It's a lovely way to kick off this question, as so much we have discussed around AI has been the concern over how we protect and hold dear those most human traits and that interpersonal dynamic between teacher and student.

Let me just drop into our thoughts at this stage a bigger question shared by **Professor Sugata Mitra**, from MIT, in a 2012 article, **"Is Education Obsolete?"** [62]. Mitra presents a scenario in which someone with AI-driven glasses pretends to be a doctor. That person might know nothing about medicine but might be able to figure out a diagnosis process entirely with online digital information. Then he asked us to imagine that this person does it repeatedly. If that pseudo-doctor's performance after a year is equal to or above the national average, might we let that person practise medicine? By the third year of pretending to be a doctor, has this person actually become one? When Mitra posted this question to his Facebook page, he heard from an accountant and an investment banker who claimed to have done just that.

It felt relevant to include, as it challenges our longer-term view of learning, how we acquire knowledge and skills through traditional learning, or by doing so with the support of technology on our shoulders.

The human factor

In terms of the bigger question of AI ever replacing that core human connection with a teacher, I do not see it; in fact, the more we see the role of technology in our lives, the more this amplifies the value and impact of human-to-human interaction. The simple truth is that most children crave a meaningful relationship with their teachers. This is a normal part of the development of our children. No matter how sophisticated they are, digital tools are just that: tools. We are looking for ways to understand more about learning and how technology can make learning more accessible, more personalised, more relevant, and hopefully more memorable.

Just like the existing tools the teacher has at their disposal. Whether it's an interactive whiteboard, a tablet, a marker pen or even a glue stick. AI is just another tool to help boost engagement and improve the delivery of teaching. As has been quoted by many, "AI will not replace teachers. But AI will replace teachers who don't engage with AI." Abid Patel

Some of our conversations around AI surrogating the role of the teacher have, of course, been led by the tech creators themselves, and naturally, when you have a solution, you want to share enthusiasm and excitement at its potential for impact. But in education, evidence-informed leads the way, so views tend to soften as our knowledge and understanding of these new tools evolve and develop. **Sal Khan**, founder of **Khan Academy** [63], is a good example; extolling the potential impact of AI for some time now has started to soften his promises of a new dawn, shifting his position and promise in an August 2024 *TES* magazine interview titled

"**Salman Khan's third attempt to change the world of education**" [64], where he shifted from his previous promise to give every student on the planet an artificially intelligent but amazing personal tutor that would result in learning gains two standard deviations above the average to where he now describes that claim and model as "unnatural." As a complete aside, I talk about **Blooms 2 Sigma Problem** [65] in a later chapter, which neatly aligns with this.

In the same interview, Khan also shifted from his previous promise to give every teacher on the planet a fantastic, AI teaching assistant to sharing in his interview that the likely outcome is that "some of a teacher's job becomes a little bit easier". The truth is we do not know the ultimate capabilities of technology and how it might be used, where appropriate, to impact teaching, learning, or school management positively.

So crystal ball gazing does need to come with a big disclaimer. I am of no doubt we will see more and more tools, many AI-based, within our schools, but the one fact, the one perception that does not rely on any crystal ball, is that children benefit from human interaction, nurture, and support.

Educator perspectives

As you would expect, much of this book is a consolidation of my thoughts and perspectives shaped and challenged by the voices of many educators from around the world, and in each section, I have reached out to those whom I know have the best, lived experience or "skin in the game" to share their perspectives, too. **Mark Anderson** shared that AI will "*[n]ever replace, but definitely emulate. We are already seeing the benefit of AI systems for assistance and support with mental health issues, guidance and relationships, when humans are time poor.*"

I mentioned **John Mikton** earlier, from the **International School of Geneva**. He has 30 years of "skin in the game," and I asked him if AI could ever replace emotional connection, personal guidance, and the inspiration of a great teacher. His response: "*At this stage, AI cannot replace the emotional connection, personal guidance, and inspiration of a great teacher. However, the issue is more about how humans engage and form relationships with AI tools. AI, especially chatbots, can provide companionship, guidance, and a sense of always having a listener who seems to understand and amplify our thoughts and beliefs. As AI evolves towards Artificial General Intelligence (AGI) and Artificial Superintelligence (ASI), this will become an even more critical question.*"

There's growing evidence that humans want AI tools to be more human-like, and although this might sound like science fiction, many current interactions with chatbots already verge on forming human-like bonds. John believes this raises important ethical questions that we need to address with students. It's not a definitive answer, as the progress to AGI (artitifical general intelligence) and ASI (artificial superintelligence) holds many opportunities and threats. Still, again, it amplifies the role of humans in shaping how and where we deploy future tools and the safeguards that we enforce.

Dr. Will Van Reyk, the deputy director of innovation at **North London Collegiate School**, shared this: "*No, AI can't replace the human touch; in some ways, AI will highlight the uniquely human skills and qualities even more. I do think, though, on the personal guidance front, AI has huge potential for offering personalised advice and resources to students and in particular in their self-study and revision time.*"

There is certainly a consensus that AI can provide a "human touch," but that is quite different. Should it, and does it add value or benefit to our children? For me, the risk outweighs the reward and can easily become a "slippery slope." **Matt Jessop** was much more succinct and direct in his perspective: "*No, and alarmed to see AI tools (like a necklace) that attempt to be a 'substitute' friend for lonely pupils – if we – society, education and education staff – ever need to rely on AI to keep a child from being friendless, having an emotional connection or being inspired by a teacher then we have failed.*"

He is, of course, right, and we need to be really clear on where AI has a role and where we need to think human, not tech, especially in those formative years of a child's development. It can be subtle. AI chatbots can be used to provide personalised advice and guidance to students, as shared earlier, but that line of the tool being perceived as a friend or sentient in any way should not be crossed.

Craig McGee, a former head teacher and current chair of governors of a primary school, who also develops tools to support school leaders in reducing workload shared that "*there's actually a place for emotional support this way. AI could provide advice, reassurance and guidance about a problem or issue that a young person (or even an adult) is embarrassed to share with someone else. It also takes the emotion out of the response. That said, I don't think it can (or should) replace the emotional connection between pupils and teachers.*" He is right on a practical level, but is this really where we want our students to go to seek support?

I can't help but reflect that all the points shared elevate the need to educate our students (and staff) on the AI tools that have been adopted and empower them to understand their roles and limitations. Natural language processing (NLP) has increasingly created an interface that can converse in an ever more human way and that can change or invoke an unhealthy emotional connection.

On that note, I think the **Turing Test** [66] is no longer an adequate measure of intelligence behaviour, courtesy of NLP advances. Those advances alone significantly blur the lines when children interact with AI tools. We should never forget that at a very simplistic level, as clever as it may seem, AI is simply the result of many computers working together, learning from the input of humans, to simulate human behaviour. It is the simulation where AI lacks that human touch or can potentially create harm.

Anyway, if we put the future gazing and associated hype to one side, that awkward question, can AI ever replace emotional connection, personal guidance, and the inspiration of a great teacher ... Nope, not in the purest sense, and nor would we want it to. It can blur some of the edges with the growing capabilities and nuance of dedicated chatbots, but it's incumbent on us to ensure those lines are not crossed and students recognise the clear boundary between digital assistance and human teachers. I think the best checklist for this question is probably as follows:

1. **AI can't replace emotional connections**: Whilst AI can assist with tasks, it will never fully replace those deeper emotional connections and personal insights that a teacher offers. Relationships with students are a fundamental part of education, which AI cannot, and in my view, should not replicate.

2. **Use AI as a tool, not a substitute**: AI should be viewed as an additional tool for teachers, helping with administrative tasks and personalised learning pathways. However, its role should be clearly defined to avoid crossing into areas like emotional support, where human interaction is crucial. Some may disagree with me on this.

3. **Be mindful of "human-like" AI risks**: AI chatbots may offer a human-like experience, but we should always be cautious of the ethical risks, if, for example, students start forming emotional bonds with AI. We should focus on making students aware of the boundaries between AI assistance and human interaction.

4. **AI for personalised learning, not mentorship**: AI absolutely has the potential to provide tailored academic support and resources, especially in independent study and revision. But, it cannot replicate the support and inspiration a teacher brings to the classroom.

5. **Educate more on AI use**: Schools need to ensure that both students and staff are educated on the strengths and limitations of AI. Understanding its role and how to use it responsibly will help prevent misuse or over-reliance on AI in situations that require human empathy and input.

ETHICS OF AI IN EDUCATION

Who controls the algorithms, and how do we prevent bias and ensure fairness?

This is a tough one, especially as whenever we see national policy groups reflecting and shaping plans for the use of AI, we always see the big tech companies at the table, something I continually warn feels like the foxes guarding the chickens. Perhaps I am unjustifiably cautious or don't give enough credit to the voices of the others at the table, but it's always the same voices who have connections and rarely those within education who can provide a much more nuanced perspective. That's probably me off a few Christmas card lists, but there we are.

I asked **Gary Henderson**, the director of IT at **Millfield School** in the United Kingdom, about this topic and he reminded me that *"we need to acknowledge the bias already exists in our text books, in our teaching, etc; We need to accept this before we seek to challenge AI on its Bias, where this bias is simply a magnification of our own human bias as shown online. There is also a challenge in how we seek* *to address bias, as evidenced by Google's failed attempt with its image generation tool. I think this will take schools to be more questioning of vendors and also vendors to be more open of seeking to address bias and inaccuracy; it will need to be a joint effort.*" He's certainly right that this isn't a new challenge and that, as with most, it will require multiple stakeholders to come to a common consensus.

When I asked **Simon Luxford-Moore**, an experienced primary school teacher of 22 years, and head of eLearning at ESMS (Erskine Stewart's Melville Schools), about this topic, he clearly had a similar view to me, suggesting instead: "*This should be developed as a United Nations–style body. Ultimately, it affects all global learners and, irrespective of varying education systems around the world, has a core set of principles that can be supported by different nations/governments/education bodies. Leading PedTech and EdTech experts should be nominated/apply for being part of this organisation and it should be for a maximum of two years before new individuals are circulated.*"

I agree 100% and can think of many who could really add value to the conversation. I think the work I referenced from **EducateVentures** is certainly shifting the dial.

The black box

On this specific topic, I was encouraged to read the book ***Big Nine*** by **Amy Webb** [67], which highlights that the algorithms behind AI are mostly controlled by a few powerful companies, particularly the "big nine" in the United States and China, which she lists as Amazon, Google, Facebook, Tencent, Baidu, Alibaba, Microsoft, IBM, and Apple and that these are the "*new gods of AI and are short-changing our futures to reap immediate financial gain.*" These companies face significant challenges related to oversight, safety, and ethics. However, driven by profits (and power), their influence within our lives is rapidly expanding.

The warning and concern she shares is that this growing control over AI impacts our lives in ways we probably do not fully understand, contributing to a "black box" feeling that obscures the effects AI has on both the ethical and practical aspects of our daily lives. This lack of transparency also exacerbates issues like misinformation and disinformation, which can spread unchecked through AI-driven platforms.

Leon Furze [68] shared with me some hint of positivity around centralised control and the growing availability of open-source code and products, saying: "*Microsoft, Google, Amazon, Apple, and Meta control the algorithms: it's not by chance that the biggest AI systems in the world are owned and operated by the incumbent corporations of social media and digital technology. Only these companies have the funds, the data, and the finances to produce truly powerful models. That being said, I'm optimistic about open source (and I mean real open source, not necessarily Meta's version). I think Open Source will lead to more transparency.*"

Linking quite nicely to that, **Carla Aerts** built on the perspective of the "black box" and lack of control but was also mindful of equity in an AI-driven system that mirrors our actions. She shared: "*This is where the power of tech and the potential for AI feudalism (we already have tech feudalism productising humanity) is going to grow and increase. The issue is that these questions are always behind the tech and that the 'black box' of AI is becoming increasingly non-transparent.*"

I agreed with her perspective and reminder that all the talk about responsible and transparent AI is good, but it is not moving the debate forward. We shouldn't forget that AI is a mirror of us and that the algorithms will amplify our biases and prejudices.

Alongside control, recognising those that pull the levers right now and the possible pathways to greater distributed control, clearly the lack of visibility of systems and tools causes some of the biggest concerns. As **Philip Alcock**, the founder of **AIxPBL**, shared with me: "*Transparency in AI development is the most important element for ensuring fairness and building trust. As the old saying goes, '***Sunlight is the best disinfectant,' and in the realm of AI***, we need to be clear about what 'sunlight' actually is. By making the inner workings of AI systems accessible and understandable through audits, we can prevent and identify biases, thereby fostering confidence in the technology. I see the educational need for a critical understanding of bias and equity as more important now than ever before. We must ensure guidelines are open to change through non-political bipartisan approaches.*"

I asked my good friend, international speaker and hugely proactive voice within the realm of school IT systems and cybersecurity, **Abid Patel**, the IT director for **Newham Community Learning** in London, for his thoughts from a school data security perspective. He shared: "*Whilst AI has generated immense interest in the education community, there is a considerable responsibility on leaders to ensure that AI is used safely within the school environment. Before the use of AI in general is authorised, there needs to be a clear understanding of the purpose of using AI or a particular tool for classroom practice.*"

He also suggested that we need to be asking:

- *Is there an understanding of what happens with the data we are inputting?*
- *Is the data being reviewed by human personnel?*
- *Where is it being held?*
- *How is it processed?*
- *Are we ensuring that we comply with local laws and that user privacy is not compromised?*
- *Have users been trained to understand the potential implications?*
- *Are users advised to check every output explicitly and to fact-check the generated output?*
- *Have users been advised that bias with AI-generated content is a very real and regular possibility?*

He also noted that guidance should be given on how to deal with any content that may be of concern and how to report it both internally to leaders and back to the application developers.

I also spoke with **Craig McKee**, who said, "*It's really important to evaluate each and every AI tool that teachers use. Who has created it, what knowledge do they have, and what information does the AI tool use to craft its answer? Answering these questions is a helpful start, but teachers will need support in understanding how answers are generated, the risk of hallucinations or just entirely made-up responses, etc.*"

Visibility

Many of these insights above consolidate into a need to better understand the tools we want to potentially use, seek greater visibility of how our data is used, and, without a doubt, require us to upskill and develop our own competence and confidence using AI tools ourselves.

Dr. Will Van Reyk, the deputy director of innovation at North London Collegiate School, shared with me: "*The best thing teachers can do in relation to ethics and AI is actually teach themselves about AI, its uses and shortcomings, before they use it with students. We cannot prevent bias and unfairness in AI as it is, in many respects, simply a reflection of the world we live in. I think a far better approach is being aware ourselves of ethical issues, pointing them out to students, and teaching students about these potential issues so they are aware of them when using AI.*"

Consolidating these insights raised together, an excellent starting point is to have a clear AI adoption plan of action for your school. A good set of actions you might consider could well be along the lines of these five:

- Develop a comprehensive AI policy that addresses data governance, privacy, equity, teacher training, curriculum integration, and ethical considerations.
- Create a clear IT infrastructure road map that outlines the necessary hardware, software, and network upgrades to support AI applications and data storage, etc.
- Establish a centralised AI guidance team to provide training and technical support to teachers and schools using AI tools.
- Scope AI tools that can impact positively on service delivery, including telephony, management information systems, and integrated AI tools like Microsoft Copilot.
- Conduct regular infrastructure and utility audits, analyses, and evaluations to assess the effectiveness of AI implementation, identify areas for improvement and mitigation, and address any challenges or concerns.

John Mikton ties in with the above list: "*To prevent bias and ensure fairness in AI; it's important for schools and educators to prioritize teaching diversity, equity, inclusion, and justice, and to model these values within school communities. This* *involves embedding these principles into our curriculum, revisiting units, and checking for bias and gender inequity."*

Fortunately, I have an amazing PLN (professional learning network) that I can lean on for support and insights. **Kavitha Ravindran**, a former secondary science teacher and co-founder of **sAInaptic**, shared her guidance on the key steps for developing equitable and trustworthy AI systems. She is quick to acknowledge that bias can enter AI algorithms in various ways, often reflecting inequalities present in training data. EdTech providers have a crucial role in ensuring that AI systems enhance human decision-making rather than perpetuating existing biases. So her two areas of guidance are summarised below and align very nicely with a 2019 report from the **McKinsey Global Institute**, **"Notes from the AI frontier: Tackling bias in AI (and in humans)"** [69], that I would also encourage you to read.

Firstly, leverage AI's strengths in decision-making:

- **Enhanced Accuracy:** AI systems can exclude irrelevant variables that may skew decisions, contrasting with human tendencies to overlook or misrepresent factors.

- **Bias Detection:** AI can analyse patterns and uncover previously unnoticed biases, providing insights into decision-making processes that may not be transparent.

- **Disparate Benefits:** AI can help traditionally disadvantaged groups by enhancing prediction accuracy, as noted by researchers like **Jon Kleinberg** and **Sendhil Mullainathan**. When properly designed, AI systems can offer fairer and more precise outcomes, potentially reducing historical biases and disparities.

And then adopt effective strategies for bias mitigation:

- **Comprehensive Procedures**: Implement robust AI deployment procedures, including technical tools and regular audits.

- **Diverse Data Collection**: Ensure training data encompasses diverse populations to prevent reinforcing biases.

- **Algorithmic Auditing and Transparency**: Conduct regular audits of AI systems and employ explainability techniques to identify and correct biases.

- **Promote Interdisciplinary Collaboration**: Work with AI researchers, domain experts, and ethicists to effectively gain diverse insights and address biases.

- **Human-Machine Collaboration:** Develop systems where human judgement complements AI recommendations, ensuring balanced decision-making.

- **Fact-Based Conversations:** Use tools to compare AI results with human decisions, enhancing understanding and accountability.

I hope we can all agree that it is the responsibility of EdTech providers that use AI in their products to invest in research and education into bias detection and ethical AI practices to foster continual improvement and awareness.

The cold comfort for this topic might well be that this isn't new. The advent of search engines created an opportunity for "the few" to coordinate what was prioritised for our consumption; social media platforms do precisely the same, both for commercial gain and now in the advent of AI we see the same challenges amplified again.

We have to have our eyes wide open. We cannot ignore or avoid due to fear or uncertainty; we need to learn and develop the best possible understanding alongside clear policies and nuanced frameworks in our schools so that we can try, evidence, and be informed of the benefits whilst always looking for ways to mitigate the risks.

Staff needs to be given resources and time to develop their own competencies and confidence, ideally as part of their teacher training from now on, and we must empower our students to be the best possible digital citizens, which will go a long way to equipping them for an AI-driven workplace.

Further Reading

- *The AI Classroom: The Ultimate Guide to Artificial Intelligence in Education*, 2023, Dan Fitzpatrick, Amanda Fox, and Brad Weinstein [16].
- *The Promises and Perils of AI in Education: Ethics and Equity Have Entered the Chat*, 2023, Ken Shelton and Dee Lanier [70].
- *My Secret #EdTech Diary: Looking at Educational Technology through a Wider Lens*, 2021, Al Kingsley [71]
- *The Theory of Educational Technology: Towards a Dialogic Foundation for Design*, 2024, Rupert Wegerif and Louis Major [72].
- *Practical AI Strategies: Engaging with Generative AI in Education*, 2024, Leon Furze [20].
- *How to Teach AI: Weaving Strategies and Activities into Any Content Area*, 2024, Rachelle Dené Poth [58]
- *The EdTech Playbook: Your Definitive Guide to Teaching, Learning and Leading with Technology and AI in Education*, 2025, Mark Anderson and Olly Lewis [73]

References

1. "ChatGPT," OpenAi, [Online]. Available: https://chatgpt.com/
2. "Introducing ChatGPT," OpenAi, 30 November 2022. [Online]. Available: https://openai.com/index/chatgpt/
3. "Hallucinations (artificial intelligence)," Wikipedia, 2024. [Online]. Available: https://en.wikipedia.org/wiki/Hallucination_(artificial_intelligence)
4. "What is AI (artificial intelligence)?," McKinsey & Company, 03 April 2024. [Online]. Available: https://www.mckinsey.com/featured-insights/mckinsey-explainers/what-is-ai

5   "Siri," Apple Corporation, [Online]. Available: https://www.apple.com/uk/siri/
6   "Alexa - Virtual Assistant," Amazon, 2024. [Online]. Available: https://en.wikipedia.org/wiki/Amazon_Alexa
7   "NetFlix," [Online]. Available: https://www.netflix.com/
8   "SRI International," Wikipedia, 2024. [Online]. Available: https://en.wikipedia.org/wiki/SRI_International
9   "Guidance for Generative AI in Education and Research," UNESCO, 16 June 2024. [Online]. Available: https://www.unesco.org/en/articles/guidance-generative-ai-education-and-research
10 "Use of Artificial Intelligence in Education Delivery and Assessment," UK Parliament, 23 January 2024. [Online]. Available: https://post.parliament.uk/research-briefings/post-pn-0712/
11 Education Endowment Foundation, "A Marked Improvement? - a review of the evidence on written marking," 04 2016. [Online]. Available: https://d2tic4wvo1iusb.cloudfront.net/documents/guidance/EEF_Marking_Review_April_2016.pdf?v=1681841884
12 "Workload Challenge: Analysis of Responses," Department for Education, 06 February 2015. [Online]. Available: https://www.gov.uk/government/publications/workload-challenge-analysis-of-teacher-responses
13 C. Bleakley, "How We've Used AI to Reduce Teacher Workloads," Schoolsweek, 04 August 2024. [Online]. Available: https://schoolsweek.co.uk/how-weve-used-ai-to-reduce-teacher-workloads/
14 "Exceed Academies Trust," [Online]. Available: https://www.exceedacademiestrust.co.uk/
15 "The AI Educator," Dan Fitzpatrick, [Online]. Available: https://www.theaieducator.io/
16 D. Fitzpatrick, B. Weinstein and A. Fox, The AI Classroom: The Ultimate Guide to Artificial Intelligence in Education, TeacherGoals Publishing, 2023.
17 M. Anderson, "The Little Book of Generative AI prompts for teachers," ICT Evangelist, [Online]. Available: https://ictevangelist.com/free-resource-the-little-book-of-generative-ai-prompts-for-teachers/
18 "The ICT Evangelist," Mark Anderson, [Online]. Available: https://ictevangelist.com/
19 L. Furze, *Practical AI Strategies: Engaging with Generative AI in Education*, Amba Press, 2024.
20 L. Furze, "Artificial Intelligence and Teacher Workload: Can AI Actually Save Educators Time?," 21 March 2024. [Online]. Available: https://leonfurze.com/2024/03/21/artificial-intelligence-and-teacher-workload-can-ai-actually-save-educators-time/comment-page-1/
21 "Educate on Purpose," Bonnie Nieves, [Online]. Available: www.educateonpurpose.com
22 "Century - AI Powered Online Learning," [Online]. Available: https://www.century.tech/
23 "SPARX Learning," [Online]. Available: https://sparx-learning.com/
24 A. Hussain, "How AI is Enhancing Assessment, Reducing Workload and Improving FE Outcomes," FE Week, 12 2023. [Online]. Available: https://feweek.co.uk/how-ai-is-enhancing-assessment-reducing-workload-and-improving-fe-outcomes/
25 "NCFE," [Online]. Available: https://www.ncfe.org.uk/
26 "AI and Education: Kids Need AI Guidance in School. But Who Guides the Schools?," World Economic Forum, 18 January 2024. [Online]. Available: https://www.weforum.org/agenda/2024/01/ai-guidance-school-responsible-use-in-education/
27 W. J. Yin, "Will Our Educational System Keep Pace with AI? A Student's Perspective on AI and Learning," Educause, 24 January 2024. [Online]. Available: https://er.educause.edu/articles/2024/1/will-our-educational-system-keep-pace-with-ai-a-students-perspective-on-ai-and-learning

28. C. f. D. &. T. CDT, "Off Task: EdTech Threats to Student Privacy and Equity in the Age of AI," 09 2023. [Online]. Available: https://cdt.org/wp-content/uploads/2023/09/091923-CDT-Off-Task-web.pdf
29. A. Kingsley, "Don't Fear AI: How to Harness its Power for Good," School News Australia, 2023. [Online]. Available: https://www.school-news.com.au/education/the-power-of-ai/
30. "Digital Futures for Children," London School of Economics and Political Science, [Online]. Available: https://www.digital-futures-for-children.net
31. "Digital Futures Commission," [Online]. Available: https://digitalfuturescommission.org.uk/
32. S. Livingstone and K. Pothong, "Education Data Futures: Critical, Regulatory and Practical Reflections," Digital Futures Commission, 5 Rights Foundation, 2022. [Online]. Available: https://educationdatafutures.digitalfuturescommission.org.uk/
33. "NORRAG Global Education Centre," Geneva Graduate Institute, [Online]. Available: https://www.norrag.org
34. S. Livingstone and G. Shekhawat, "AI and Children's Rights," 29 May 2024. [Online]. Available: https://www.norrag.org/ai-and-childrens-rights/
35. "Data Protection Impact Assessment - DPIA," Information Commissioners Office (ICO), 19 May 2023. [Online]. Available: https://ico.org.uk/for-organisations/uk-gdpr-guidance-and-resources/accountability-and-governance/guide-to-accountability-and-governance/data-protection-impact-assessments/
36. "Convention 108+. Guidelines for the protection of personal data in educational settings," Council of Europe, 2020. [Online]. Available: https://www.europarl.europa.eu/meetdocs/2014_2019/plmrep/COMMITTEES/LIBE/DV/2018/09-10/Convention_108_EN.pdf
37. TeachAI, "AI Guidance For Schools Toolkit," 2024. [Online]. Available: https://www.teachai.org/toolkit
38. "What is the Impact of Artificial Intelligence on Students?" eSchool News, 05 February 2024. [Online]. Available: https://www.eschoolnews.com/digital-learning/2024/02/05/what-is-the-impact-of-artificial-intelligence-on-students/#:~:text=Overall%2C%20the%20positive%20impact%20of,dynamic%20and%20adaptive%20educational%20experience
39. "Social Science Research Network," SSRN, [Online]. Available: https://www.ssrn.com/index.cfm/en/
40. P. Kaledio, A. Robert and L. Frank, "The Impact of Artificial Intelligence on Students' Learning Experience," 1 February 2024. [Online]. Available: https://doi.org/10.2139/ssrn.4716747
41. D. R. Darwin, N. Mukminatien and N. Suryati, "Critical Thinking in the AI Era: An Exploration of EFL Students' Perceptions, Benefits, and Limitations," *Cogent Education*, vol. 11, no. 1, 2024. https://www.tandfonline.com/doi/ref/10.1080/2331186X.2023.2290342?scroll=top
42. "Scaling up Digital Learning and Skills in the World's Most Populous Countries to Drive Education Recovery," UNESCO, 20 April 2023. [Online]. Available: https://www.unesco.org/en/articles/scaling-digital-learning-and-skills-worlds-most-populous-countries-drive-education-recovery
43. "Lack of Progress on Closing Educational Inequalities Disadvantaging Millions Throughout Life," Institue of Fiscal Studies, 16 August 2022. [Online]. Available: https://ifs.org.uk/inequality/press-release/lack-of-progress-on-closing-educational-inequalities-disadvantaging-millions-throughout-life/
44. M. Trucano, "AI and the Next Digital Divide in Education," Brookings Institute, 10 July 2023. [Online]. https://www.brookings.edu/articles/ai-and-the-next-digital-divide-in-education/

45. S. H. Patel, "Five Policies to Make AI-Enabled Learning Safe and Equitable," SchoolsWeek, 23 February 2024. [Online]. Available: https://schoolsweek.co.uk/five-policies-to-make-ai-enabled-learning-safe-and-equitable/
46. "Digital Poverty Alliance," [Online]. Available: https://digitalpovertyalliance.org/
47. A. Kingsley, "6 Considerations For A School District's AI Strategy," Forbes, 17 July 2024. [Online]. Available: https://www.forbes.com/sites/forbestechcouncil/2024/07/17/6-considerations-for-a-school-districts-ai-strategy/
48. "Shape the Future: How Educational System Leaders can Respond to the Provocations of Artificial Intelligence," Educate Ventures, 2024.
49. A. Smolansky, A. Cram, C. Raduescu, S. Zeivots, E. Huber and R. Kizilcec, "Educator and Student Perspectives on the Impact of Generative AI on Assessments in Higher Education," 2023.
50. R. Kizilcec, E. Huber, E. C. Papanastasiou, A. Cram, C. Makridis, A. Smolansky, S. Zeivots and C. Raduescu, "Perceived Impact of Generative AI on Assessments: Comparing Educator and Student Perspectives in Australia, Cyprus, and the United States," 2024. https://doi.org/10.1016/j.caeai.2024.100269
51. T. N. Hopfenbeck, Z. Zhang, S. Z. Sun, P. Robertson and J. McCrane, "Challenges and Opportunities for Classroom-Based Formative Assessment and AI: A Perspective Article," Frontiers in Education, 2023.
52. T. N. Hopfenbeck and G. Stobart, "Large-Scale Implementation of Assessment for Learning," *Assessment in Education: Principles, Policy & Practice*, 22, pp. 1–2, 2015.
53. J. Gardner, M. O'Leary and L. Yuan, "Artificial intelligence in educational assessment: 'Breakthrough? Or buncombe and ballyhoo?" *Journal of Computer Assisted Learning*, vol. 37, no. 5, pp. 1207–1216, 2021.
54. J. Rudolph, S. Tan and S. Tan, "ChatGPT: Bullshit spewer or the end of traditional assessments in higher education?" *Journal of applied learning and teaching*, vol. 1, no. 6, pp. 342–363, 2023.
55. M. Perkins, L. Furze, J. Roe and J. MacVaugh, "The Artificial Intelligence Assessment Scale (AIAS): A Framework for Ethical Integration of Generative AI in Educational Assessment," *Journal of University Teaching and Learning Practice*, vol. 21, no. 06, pp. 1–18, 2024.
56. L. Meakin, "AI and assessment: Rethinking assessment strategies and supporting students in appropriate use of AI," Chartered College, 13 May 2024. [Online]. Available: https://my.chartered.college/impact_article/ai-and-assessment-rethinking-assessment-strategies-and-supporting-students-in-appropriate-use-of-ai/
57. D. Christodoulou, *Seven Myths about Education*, Routledge, 2014.
58. R. Dene Poth, How to Teach AI: Weaving Strategies and Activities into Any Content Area, International Society for Technology in Education, 2024.
59. "NetSupport - Award Winning Education Solutions," [Online]. Available: www.netsupportsoftware.com
60. A. Hamilton, D. Wiliam and J. Hattie, "The Future of AI in Education: 13 Things We Can Do to Minimize the Damage," 2023.
61. H. L. Fred, "The True Teacher," *Texas Heart Institute Journal*, vol. 37, no. 3, pp. 334–335, 2010.
62. "Is Education Obsolete? Sugata Mitra at the MIT Media Lab," Civic Media, 16 May 2012. [Online]. Available: https://civic.mit.edu/index.html%3Fp=804.html
63. "Khan Academy," [Online]. Available: https://www.khanacademy.org/
64. E. Peirson-Hagger, "Salman Khan's third attempt to change the world of education," TES Magazine, 12 August 2024. [Online]. Available: https://www.tes.com/magazine/analysis/general/salman-khan-how-ai-can-transform-education

65. B. S. Bloom, "The 2 Sigma Problem: The Search for Methods of Group Instruction as Effective as One-to-One Tutoring," *American Educational Research Association*, vol. 13, no. 6, pp. 4–16, 1984.
66. A. Turing, "The Turing Test," 1950. [Online]. Available: https://en.wikipedia.org/wiki/Turing_test
67. A. Webb, *The Big Nine: How the Tech Titans and Their Thinking Machines Could Warp Humanity*, PublicAffairs, 2019.
68. "Leon Furze," [Online]. Available: https://leonfurze.com/
69. J. Silberg and J. Manyika, "Notes from the AI frontier: Tackling the bias in AI (and in humans)," McKinsey Global Institue, 2019.
70. D. Lanier and K. Shelton, The Promises and Perils of AI in Education: Ethics and Equity Have Entered The Chat, Lanier Learning, 2024.
71. A. Kingsley, "*My Secret# EdTech Diary: Looking at Educational Technology through a wider lens*", Hachette UK, 2021.
72. R. Wegerif and L. Major, *The Theory of Educational Technology: Towards a Dialogic Foundation for Design*, Routledge, 2023.
73. M. Anderson and O. Lewis, The EdTech Playbook: Your Definitive Guide to Teaching, Learning and Leading with Technology and AI in Education, John Catt, 2025.
74. "Bloom's 2 sigma problem," Wikipedia, 2010. [Online]. Available: https://en.wikipedia.org/wiki/Bloom%27s_2_sigma_problem

Improving attendance in education – do we need more and different "spaces"?

Congratulations, you made it through the complex and tricky topic of artificial intelligence (AI), only to find yourself reading about the equally tricky topic of improving attendance. Well, on a plus, you are halfway through the topics in the book, so after this, you are on the home straight, but it's fair to say this is one of the most pressing and "current" topics I could have included.

I could have made this a really short chapter and just agreed that we need to get our children back into school. Their attendance is vital for the learning journey, and this is simply a conversation about approaches to get them across the school threshold each morning. Naturally, if that was the end of it, it probably doesn't qualify as an "elephant in the room" type of discussion, so for the purpose of this healthy discussion, is the problem the child, the parent, or the room we are trying to ask them to enter?

Unless you have been on an extended sabbatical, I have no doubt you will be aware that post-COVID attendance levels in our schools have significantly fallen. I'm used to seeing my own schools with attendance levels sitting at 97% to 98% with a few seasonal blips, and I am now pleased to see that our stats start with a 9. Clearly, something is going wrong. We have quite a few factors at play: social, emotional, and mental health (SEMH) factors and anxiety surrounding being at school, parents increasingly working more from home, negative media perceptions around the value of education, schools beyond capacity and struggling to recruit and retain, the list goes on.

Research conducted in 2019 **"Risk Factors for School Absenteeism and Dropout: A Meta-Analytic Review"** [1] found that *"for school absenteeism, significant and substantial effects were found around risks such as the physical and mental problems of the child, substance abuse, antisocial or risky behaviour, problems at or with school, characteristics of the school, parenting problems and difficulties, and family problems. Regarding school dropouts, similar risks were identified, along with risks related to peer group characteristics and social status within a peer group."* They also indicated that post-pandemic illness was a natural driver for absenteeism alongside a shift in parental attitudes towards attendance. That sounds pretty in line with my comments above.

So, as I have done in earlier chapters, let's start with a bit of a state of the nation.

Where are we now?

Using data from the **Department for Education (DfE)** for the full academic year 2023/24 up to 19 July 2024 (the latest data available at the time of writing) [2], overall absence rates for the academic year stood at **7.2%**, with 4.7% authorised and 2.5% unauthorised. The persistent absence rate for the academic year was also **20.7%**.

By school type, the absence rates across the academic year were 5.5% in state-funded primary schools (3.9% authorised and 1.6% unauthorised), 9.1% in state-funded secondary schools (5.5% authorised and 3.6% unauthorised), and 13.0% in state-funded special schools (9.7% authorised and 3.3% unauthorised).

When we look by pupil characteristics, the absence rates were 11.1% for pupils who were eligible for free school meals versus 5.8% for pupils who were not eligible for free school meals and 13.3% for pupils with an education, health and care plan (EHCP), 10.9% for pupils with Special Educational Needs (SEN) support compared to 6.5% with no identified SEN.

There are some big numbers there, especially when we look at some of our more vulnerable cohorts, but we all know a number in isolation doesn't have much context to allow us to draw any conclusions. I did, of course, check back for similar data for the 2018/19 academic year [3], the last pandemic-free period where overall absence rates for the academic year stood at 4.7%, with 3.3% authorised and 1.4% unauthorised. Alongside that, the persistent absence rate for the academic year was almost half what it is now at "just" 10.9%.

So, I guess we can quickly conclude that this is a problem just in England? Our data shows this significant downward curve in attendance. Well, no, this is happening everywhere. In the United States, the **National Center for Education Statistics (NCES)** [4] reported in January 2024 [5] *"that their average daily attendance rate for students was 90 percent, according to new data from the School Pulse Panel (SPP)"* and that just 37% of public schools had an average daily attendance rate of 95% or higher.

On a global scale, the Organization for Economic Cooperation and Development (OECD) [6] released a policy paper **"Evaluating post-pandemic education policies and combatting student absenteeism beyond COVID-19"** [7] showing a broadly consistent trend (with a few notable exceptions including Sweden), and also highlighting in their Programme for International Student Assessment (PISA) 2022 data that for students who are on long-term absence, *"the most common cause reported by students who missed school for more than three consecutive months at any education level was sickness (70.5%). The second most commonly cited reason was a lack of safety at school (18.5%) and the third was boredom (18.5%)."* Those last two categories certainly stand out.

Recognising the attendance challenge we are seeing right now, England's somewhat self-professed world-leading attendance drive sounded like a step in the right direction. In a May 2024 press release **"England's World Leading Attendance Drive Continues"** [8] announced that the next phase of DfE's world-leading attendance drive will provide new data for schools to help them spot trends in children's attendance for earlier intervention. There are a lot of "world-leading" references through their communications, which does make me smile somewhat. This focus on data was a second phase after the earlier introduction of attendance hubs to provide tailored support to students and their families to help reduce absence which is run by schools with strong track records in boosting attendance.

In fact, on the subject of data, then–Education Secretary Gillian Keegan, announced in the aforementioned press release: *"Attendance is my number one priority. Alongside schools, I am one of the only Education Secretaries in the world to now have in-depth daily attendance data at their fingertips, giving the government, councils and schools the insights needed to target pupils who need the most support."* Is that data to provide support or challenge?

Now bear with me, we need data to be better informed, but if you have read much of the comms from the DfE, it gives the clear inference that they are providing tools and guidance to help schools better manage attendance and "fix" the problem, yet many of us I believe, whilst appreciative of any resources, also know that much of the problem lies at home and with the child, and we need to tackle the SEMH issues and disconnect nationally first, otherwise, no strategy will be fundamentally effective in school. Perhaps I have prejudged and my conversations in this chapter will refine my perspective, and if it does, I'll be the first to say so.

For the benefit of balance, the government's attendance ambassador, **Rob Tarn**, CEO of **Northern Education Trust**, shared his experiences, saying, *"We used this data to identify patterns of absence in one cohort of Year 7 students in one of our academies. This has allowed us, working closely with the LA, to target intensive intervention to reduce the number of this cohort who are persistently absent."*

Much of the above is linked to the 2022 **Department for Education** guidance **"Working together to improve school attendance"** [9], which provides detailed expectations and statutory guidance for maintained schools, academies, independent schools, and local authorities (LAs).

So, we have a wide range of strategies and guidance to help improve attendance in our schools; it's holistic, and we find what best supports each child. But what about the school itself? Isn't there also an argument that either the structure and formality of a mainstream school or the limits on the curriculum offered could also be an equally relevant factor in why a child does not feel motivated, safe, or engaged enough to come to school?

We must acknowledge that the government will not be inclined to accept or voice that view at the highest level. As you will appreciate, throughout this book, I intentionally choose to play devil's advocate when asking many of these questions. **The Education Development Trust** reports [10] their key recommendations, and highlighted that one strand should be: *"Reviewing the curriculum to ensure it remains representative, inclusive, and accessible for all pupils through its content and delivery."*

Now that we have set the scene, let's discuss a few key questions I wanted to unpick.

BEYOND THE CLASSROOM WALLS

Is there a place for alternative hybrid and online schools?

At the heart of this question, we have to be open to the idea that something "beyond" the normal classroom may actually add value for some of our students. That can be an awkward question to answer at the governmental level as it becomes a very small leap into a media headline that our schools are not fit for purpose.

Now, I, like many, have issues about our current curriculum, our ever-narrowing subject focus, and assessment addiction, but for the vast majority of children, our schools are a safe and nurturing space that allows them to thrive and excel, supported by dedicated and committed professionals. That does not mean it's suitable for all, and there won't be a member of a Senior Leadership Team (SLT) anywhere who has not discussed the suitability of their setting for some children or, more likely, the lack of availability of a suitable specialist setting. I can talk from the perspective of working in the English education system, but to suggest we are in a unique position would be misleading.

In writing this book, I have been very mindful of not simply providing an opinion piece but trying at each stage to reference articles, research, and reports that substantiate those perspectives and, where I can, challenge them too. The 2023 article by the **SEND network "The over-subscription of specialist schools: Too many children are being failed"** [11] highlighted that every child with Special educational needs and disabilities (SEND) has a right to be educated within a mainstream school and equally has the right to be educated within an alternative, specialist school. However, for many children with SEND, this right is not being enacted because of a nationwide crisis in the amount of specialist school places available.

Research at the same time undertaken by the **BBC** [12] cited that half of state-funded schools in England for children with SEND are oversubscribed. So, we are on message when it comes to the need for more capacity in our system for children with complex needs, typically specialist provision, but sometimes short interventions in an alternative provision, hopefully with a wrap-around plan for returning to mainstream when appropriate. Sadly, we often fail on the latter, but that is a whole different chapter.

For the purpose of simplicity (my specialist subject), I am going to park the obvious around supporting children with physical or complex SEND, but why do we think this provision is needed? A good provision provides a specialist capacity to provide support, interventions, and nurturing in a format that best suits the child. So, we have capacity and time unlocked in that setting (hopefully) that couldn't be offered in a mainstream setting. What about teacher skills? We have seen the remit of the role as a teacher grow exponentially over decades; as a job description, implied if not always explicit, it's a huge list. Do we train our newly qualified teachers (NQTs), or as now identified, early career teachers (ECTs), with the skills to support learners with complex needs, and sometimes not complex, but ones that require quite specialised support?

This isn't unique, by the way; you'll find a similar conversation in the police service, for example. Research was undertaken in the United States with teachers in general education, (GE) an equivalent term to the mainstream, in the article, **"Barriers general education teachers face regarding the inclusion of students with autism." Al Jaffal** [13] found: *"The findings showed that GE teachers lack training in how to work with students with ASD in their GE classrooms, lack collaboration opportunities with their special education colleagues to better support their students with ASD, and are not provided sufficient resources by their schools and programs to create an appropriate inclusive environment in their GE classrooms."* Sound familiar?

That is not to say that educators don't try. **Kat Cauchi**, a former primary school teacher, shared: *"With the continuous pressures on teachers, along with behaviour policies that often focus on reactive behaviour management strategies rather than reactive sometimes the focus does end up too much on the 'stick'. Taking the time* *to help learners build skills such as self-regulation and equipping them with the emotional literacy to express themselves in a safe and healthy way can go a long way to improving engagement and behaviour."* She's right, but that feels like sometimes it is a bandage over the child's root issues that need specialist intervention. Again, schools try to deliver those, too, but specialist capacity is often stretched beyond belief.

Now, I wanted to highlight that the challenges in our mainstream settings are not just about suitable environments; we don't have enough suitably trained professionals to provide the support some of our learners need. That may be a constraint largely exasperated by insufficient funding, but there is also a shortage of suitably qualified professionals within the broader system, from educational psychologists onward. The net outcome is that all learners, in general, are required to "fit" into the mainstream schedule and experience, often when that is acknowledged not to be the optimum pathway for the child.

A sliding scale

Let's slide our scale, shall we, from the child with the most complex specialist needs, toward the most median child. Is there a fixed line where suddenly a mainstream setting is a perfect fit, or do we have a grey area where it's not so clear? Alternative provisions, sometimes referred to as pupil referral units, have always been seen as the place where permanently excluded children go, typically for behavioural issues. These "naughty schools" should be a temporary place for children to get specialist support to get them back on track and then help them with successful reintegration. The good ones do that with a very personalised approach, often with a restricted timetable (initially) and one-to-one support.

Many of these children have seen successive academic failures as a reason to disengage from education and need opportunities to rebuild confidence and not be set up for failure. Personalised support is the pathway to re-engaging them, removing their anxieties and broadening the curriculum offered to allow them to achieve. Their challenging behaviour in the mainstream often made them stand out, and they began this pathway to an alternative provision.

On that sliding scale, as we move further away from the obvious children in need of interventions, that grey area gets much harder, but as we have discussed in the introduction to this chapter, with the huge rise in SEMH cases across our children, more and more are struggling to fit and flourish in the mainstream. Let's be clear: The rigidity of our current curriculum and the expectations of our schools have made them less and less suitable for students in the grey zone.

I always like to capture specialist insights and asked **Matt Pitman** [14], head of secondary, **Global Village Learning**, Australia, some of these questions. I asked him about the benefits and differences of alternative learning spaces, and he summarised the following: *"These spaces have the power to assist us in rediscovering the difference between education and learning. Alternative and hybrid schools are* able to meet the needs of their students because at their core, they create space for exploration, play and independent learning. When we over-structure our curriculum, we strip the autonomy away. By addressing this need for vulnerable students, these schools highlight the gap between the issues associated with education in its current form and any issues with learning."

Now, this chapter has a focus on attendance. I can recall one of my roles as chair of an alternative provision (AP) school. After a very challenging Ofsted inspection, I was asked by the LA to come and join as an acting chair and support stabilising it. I was happy to (*and stayed for nearly three years*). Alongside issues with children being on part-time timetables for far too long and limited interventions or support for moving back to the mainstream, one of the biggest challenges was attendance. As the 2021 article from **Edutopia**, **"Reimagining Alternative Education"** [15], highlighted, *"Alternative education should be framed not as a last resort for 'bad' students but as a way to provide positive, intentional supports."*

I can confirm many of our learners were disengaged, were always seen as failing within the mainstream settings, and had lost any visibility of what an education could tangibly offer them. Attendance started with creating a purpose, offering courses, alongside literacy and numeracy, that students could relate to and had a good opportunity to succeed at, alongside trying to reignite enjoyment. Right now, a mainstream setting doesn't have the capacity to provide the breadth of curriculum that "fits" every child. Ironically, during the pandemic, the AP had a higher engagement in online learning than in getting those same students to cross the threshold into the classroom, and yes, they engaged in the learning more, too. My point is that we have to adapt our offer to suit some children's needs, and real adaptability is hugely compromised in our education settings as a rule.

Changing spaces

Courtesy of the pandemic accelerating virtual learning as a needed alternative, many educators highlighted that for some learners, it was a better fit for them. An article in **Education Week** [16] shared teacher feedback from the period where we shifted to online learning, with an expected assessment that *"most students didn't make much progress—or flailed—in online learning during the pandemic."*

It was new, not always well structured, and everyone was learning, so this is familiar feedback. However, what really stood out was that *"a subset who may have struggled with in-person learning in the past actually thrived, some of whom have learning and thinking differences or mental health conditions like social anxiety."* Adapting our offer to meet differing needs rings true again.

If you have had the pleasure of reading **Daniel Willingham**'s book *Why Don't Students Like School* [17], then you will be familiar with him discussing that understandably dejected feeling that a teacher has when they realise that some of their students do not enjoy school much and they struggle to inspire them. He explains that contrary to popular belief, the brain isn't designed for thinking; it is designed to save you time from having to think, as it's not very good at that. Phew, I feel exonerated! Anyway, he explains that while thinking is slow and unreliable, people enjoy mental work if it is successful. They like to solve problems, but not work on unsolvable problems. In the same way, he explains (no revelations here), if schoolwork is always a bit too difficult (or too easy, for that matter), it should be no surprise if a student doesn't like school much.

That simple point, which I know everyone will be acutely familiar with, is why, in a one-size-fits-all delivery of education, we will always have children going too fast or too slow for their needs, and our ability to adapt to support them is restricted. A more personalised offer can potentially be better met. We could, of course, fund a lot more staff in our schools to allow greater flexibility. (I know, crazy idea.)

People are naturally curious, but we are not naturally good thinkers; unless the cognitive conditions are right, we will avoid thinking. Daniel T. Willingham

We have seen a growth in children and parents feeling that the mainstream offer does not meet their needs, and settings designed to provide more personalised learning pathways, in person or online, have become an increasingly credible alternative. Sometimes cost is a barrier to this provision, and that's a shame, but over time, availability versus demand will hopefully shape those provisions and their accessibility.

The argument presented to support an online provision is multi-faceted; one strand is around mitigating some of the growing anxiety we are seeing with our children. This suggests that online schools benefit children suffering from anxiety in several ways: Children can make progress at their own pace, and they can learn in an environment that is free from any distractions or problematic behaviour. They also suggest: "*While virtual classrooms give anxious youngsters social interaction, which is essential, even for children with anxiety, the experience is considerably less stressful than in-person teaching*" [18]. It has also frequently been highlighted that anxious students can benefit from more one-to-one contact with their teacher, as typical virtual class sizes are considerably smaller.

Like every education space, there are good and, how shall I say, less good provisions, so a virtual school isn't automatically the panacea. A 2017–2018 study in the United States by the **University of Colorado** [19] reviewed 300,000 students attending over 500 virtual schools, which showed that 50.1% of their virtual high school students graduated within four years, compared to 84% of high school students nationally. At first glance, it is not so good, but let us also remember the cohort of children that may have elected for a different educational journey; for some, academia may not have been their strength, but they may have had a different and equally successful learning journey. Seven years after this study, the tools and technology available now to deliver an immersive learning experience have also hugely evolved, but clearly, there is a way to do so. If you want to see a really good example, then take a look at **Sophia High School** [20] the United Kingdom's first accredited online school, which is hugely innovative with their approaches to delivering learning.

I'm increasingly of the view that without significant change at the national level, online is potentially the best pathway for some learners. Whilst it is not my intent to judge, I feel like any offer, with the right pedagogical lead and steer, has to be a better pathway than homeschooling, where we rely solely on the capabilities and capacity of parents, well intentioned as that always is.

I can summarise the context of this question into these five primary takeaways, which I hope help consolidate:

1. **There is not a "one-size-fits-all" solution**: Mainstream schools work well for most children, but they aren't suitable for everyone. Hybrid and online schools offer perfectly credible alternatives, particularly for children whose needs aren't being fully met in those traditional settings.

2. **We have specialist provision shortages**: There's a significant lack of specialist and alternative provision, especially for children with SEND and SEMH needs. Hybrid and online schools can help fill this gap, offering tailored support for students who struggle in mainstream environments.

3. **We need personalisation and flexibility**: Alternative schools, whether hybrid or online, create opportunities for personalised learning. They can provide the flexibility to adapt to individual students' needs, potentially helping them build confidence and reengage with their learning.

4. **Priority on addressing student anxiety**: Online learning can be a better fit for students dealing with anxiety or other mental health challenges, offering a less stressful environment and more focused, one-to-one support from teachers.

5. **Mainstream and alternative models can coexist**: Rather than viewing hybrid and online schools as lesser alternatives, we should see them as complementary options that can coexist with mainstream education. When done right, these alternatives can unlock a child's potential where traditional models may just not be the right fit for the child.

Let's be clear: I asked this question to prompt challenge and discussion, as with all of those I selected in the book. It is always seen as a choice of mainstream education or a lesser option.

We need to change our mindset, not in any way to degenerate our mainstream provision but to acknowledge, due to the ever-changing needs of our children, that there are other credible pathways, when done right, that can unlock the confidence and engagement of a child that would otherwise sink in our traditional offer. That is not a criticism of those doing their utmost to support each child; it is just a simple recognition that one size doesn't fit all. Different provisions can coexist healthily. The more we find ways to adapt and reform our mainstream, the more children will find a place to flourish.

ADDRESSING THE UNDERLYING CAUSES

Do we focus too narrowly on the stick, rather than understanding why students disengage?

Your child wasn't in school last week, so here's a fine. Problem sorted. Really?

As I hinted in my introduction, if you look at any national press or publications, the government is providing support for schools to help get their children to attend. So it's the schools that have the problem, yes? I would argue that schools are dealing with the outcome of a much broader societal issue in many cases. It's unsurprisingly linked to some of the points discussed in the previous question.

The government can use their new data captures to help inform, but as this June 2024 article in **The Guardian** highlighted, **Special Educational Needs and Disabilities** [21], with nearly nine out of ten heads reporting a marked rise in students missing school due to mental health issues since the COVID-19 pandemic. I noted a quote by **Lorriane Yates**, the assistant principal at the **Astrea Academy Trust**, in the article, who said that children in years 9 and 10 faced the most significant challenges *"as they are the cohort of young people that were most disrupted by Covid and that were impacted by Sure Start centres and children's centres being closed."*

I spent ten years as the one "non-political" co-opted member of my LA **"Children and Education"** scrutiny committee, and remember how unpopular I was when I voiced my disapproval and voted against their decision to close our **Sure Start centres** [22], and warned, like many others, that this would have a much higher cost to pay in the long run.

Anyway, linked to home factors, the article also highlighted that in feedback from over 500 schools, they found that parents had become "unduly cautious" in keeping their children off school, with some away for weeks instead of one or two days. **Geoff Barton**, then–general secretary of the **Association of School and College Leaders (ASCL)** [23], wrote in an article [24] for *SecEd Magazine*, while welcoming government initiatives: *"The most effective solution to poor attendance is to have attendance officers knocking on doors and talking directly to families about why children are missing school, what barriers there are to attendance and how these can be solved."* In parallel, **Paul Whiteman**, general secretary at the **National Association of Head Teachers (NAHT)** [25], said that recent data *"underlines the need for the government to invest far more in tackling persistent absence and the reasons for it, which may include everything from issues at home, to poverty, mental ill-health and a failure to fund adequate support for many children with SEND."* Having such a wide-ranging causation, you could suggest we are left tinkering at the edges without a change, at scale, in funding.

Moving very slightly westward, a May 2024 article published by the **BBC**, **"Mental health cited for pupils missing school"** [26], indicated that data showed 40% of secondary school students in Wales missed, on average, one afternoon per week over the previous academic year. The reasons given by children for avoiding going to school were panic attacks, anxiety, and problems with mental health, among other reasons.

Parental disconnect

Across the pond in the United States, the **Brookings Institute** research article [27], in March 2024, found: *"A lot has been written about the disconnect between parents and experts when it comes to COVID-19 learning loss and recovery. Our most recent results suggest this same disconnect also seems to hold when it comes to attendance. Our results point to low overall levels of concern, which seemingly flies in the face of the evidence about how much school U.S. children are actually missing."* In fact, their key finding was that less than half of parents/caretakers with children at risk of being deemed chronically absent reported being concerned about it.

The **Education Development Trust** [28] shared in their **"Improving school attendance by fostering a sense of community belonging"** [10] article that a recent report by the **Education Select Committee** on persistent school absence [29] had identified barriers linked to poverty as a key driver in post-pandemic attendance issues. This is alongside a higher rate of absence for pupils with SEND, who are more likely than their peers to miss school, especially where their specific individual needs are not being met.

We can come full circle from the school to the child, to the family, to the system back to the school; in truth, we all accept there are marginal gains to be had at all stages of that cycle by reviewing the excellent **"Understanding Attendance: Findings on the drivers of pupil absence from over 30,000 young people in England"** [30] report by **ImpactEd** [31]. In January 2024, a meta-analysis of 51 separate studies about school belonging concluded that, ahead of peer and parental influences, teacher support had the strongest correlation with a pupil's sense of belonging. It highlighted that effective school–pupil relationships which prioritise caring relationships and friendliness can also provide better insights into individual motivators (and barriers) to attendance.

We should all acknowledge that being more familiar with a child's context helps schools and other stakeholders (Educational Psychology Service or family support workers) to be more effective at tailoring support to the child's needs.

The only issue with the above would be the need for adequate funding, services, and capacity to provide that support. Getting the services of an educational psychologist in my area can, at times, carry similar odds to a lottery win. I may have exaggerated that for effect!

So, my opening sentence on this alluded to issuing a fine to fix the problem. I am not a supporter of this. At a simple level, it can disproportionally punish parents on lower incomes but fundamentally avoids us tackling much of the discussion above. I get it that sometimes the decision on attendance is a simple cost-benefit analysis on a term time holiday, and perhaps that's easier to critique. **Geoff Barton**, of the **Association of School and College Leaders** [32], said in a quote for the BBC, *"If everybody took term-time holidays, it would be "chaos" in schools – and fines gave a clear signal they were unacceptable."*

Ed Dorrell, director of **Public First** [33], shared a different perspective in a *Schools Week* article, **"Attendance: Another fine mess the government's got us into,"** saying that punishing struggling families by making them struggle more is outdated, regressive, and completely counter-productive. He didn't mince words, saying, *"Some things just make my urine boil. In education, fines for non-attendance are one of those things. It's a crap policy. It's so crap, in fact, that it achieves the opposite of what it is designed to achieve."*

Public First held focus groups across England to investigate the rise in pupil absences since 2019 [34], and found a *"fundamental breakdown in the relationship between schools and parents across the socioeconomic spectrum."* They found an "increased willingness among parents to take children on holiday during term time," a rise in mental health problems, and the cost of living crisis were among the factors driving lower attendance. They signposted some recommendations that resonate within the context of this chapter, namely:

- A review of how schools and the education system communicate with parents and broader national messaging.

- Support for schools to provide intensive, nuanced support to families for whom attendance is a significant issue.

- Better joined up working and signposting to para-educational agencies, including those in mental health.

- Fund schools better, because other strains on the education system are manifesting in the attendance crisis.

- Invest in SEND and CAMHS (Child and Adolescent Mental Health Services) to significantly improve attendance.

There were a few others, but these were the most salient ones. It's a much broader ecosystem that needs investment to deliver sustained change in behaviours and provide the right support to families. Surely, it is time to move beyond policies that most leaders don't think work. If we want to reverse the attendance crisis, we must rebuild both trust and the resources that support families in getting their children into school, alongside a better understanding of the value their children derive.

As **Matt Pitman** shared with me, we can discuss the accessibility and personalised nature of the curriculum offered to meet a disengaged child's need, but *"that* *cannot lead to increased attendance alone, in needs to be in consultation with the young person and their families which certainly could assist with creating an environment in which the student feels safe and has a sense of ownership over their learning."*

I think we need to be really explicit on this. We absolutely can adapt our learning spaces and most definitely need to look at a broadening of our curriculum and approaches to learning so that our schools are more inclusive, but we have a societal issue that also needs to be addressed at a national level to ensure the right support for children and families well before they arrive for the first time at our school gates. If I have to condense down the key factors right now that we need to be both be mindful of and look to address, they are as follows:

1. **Mental health and home pressures**: A significant rise in absenteeism is linked to mental health issues, particularly among students who were heavily impacted by the pandemic. Factors such as anxiety, panic attacks, and broader societal issues like poverty and home instability are driving absences, highlighting the need for holistic support beyond the school gates.

2. **Parental disconnect and engagement**: There is a disconnect between schools and parents when it comes to attendance. Some parents have become overly cautious, keeping children home longer than necessary, while others lack concern about chronic absenteeism. Schools need to improve communication with parents to rebuild trust and help them understand the long-term impact of absenteeism.

3. **Fines aren't a solution**: Punitive measures like fines for absenteeism often disproportionately affect lower-income families and fail to address the root causes of the issue. Instead, a more supportive approach – one that focuses on understanding and addressing underlying barriers to attendance – is needed.

4. **The need for tailored support**: Addressing absenteeism requires personalised interventions that consider each student's unique circumstances, especially for students with SEND. However, schools face challenges in accessing sufficient resources like educational psychologists, which limits their ability to provide the necessary support.

5. **More investment in services**: Schools alone cannot solve the attendance crisis. There needs to be greater investment in mental health services (e.g., CAMHS) and SEND support. Collaboration amongst schools, families, and para-educational agencies is crucial for tackling the complex web of factors contributing to absenteeism.

6. **Rebuilding trust with families**: Rebuilding trust and relationships with families is key. Schools need to work closely with parents and students to create an inclusive environment where students feel safe and have a sense of ownership over their learning, hopefully encouraging better attendance.

THE ROLE OF PARENTS

How do we re-engage families to recognise the importance of a collegiate education?

The pandemic threw up all sorts of previously minimal challenges with education. It was a catalyst for parents to have to take a significantly closer involvement in their child's education, especially during the period of remote learning. The workplace changed, too, with more families having access to a hybrid workplace, spending some days of the week working from home. For some, the huge disruption to our lives amplified anxieties and fears about their child's safety and so much more.

One of the recent drivers to great long-term absence from school has been a shift in parental perspectives alongside now being able to more easily accommodate a child that doesn't want to go to school. It's easier for more sick days to accumulate now, and for some, courtesy of what I would classify as negative "teacher bashing" messaging and lack of government support, a diminished perception of the value of education and educators.

How do we re-establish or improve engagement with that cohort of currently disconnected families? Well, it absolutely needs to start at the top, with government support for teachers and the school system, stopping the blaming of schools for poor policy and leadership decisions centrally, and recognising that many of the challenges schools now face is due to underfunding of broader social care initiatives.

Beyond that within our schools, it's a refocus and continuity of efforts for better engagement. That means reflecting on and ensuring we have a school environment where parents feel comfortable coming and going and that their voices are heard and valued. Being seen to listen and share goes a long way, perhaps through holding regular parent-teacher conferences, hosting parent events, and making sure all activities are accessible for our non-English-speaking (EAL) parents.

No points are awarded here in stating the obvious, but it's also important to make it as easy as possible for parents to get involved with their child's education and encourage them to do so. I'd argue our increasingly flexible digital platforms provide far greater opportunities for visibility and input from parents alongside hybrid parent evenings to ensure all parents and carers are able to engage.

I'm really mindful in summarising these next steps so that many of the readers will be better informed than I am, but it feels appropriate to include them for completeness, so forgive me. It is, for example, consistently highlighted that it's important for schools to be flexible and understand the specific needs of both parents and their children when identifying what additional type of support they might need. I will clarify that I have yet to experience a school that does not make every effort in this regard, and topics around persistent or severe absence and behaviours fall into this bucket. However, pressure and time commitments can sometimes impact best endeavours.

Over the years, I have spent many hours early at the school gate or at parents' evenings and open evenings meeting and chatting with parents, something our SLT teams across the schools are hugely focused on. We all acknowledge that building rapport, hopefully building some trust in the relationships between the school and parents, is essential, especially down the line if challenges occur. Time permitting, the more we get to know our families and can engage with them in their activities, the more they will feel valued and inclined to be more engaged when the school reaches out.

Sharing advice on how new parents can best engage with staff and leadership in a productive way is also something we often assume is understood but could be more formally signposted.

I am very conscious that school staff often have one hand tied behind their backs when it comes to supporting parents in accessing additional services and support for their child, the broader system has little to no capacity, and wait times are excessive. While it is out of the school's control, it is fair to say that sometimes the staff still becomes the lightning rod for parental frustration. It's understandable (sometimes), and while there is no magic fix to this, being transparent about where the lines of demarcation sit and making the system visually accessible can help diminish wrongly directed frustrations. It will still happen, though.

So, whilst being really mindful of not teaching any readers to suck eggs, in summary, there isn't an easy fix, which you already know. However, better communication, being transparent, being visible and accessible, bringing parents into the school, crafting more volunteer opportunities, using governors, building social capital (using positive opportunities for engagement with difficult parents), and spreading positivity via social media platforms are very much the strands that we need to focus on with a view to marginal gains from each. I have tried to summarise this into five key points below.

1. **Government support and positive messaging**: Re-engagement must start at the top, with stronger government support for schools and teachers. Moving away from negative rhetoric of late about schools and educators will help rebuild trust and reinforce the value of education in the eyes of disconnected families.

2. **Create a welcoming school environment**: Schools need to focus on fostering an environment where parents feel comfortable and valued (most already do). We can always improve communication; ensuring parents' voices are heard; and making the school an accessible space for all, including non-English-speaking families.

3. **Leverage digital tools for engagement**: The increased use of digital platforms provides an opportunity for schools to engage parents more easily. Schools could offer hybrid parent–teacher meetings and make it simple for parents to stay involved in their child's education, providing flexibility for all families.

4. **Build relationships early**: Establishing rapport and trust between schools and families is always a priority. By being visible, engaging with parents at school events, and creating regular opportunities for interaction, schools can continue to build long-term relationships that will help when challenges arise.

5. **Being transparent and managing expectations**: Schools must be clear about the limitations they face, particularly when external support services are unavailable or slow to respond. Transparency about the boundaries of the school's responsibilities and providing clear information about additional services can help reduce parental frustration, at least with the school anyway.

We don't have to engage in grand, heroic actions to participate in the process of change. Small acts, when multiplied by millions of people, can transform the world. Howard Zinn

References

1. J. Gubbels, C. E. van der Put and M. Assink, "Risk Factors for School Absenteeism and Dropout: A Meta-Analytic Review," *Journal of Youth and Adolescence*, vol. 48, pp. 1637–1667, 2019.
2. "Pupil Attendance in Schools - Headline Facts and Figures," Department for Education, 08 August 2024. [Online]. Available: https://explore-education-statistics.service.gov.uk/find-statistics/pupil-attendance-in-schools
3. "Pupil Absence in Schools in England," Department for Education, 2020. [Online]. Available: https://explore-education-statistics.service.gov.uk/find-statistics/pupil-absence-in-schools-in-england/2018-19
4. "National Center for Education Statistics (NCES)," [Online]. Available: https://nces.ed.gov/
5. "Public School Leaders Report 90 Percent Average Daily Student Attendance Rate in November 2023," NCES, 18 January 2024. [Online]. Available: https://nces.ed.gov/whatsnew/press_releases/1_18_2024.asp
6. OECD, "Organisation for Economic Co-operation and Development (OECD)," [Online]. Available: https://www.oecd.org/
7. "Evaluating Post-Pandemic Education Policies and Combatting Student Absenteeism Beyond COVID-19," *OECD Education Policy Perspectives*, vol. 101, 2024. https://doi.org/10.1787/a38f74b2-en
8. "England's World Leading Attendance Drive Continues," Department for Education, 10 May 2024. [Online]. Available: https://www.gov.uk/government/news/englands-world-leading-attendance-drive-continues
9. "Working Together to Improve School Attendance," Department for Education, 07 March 2024. [Online]. Available: https://www.gov.uk/government/publications/working-together-to-improve-school-attendance
10. "Improving School Attendance by Fostering a Sense of Community Belonging," Education Development Trust, 2024. [Online]. Available: https://www.edt.org/research-and-insights/improving-school-attendance-by-fostering-a-sense-of-community-belonging/. [Accessed 02 04 2024]

11. H. McCormack, "The Over-Subscription of Specialist Schools: Too Many Children are Being Failed," SEND Network, 23 February 2023. [Online]. Available: https://send-network.co.uk/posts/the-over-subscription-of-specialist-schools-too-many-children-are-being-failed-87e94f5c-4bb8-4e05-bb65-21dad853500c
12. E. Dunkley, K. McGough and H. Agerholm, "Overcrowded Specialist Schools: 'We're Teaching in Cupboards'," BBC, 20 February 2023. [Online]. Available: https://www.bbc.co.uk/news/education-64418797
13. M. Al Jaffa, "Barriers General Education Teachers Face Regarding the Inclusion of Students with Autism," *Frontiers in Psychology*, vol. 13, p. 873248, 2022.
14. M. Pitman, *The Connection Curriculum: Igniting Positive Change in Schools Through Sustainable Connection*, Amba Press, 2024.
15. T. Robinson, "Reimagining Alternative Education," Edutopia, 02 August 2021. [Online]. Available: https://www.edutopia.org/article/reimagining-alternative-education/
16. A. Klein, "Virtual Learning Was Better for Some Kids. Here's What Teachers Learned From Them," Education Week, 18 August 2021. [Online]. Available: https://www.edweek.org/teaching-learning/virtual-learning-was-better-for-some-kids-heres-what-teachers-learned-from-them/2021/08
17. D. T. Willingham, Why Don't Students Like School?: A Cognitive Scientist Answers Questions About How the Mind Works and What It Means for the Classroom, Jossey-Bass, 2021.
18. "How Homeschooling at Online School Can Help Children With Anxiety," Cambridge Home School Online, 02 2021. [Online]. Available: https://www.chsonline.org.uk/blog/homeschooling-at-online-school-can-help-children-with-anxiety
19. A. Molnar, "Virtual Schools in the U.S. 2019," 05 2019. [Online]. Available: https://nepc.colorado.edu/sites/default/files/publications/Virtual%20Schools%202019.pdf
20. "Sophia High School," [Online]. Available: sophiahigh.school.
21. "Mental health is main cause of rising absences in England, say headteachers," The Guardian, 14 June 2024. [Online]. Available: https://www.theguardian.com/education/article/2024/jun/14/mental-health-anxiety-absences-pupils-schools-covid-pandemic-headteachers
22. "Sure Start Centres," Wikipedia, 1998. [Online]. Available: https://en.wikipedia.org/wiki/Sure_Start
23. "Association of School and College Leaders (ASCL)," [Online]. Available: https://www.ascl.org.uk/
24. "School attendance crisis: One in four secondary students persistently absent," SecEd Magazine, 30 January 2024. [Online]. Available: https://www.sec-ed.co.uk/content/news/school-attendance-crisis-one-in-four-secondary-students-persistently-absent/
25. "National Association of Head Teachers (NAHT)," [Online]. Available: https://www.naht.org.uk/
26. M. Williams and M. Davies, "Mental health cited for pupils missing school," BBC, 27 May 2024. [Online]. Available: https://www.bbc.co.uk/news/articles/cd11g7jz92ro
27. A. Saavedra, M. Polikoff and D. Silver, "Parents are not fully aware of, or concerned about, their children's school attendance," Brookings Institute, 26 March 2024. [Online]. Available: https://www.brookings.edu/articles/parents-are-not-fully-aware-of-or-concerned-about-their-childrens-school-attendance/
28. "Education Development Trust," [Online]. Available: https://www.edt.org
29. "Persistent absence and support for disadvantaged pupils – Report Summary," UK Parliament, 27 September 2023. [Online]. Available: https://publications.parliament.uk/pa/cm5803/cmselect/cmeduc/970/summary.html
30. "Understanding Attendance: Findings on the drivers of pupil absence," ImpactEd Evaluation, 01 2024. [Online]. Available: https://www.evaluation.impactedgroup.uk/research-and-resources/understanding-attendance

31 "ImpactEd Evaluation," [Online]. Available: https://www.evaluation.impactedgroup.uk/
32 B. Jeffreys, N. Standley, V. Park-Froud and B. Kris, "School absence fines for parents to rise by £20 in England," BBC, 29 February 2024. [Online]. Available: https://www.bbc.co.uk/news/education-68420275
33 "Public First," [Online]. Available: www.publicfirst.co.uk
34 "'I don't really care anymore': Parent apathy on attendance laid bare," Schools Week, 30 August 2024. [Online]. Available: https://schoolsweek.co.uk/i-dont-really-care-anymore-parent-apathy-on-attendance-laid-bare/

Is the future of education going to become hybrid or online?

Goodness, this is a topic that I have either been asked about or heard about in so many discussions post-pandemic. Let us zoom right out to a global view and a new role in delivering a brand-new education system for everyone. Yes, it's a fantasy role, but we can have a play with that concept for a bit to kick off the conversation. If we looked at a global population, disparate in geography, economic equity, and opportunities, then it's not a big leap to think the solution for our new "global education" offer would be one that was made available to every child online. That would certainly be cheaper than trying to build a school in all four corners of the globe to meet every child's needs.

At this point, I am not in any way suggesting this is a like-for-like swap, but in my fantasy model, it would be a logical and most practical way of delivering education to the masses. I could probably assign a tick in the box for accessibility of educational offer, possibly another tick for offering flexibility in learning, perhaps allowing children to adapt the pace to suit their needs. It would be much more cost effective than brick-and-mortar provision, and being accessible to all, could foster diversity and help mitigate global educational disparities.

OK, I may have skipped over digital equity in this scenario and ensuring all children have a suitable device and connection to access the provision (no small task); I might have also skipped over the value of face-to-face interaction with teachers and peers too, but we unpick that in later chapters.

So, the big questions, which, to be clear, somehow get distorted into being a critique of what we do now, rather than a conversation about what we might need to think about for the future, are being supported by the premise that a blended learning model is fit for purpose. How do we ensure equity for all of our children, and how do we measure and not lose sight of the core benefit of human-to-human interaction? I also want to touch on a bit of a potential self-fulfilling prophecy: If we continue to see a decline in educator numbers alongside a growing student cohort, might we be forced to offer a more virtual "at scale" solution to meet needs?

So, lots to unpick, but as you can see, in the first two paragraphs alone I have "fixed" the world with a simple online education system for all. If only it was that simple!

Global perspectives

I need to be a bit more specific here in my remit, as if this discussion was exclusively about higher education, it is fair to say we are already on that journey, courtesy and perhaps accelerated by the 2020 pandemic. However, the direction of travel (in some contexts) was already there. If we step another notch up on our personal learning pathway, then as adults, online learning is not a concept, it's a practical and popular pathway for all the practical reasons. **The World Economic Forum** shared an article in January 2022 titled **"These 3 charts show the global growth in online learning"** [1], which highlighted student course enrolments through the learning platform **Coursera** had grown from 26 million in 2016 to 189 million in 2021. In a May 2024 *Forbes* article, **"2024 Online Learning Statistics"** [2], they highlighted that over 10 million U.S. college students now take distance education courses and that primarily online-based colleges enrol approximately 1.1 million new students a year. I wanted to share these stats to highlight some of the earlier points about accessibility and equity, where in this report, they also highlighted that Black students made up 23.3% of the cohort at online colleges versus only 12.5% as "traditional" college students. We will come back to this in more detail, but to round off the numbers, in 2022, there were 279,162 degrees conferred by primarily online colleges in the United States.

In the United Kingdom, there is a similar trend within adult education and access to skills and accreditations, alongside a growth in accessing higher education provisions. **Oxford Learning College** research [2] highlighted in 2022 that there were 184,405 U.K.-based online undergraduate students, and a report by **Statista** in July 2024 [3] reported that between 2007 and 2019, the percentage of people who accessed online courses rose from 4% to 17%. Interesting, but with better connectivity and technology over that period, again not a huge surprise.

I don't expect any of this to be revelationary, but acquiring skills and certifications as an adult learner is quite different from delivering mainstream education for the ages of 4–18 or K–12. Like most things as adults, it is also delivered to us as a cost proposition. According to Statista research, the online education market was valued at £7.66 billion in 2024, so there are other, more commercial, drivers in this sector to be mindful of.

In parallel to the core education conversation, there has also been a global focus on sustainability and the environmental impact of face-to-face training and learning, which seems to paraphrase into a position that traditional training requires a vast number of resources to run effectively, such as classroom space, energy, content materials, and transportation. And so consequently, delivering online learning lowers environmental impact by saving energy, reducing resource use, and reducing pollution. So, online learning can be an essential tool in the global fight against climate change, too?

Clearly, this discussion around adult online courses and meetings, and the decision between in-person and face-to-face learning is a conversation for a very different book and perhaps overstated in a far too simplistic way from an eco-perspective. Nonetheless, it is important to note the direction of travel we are seeing for our children once they leave school, in order to have a healthy conversation about what they might experience at school.

What about at school age?

OK, so let's move our focus to our target age group of 4- 18-year-old children, "school age," and see where we stand today. We have children in a school (of many types), and in the physical attendance sense, we have children enrolled in an online provision, we have children who are homeschooling, and we have disengaged children. I have very much condensed the categories there, but don't forget this is just an introductory chat to set the state of the nation before we dive into the important questions.

According to a May 2024 article, **"The Increase in Homeschooled Children"** [4], the latest **Department for Education** data showed: *"In fact, more than one in 100 children were reported to have been homeschooled during the last summer term, with parents citing lifestyle or 'philosophical reasons' for their decision. The data* *also revealed a significant increase in the number of homeschooled children, with 97,000 children being educated at home in 2023.*" At the same time, the **Department for Education** also released their persistent absence data within their 2024 **"Pupil Attendance in schools"** report [5] highlighting that the number of children persistently absent from school remained stubbornly higher than pre-pandemic levels, especially among older children at secondary school and those with special needs.

I could have cited another 50 articles reflecting a similar message, but I think we all recognise a growing cohort of children (and parents) that do not see the value or relevance or suitability of a traditional school experience. We have more and more learners disconnecting from education and struggling with the inflexibility of the experience and we have a world where past the age of 18, learning online is becoming the norm with evidenced impact of its suitability. So why, then, can we not consider the same with our current "in-school model"?

Human interaction

I'm going to kick things off with a clear non-negotiable – there is value in human-to-human interaction; there is value in children developing skills to work with and interact with peers; and at any age, human-to-human relationships are often more impactful from virtual ones. If we can't mitigate all these factors, and more, then does not a blend of in-person and digital learning sound like a perfectly sensible trajectory? But, is that for some children or for all children?

Educators around the world have often quoted the late **Sir Ken Robinson** [6] on the need for a shift in educational paradigms. So, isn't it time we actually made that change? Many of the chapters in this book would advocate the same. Sir Ken Robinson believed that the current education system is outdated, built for the industrial age, and no longer serves the needs of today's fast-evolving world [7]. He called for a fundamental transformation towards a more personalised, creative approach that nurtures each student's unique talents and interests. Robinson argued that creativity and innovation should be at the heart of education, preparing young people for the challenges of the 21st century.

Robinson indeed championed a much more holistic system that values creativity, critical thinking, and problem-solving. His vision was an education that's flexible, personalised, and designed to develop each student's abilities, with which he believed we could equip students for success in a rapidly changing and complex world. An education system that can flex in the way that it delivers teaching and learning seems to fall very much into that space.

As long as we can mitigate some of the key concerns, we should be open and receptive to innovating our learning space: physical or online. Something has to change and if we truly respect the diversity of our children's needs, then we can't keep trying to squeeze them into our singular model for education.

ENSURING EQUITY

How do we bridge the digital divide and guarantee all students have the necessary access and support?

Much of this topic can be divided into discussions of national digital infrastructure, access to devices, access to digital skills, and effective digital adoption. I introduced myself a good few chapters ago as a man who wears many hats. For some years now, one of these has been an ambassador for the Digital Poverty Alliance [8]. They are an amazing organisation with a main focus on policy and advocacy, gaining the evidence needed to bring the community together and drive the social change needed to end digital poverty by 2030. Digital poverty, as they succinctly state, its "The inability to interact with the online world fully, when where and how an individual needs to."

There are three key areas that influence digital poverty, starting with the obvious circumstantial determinants: people's living conditions, their economic stability, family and social context, as well as health and lifestyle. Alongside that, though, the bigger determinants fall on a much broader national discussion, namely device and connectivity availability and affordability, infrastructure, capability, the skills to use, as well as support, those enablers and influences that support a need to acquire skills with technology, and sometimes it's a limit on access, because of the accessibility and design of digital services.

I know this isn't the primary purpose of this chapter, but discussing the relative merits of online or hybrid education is based on a foundation of all children having the choice to access. Digital poverty impacts every country, and the ramifications go beyond the obvious, so whether it is accessing education, the Social Security system, job opportunities, or cheaper energy, it's a core part of how we live.

On a home country basis, in England, for example, one in five children homeschooling during the pandemic did not have access to an appropriate device like a laptop, and during, 26% of young people did not have access to a laptop or similar device. Does that sound bad? Then how about 53% of people offline can't afford an average monthly broadband bill? All of these statistics are sourced from the Digital Poverty Alliance, but the clock is ticking; with each new development in technology, more people are left behind. Our conversation on the potential for future digital learning stops right here without a level playing field for all our children.

In my local region, Cambridgeshire, an international jewel in the crown of research, biomedical technology, and more, our economic growth plan requires a skilled workforce. How do we prime the pump if our families across the region don't have the digital equity to acquire the skills we need?

This is a global challenge, albeit, in each country, that will be extended or closed depending on the aforementioned factors. A 2023 report, **"Closing the Digital Divide for the Millions of Americans without Broadband"** [9], from the **U.S. Government Accountability Office** [10], focused on work to help close the digital divide for the millions of Americans without broadband. It highlighted that the **Federal Communications Commission** has a goal of universal service for all Americans – and Congress recently approved over $42 billion to accelerate efforts to expand access. However, addressing the digital divide continues to be a challenge, with a third citing cost as the continued barrier.

With similar ambitions to the **Digital Poverty Alliance**, the **Pew Charitable Trust** in the USA, highlighted in a 2019 report in **"America's Digital Divide"** [11] that data from the **Federal Communications Commission** estimated more than 21 million people [12] in the USA didn't have a broadband connection, including 27% of people living in rural settings. So much for our developed nations being at the front of digital equity. How about we revise our baselines and set a minimum provision for every person to be able to access to a place to live, food, healthcare, education, and a digital connection, not as an expectation but as a guarantee.

A 2024 article [13] in *Government Technology Magazine*, shared a perfectly concise summary: *"Bridging the digital divide offers a pathway for families to become more self-reliant and reduce dependence on government assistance. Access to digital education and online job opportunities empowers individuals to seek better economic prospects, improve their skills, and pursue gainful employment. As families grow more self-sufficient, they contribute to a stronger economy and reduce the burden on social support programs, ultimately benefiting our entire nation."*

Let's move on and assume our global magic wand has provided digital connectivity and a suitable device in the hands of every student. Age and stage are somewhat immaterial, but the real lever that shifts this from opportunity to impact is providing the skills to access the resource; this is what delivers agency.

Digital skills

I am a huge fan and supporter of the concept of digital citizenship, which also embraces skills. It is fair to say that the world has changed dramatically in the last 30 years. The growth of the internet means that much of our lives now take place online, and the process of digitising society only seems to be accelerating, especially with the arrival of AI. With this rapid change comes the need to know about digital citizenship – the roles, responsibilities, and skills for navigating a new digital life. I certainly resonate with the simple summation by Susan Halfpenny from the University of York [14] when she said, *"On a simplistic level, we might take digital citizenship as the ability to access digital technologies and stay safe... However, we also need to consider and understand the complexities of citizenship as we start to become a digital citizen, using digital media to actively participate in society and political life."*

When we consider that essentially everyone with an internet connection is a digital citizen, the concept of digital citizenship becomes a critical part of our lives. No matter what age a person is, knowing how to stay safe, respect others, and participate meaningfully in our ever-evolving digital society becomes a necessity.

This isn't something new, but in delivering equity of access to the tools and resources we need, this is, or certainly should be, a foundation of a digital society. **The Council of Europe** provides resources for **Digital Citizenship Education (DCE)** [15], saying they can be described as *"individuals able to use digital tools to create, consume, communicate and engage positively and responsibly with others."* This is very much in two parts, firstly to develop the essential **skills** and **knowledge** needed in today's connected world, and then secondly to encourage and foster the **values** and **attitudes** that will ensure they are used respectfully and purposefully.

So, our simple sum for equity is very clear:

Connectivity + Device + Digital Citizenship + Support = Digital Equity

We could go a long way toward establishing these foundations by ensuring as a statutory provision that every school-age child has guaranteed access to each of the above, and then we can build. Often, it's about those marginal gains and extra interventions we can offer to nudge the digital divide that little bit closer.

THE SOCIAL ELEMENT OF SCHOOL

Can online models replicate the essential socialisation and sense of community found in traditional schools?

Hmm, this is a tricky one, I really wanted to share a very clear no to this question. Unlike adult learning, where we acquire skills, the role of our childhood educational journey is two parallel pathways, one to acquire skills and knowledge and a second to grow the whole person and develop and nurture their social and emotional development, and that really feels like an in-person proposition. Then I reflected during the pandemic on how we engaged with our SEND students in our mainstream settings and how we engaged with disengaged learners at our alternative provision setting, and we found that the 1:1 digital engagement was often better suited to those learners and fostered better engagement. It's not built on clear evidence mind you; that's personal perspectives, and that doesn't feel like enough.

The advent of technology within education (EdTech) has unlocked opportunities and approaches to learning and engagement that simply weren't on the table ten years ago. We have a digital workplace where people interact, introduce, and conclude opportunities all from a series of tiled faces on a screen. It doesn't stop us from not being in the same room. Somehow, though, I am still always left with the knowledge that the subtle bits on how a person is doing, what is happening in their lives, and discussing pressures and challenges is something that happens in person five minutes before or after a meeting, so that same void feels like a challenge to mitigate in a fully digital learning experience. Of course, that's the challenge with a teacher–student relationship, but we also have to factor in the value of the social interactions between students, the building of friendships, and the skills of co-working and team building.

I suspect I am slightly influenced by our pandemic experiences and the continued discussions around subsequent learning loss and SEMH challenges. They are all negatives, but are they actually a fair comparison? The pandemic required an immediate approach. Instead of being introduced to online learning inch by inch, piece by piece, students were thrust into it almost overnight. It's not unreasonable to suggest it was the speed of the switch that most affected their learning alongside unprepared or skilled teachers to deliver lessons.

An established online school today would ensure students are eased into online classes and provided with the support, time, guidance, and reassurance they need to adjust to something they're largely unfamiliar with. It's really not the same, and I can see good examples showing just as impactful learning from an online school. Perhaps it's also about being an environment that suits some learners where a mainstream setting causes anxiety or where it offers consistency when families who are moving on a regular basis for example. Sometimes it's about unlocking access to a quality learning experience that isn't available locally, and I'm certainly all for choice.

Let's either agree or disagree on the curriculum side, but assume that both pathways allow access to a quality education. What about the development of the child in a broader sense? Is it fair to say that school provides an essential environment for children to make friends, interact with others, and develop social skills? Is it also fair to say that without this interaction, they may struggle with communication and emotional intelligence as they grow up?

In the 2021 report from the **Sutton Trust** [16] titled **"Views on the ground from parents, providers and teachers,"** they cited that post-pandemic, 20% of parents felt that their child's physical development had been impacted negatively, and 25% felt similarly about their language development. Over half (52%) said their child's social and emotional development had been harmed. So was that all due to the broader limitation on a child's interactions during the pandemic, or partly from missing the physical activities and social interactions from within school? It's not clear, but it feels like potentially it's a blend. I couldn't help feeling that the biggest concern for online/home learning is the risk of social isolation and missing opportunities for social interactions.

Reading an article on **"Understanding Socialisation"** from the **Coalition for Responsible Home Education** [17], they summarised the following: *"The term socialisation refers to the process through which a child gains the social skills they need to effectively navigate the social norms and behaviours of the broader society. Children who are homeschooled (like all other children) need to build the 'social fluency' that will enable them to negotiate a variety of different social situations, develop and maintain strong relationships, and work well with others in varying contexts."*

I took a look at some of the resources from **Connections Academy** [18], an online school by **Pearson**, discussing **"Online School as an Agent of Socialisation,"** where they recognise that *"a high-quality online school ensures that school socialisation* *and the development of social skills is a key component in every student's experience"* [19]. Like many others, they offer a raft of clubs and activities, including, where distance allows, in-person trips. They also shared: *"Research suggests that for students with social anxiety, socialising online is easier than in person. Socialising online vs. in-person reduces communication apprehension, helping students with social anxiety feel more comfortable communicating and engaging with their peers and teachers"*. I will note however, that the research used to support this was for college students, **"Social Anxiety in Online and Real-Life Interaction and Their Associated Factors"** [20], so is not a perfect match for all age groups as evidence.

I can share firsthand the excellent and innovative work of **Melissa McBride** and her team at **Sophia High School** [21], in offering a broad and forward-thinking curriculum. They are fully Ofsted accredited, and are a good example of what can be offered online.

It feels like it should be significantly harder to build a virtual sense of community compared to the physical environment, but on reflection, isn't that ultimately about quality of leadership and focus? There isn't a fixed definition of a child accessing an online school; they might still have regular and physical sports clubs, drama, music, and more, or they might be quite isolated. It does seem to resonate that if you have access to excellent, quality, and holistic education on your doorstep, then it makes sense to access it, but if you don't, for geographical reasons or your child struggles in that environment, then increasingly, quality provision is now available, albeit limited to the independent sector. Times are changing, though; demand and competition will drive quality and breadth of offer, and ultimately, that can only be a good thing.

The key elements to be mindful of, and where we need to further develop evidence, are shaped around these five pillars:

1. **In-person interaction supports all-around development**: Traditional schools foster both academic growth and core social and emotional development, which feels inherently tied to face-to-face interaction. This aspect of building friendships and social skills still feels harder to replicate in a fully online settings.

2. **Online learning can suit some students**: Some learners, especially those with SEND or who struggle with anxiety, may benefit from the personalised and less stressful environment of online learning. For these students, virtual engagement can potentially offer better opportunities for connection and progress than traditional classrooms.

3. **Technology has hugely expanded the possibilities**: The advent of EdTech has made it possible to create vibrant digital learning environments, though the challenge remains in fostering the subtle, more spontaneous interactions that happen naturally in physical spaces. The gap is definitely closing mind you.

4. **Socialisation still needs priority**: While good online models have the potential to provide "academic excellence," there are still risks of social isolation. Online schools often intentionally create opportunities for students to build social fluency, through virtual clubs, extracurricular activities, and, where possible, in-person events. Some do this really well.

5. **Leadership and quality matter**: The effectiveness of an online school's ability to foster a sense of community depends heavily on leadership and the quality of the program. Just like a physical school. As always, we can't group all online schools together and simply treat them as the same, but strength of leadership is likely to be a bigger factor on the success of an online provision.

Does the pressure on teacher numbers dictate the path we follow?

Apologies, but this is just a short food for thought at the end of this chapter to set us up for the topic coming next. If our population continues to grow and naturally, our student cohort follows a similar trajectory, and in parallel, we have fewer teachers due to higher departures than arrivals (see the next chapter), don't we reach a tipping point where we need to think about a hybrid model so that more children can access the skills of those available educators? Couldn't education move to some days in school, some not? Could online learning allow more children to access those subject specialists? You will have a view, but it is a completely new concept for our governments.

Gary Henderson, director of (information technology) IT at **Millfield School,** shared his perspective: *"I feel the pressure on teacher numbers and on workload are pushing towards a greater need to use online technologies. For me, the key is to use tech where it has the greatest impact rather than trying to see it as a replacement. So could tech tools be used to support students in more rote and memorisation areas of the curriculum, freeing up the teachers to focus on the discursive areas possibly?"*

So come on, shouldn't we at least consider and plan for some of these online or hybrid options? As you'll see in the next chapter, I'd prefer if we could recruit and retain more educators. Hopefully, I have left you with a hook to read on!

References

1 "These 3 Charts Show the Global Growth in Online Learning," World Economic Forum, 27 January 2022. [Online]. Available: https://www.weforum.org/agenda/2022/01/online-learning-courses-reskill-skills-gap/
2 "Online Education & E-Learning Statistics UK," Oxford Learning College, 2023. [Online]. Available: https://www.oxfordcollege.ac/news/online-education-statistics/
3 D. Clark, "Digital Learning in the UK - Statistics & Facts," Statista, 03 July 2024. [Online]. Available: https://www.statista.com/topics/8518/digital-learning-in-the-uk/

4 "The Increase in Homeschooled Children," Benbridge Academy, 27 May 2024. [Online]. Available: https://www.benbridgeacademy.co.uk/the-increase-in-homeschooled-children/
5 "Pupil Attendance in Schools - Headline Facts and Figures," Department for Education, 08 August 2024. [Online]. Available: https://explore-education-statistics.service.gov.uk/find-statistics/pupil-attendance-in-schools
6 "Sir Ken Robinson," [Online]. Available: https://www.sirkenrobinson.com/
7 S. K. Robinson, "Changing Education Paradigms," TED Talks, October 2010. [Online]. Available: https://www.ted.com/talks/sir_ken_robinson_changing_education_paradigms
8 "Digital Poverty Alliance," [Online]. Available: www.digitalpovertyalliance.org
9 "Closing the Digital Divide for the Millions of Americans without Broadband," U.S. Government Accountability Office, 01 February 2023. [Online]. Available: https://www.gao.gov/blog/closing-digital-divide-millions-americans-without-broadband
10 "U.S Government Accountability Office," [Online]. Available: www.gao.gov
11 J. Winslow, "America's Digital Divide," The Pew Chaitable Trust, 26 July 2019. [Online]. Available: https://www.pewtrusts.org/en/trust/archive/summer-2019/americas-digital-divide
12 "21 Million Americans Still Lack Broadband Connectivity," The Pew Charitable Trust, 10 July 2019. [Online]. Available: https://www.pewtrusts.org/en/research-and-analysis/fact-sheets/2019/07/21-million-americans-still-lack-broadband-connectivity
13 M. Egwuekwe, "Opinion: We Must Close the Digital Divide in America," Government Technology Magazine, 27 February 2024. [Online]. Available: https://www.govtech.com/network/opinion-we-must-close-the-digital-divide-in-america
14 "What is Digital Citizenship? – A Guide for Teachers," Future Learn, 03 September 2021. [Online]. Available: https://www.futurelearn.com/info/blog/what-is-digital-citizenship-teacher-guide
15 "Digital Citizenship Education (DCE)," Council of Europe, [Online]. Available: https://www.coe.int/en/web/digital-citizenship-education/the-concept
16 R. Montacute and E. Holt-White, "Views on the Ground from Parents, Providers and Teachers," The Sutton Trust, 2021.
17 "What the Research Says on Socialization," Coalition for Responsible Home Education, [Online]. Available: https://responsiblehomeschooling.org/research/summaries/homeschooling-socialization/
18 "Connections Academy by Pearson," [Online]. Available: www.connectionsacademy.com
19 C. Hennessey, "Socialization for Online School Students," Connections Academy by Pearson, 31 March 2022. [Online]. Available: https://www.connectionsacademy.com/support/resources/article/socialization-for-online-school-students/
20 J.-Y. Yen, C.-F. Yen, C.-S. Chen, P.-W. Wang, Y.-H. Chang and C.-H. Ko, "Social Anxiety in Online and Real-Life Interaction and Their Associated Factors," *Cyberpsychology, Behavior and Social Networking*, vol. 15, no. 1, pp. 7–12, 2012.
21 "Sophia High School," [Online]. Available: www.sophiahigh.school

7 Recruitment and retention – do we undersell the profession?

Hopefully, nobody will be surprised to see this topic appear in my book. It's probably one of the most pressing and challenging topics of all. Reflecting on this topic, and not least seeing the challenges we have within my own trust to recruit good teachers, we can see it's a problem that is growing rather than even remaining at a constant level. The biggest challenge on a day-to-day basis is finding strong replacement teachers, especially on the strength in depth when we look at applications for senior positions. We might conclude later that there is less appeal in senior leadership roles given the breadth of responsibility and workload, but there is certainly a sense that too many good and experienced people are leaving the profession at one end, and too few are arriving to supplement and replace at the other end.

In an ideal world, we would be discussing a singular problem, one that might have somewhat obvious interventions that could addressed, but it's clear to me that there are quite a few conveniently aligned issues that combine to cause the current pressures on our system. If we want to return to a sustainable system, first and think more long term, we need good people looking to education as an appealing and rewarding profession. Once we have a sufficient inflow of new teachers, we then need to reflect on making the job sufficiently manageable, rewarding, and motivating to ensure that we can keep these same folks for the duration of their careers. Finally, we need to then ensure that the most able, and those most experienced are rewarded with pathways for progress into leadership that are attractive, doable, and rewarding to better retain their skills in the system. How hard can that be? (*note the intended tone of sarcasm here*).

Now, I am going to preface this topic with a clear recognition that people far better than me have discussed this topic for some time, and the truth is, some of the necessary interventions are not within the control of the education system, they sit far higher up the food chain, but that absolutely doesn't mean we can't signpost these challenges better or advocate in a more cohesive way how change might be delivered, and why it might be a saving for any government in the long run. I talk more about this in the next chapter, but one of the biggest barriers to system-wide change is that governments, and in particular ministers, like interventions that deliver outcomes within a singular electoral cycle, it feeds into the "look what we did" PR of subsequent elections, that's a problem because many of the core interventions we could (and I argue should) do, have a longer life span before you reap all of the rewards. So, it requires governments, wherever they are in the world, to put education over politics and have the kahunas to make long-term decisions.

The topics I focus on in the chapter start with the perception of the value of educators, do we sell the profession short at a national level, then the slightly tricky and sensitive topic of Pay (buckle up) and then how we better support the profession and educators in a sustainable system. I may have bitten off more than I can chew in this chapter, but you have to think big if you want to talk about change.

Where are we now?

As with all of the chapters in this book, I like to start with a bit of a state of the nation. It's easy to get sidetracked with anecdotal references, but I doubt my publisher would support me following that trajectory, especially on this topic. I am going to try and focus on three parts of the journey: recruiting new, retaining and developing, and reducing departures.

A June 2024 **TES magazine** article, **"The scale of the teacher retention crisis revealed"** [1], highlighted that over a 12-year period, just over 40,000 state school teachers left within just one year of teaching. That equates to approximately 11 out of each 100 new recruits stepping away after one year. By year three, 26 will have left, and by year 10, it's 42. That's a significant attrition rate for any sector. It's a new issue, though, isn't it? Well, actually, no. The data shared for England by the **Department for Education** in their November 2023 census data indicated that while in 2022, 11.3% of teachers left after a year, back in 2016, that number was 15.1%.

I was about to say that this shows either a gap in training before arriving in the classroom or the job isn't quite what they expected as new recruits. Fortunately, in the same article, **Emma Hollis**, chief executive of the **National Association of School-Based Teacher Trainers (NASBTT)** [2], said, *"one key issue is that many early career teachers experience a "dissonance" between what they expect when they apply for initial teacher training and the reality when they enter the classroom."*

The article also highlighted a perspective that primary teachers typically choose to go into teaching motivated by developing children holistically; secondary teachers arrive with a passion and opportunity to share their specialist subject, but both find their time spent number crunching and dealing with a much wider set of issues.

A 2022 article by *EducationWeek*, titled **"Here's how many hours a week teachers work"** [3], highlighted that a typical teacher works about 54 hours a week – with just under half of that time devoted to directly teaching students. Now, I know this will be contentious, but self-reporting by surveying how many hours anyone works, in my humble opinion, does tend to encourage an overestimate rather than underestimate of how busy anyone is, but I'm not sure there is an alternative measure of capturing this effectively, and my firsthand experience shows there is validity in the numbers being reported. While teachers cited the need for better pay to match the amount of work they put in each week, they also said support systems to help manage their workloads are crucial. They also highlighted that it will take logistical changes such as reworking school calendars and prioritising the social-emotional needs of both students and teachers.

I was expecting many of the topics I chose for this book to be interconnected, so I wasn't surprised when they also referenced the closure of many wraparound services over recent years that put more social worker and mental health support kinds of responsibilities onto the shoulders of teachers alongside their academic duties.

Reinforcing that perspective on the primary motivators to become teachers, a report by the **National Foundation for Education Research** [4] in 2024, **"Shifting career motivations are not to blame for worsening teacher shortages"** [5], said that by the very nature of teaching, it is for many graduates highly attractive as a career where you can have a positive impact on others, and evidenced this by noting: *"This 'pro-social' aspect of the teaching profession is a strong motivator for graduates to become teachers. Data from the 2018* **Teaching and Learning International Survey (TALIS)** *[6] showed that nearly all teachers in* **OECD** *[7] member countries, including*

England, said that they were motivated to become a teacher in part to 'influence the development of children' and 'provide a contribution to society."

For a wider global perspective, similar research was done in the United States, in this case, applications for teaching qualifications in Texas between 2009 and 2020. The research **"From Interest to Entry: The Teacher Pipeline From College Application to Initial Employment"** [8] also identified a sharply declining interest in teaching applications over the period. As an aside, they also showed that students of colour, men, and students with higher academic scores were substantially under-represented in applications for teacher qualifications, but for now, that is a separate topic.

An excellent research paper, **"Nuance in the Noise: The Complex Reality of Teacher Shortages"** [9], published in 2019, highlighted the following: *"Generic, national teacher shortage narrative is pervasive. This narrative has likely taken hold because there is no single, comprehensive data source on teacher shortages. The way districts and states collect this data is unique to local contexts, and the way they report to the U.S. Department of Education varies by state. Many who tell the teacher shortage story often consider teacher shortage data sources in isolation and tend to overgeneralize specific problems to the profession as a whole. When all data connected to teacher shortages are considered together, the specificity of problems emerges."* There was data over a five-year period from 2011 through to 2016, and that year over year, the number of students enrolling in and completing teacher preparation programs had decreased. Falling from 685,000 enrolled in teaching qualifications in 2011 to 441,000 in 2016. The successful completion numbers also fell from 217,000 to 160,000 in 2016.

The recruitment challenges may be similar in different countries around the world, but the teaching landscape most definitely isn't. The research also highlighted that in the United States in 1955, the average student/teacher ratio was 27 to 1; by 2012, that ratio was down to 16 to 1. In essence, they might have fewer graduates completing their teaching qualifications in the United States than before, but as the report states, *"there are still more teachers produced than classrooms to fill, even as the number of students served per teacher has declined."* A 2017 article in **Education Week**, titled **"Teaching Force Growing Faster Than Student Enrolment Once Again"** [10], highlighted that even with lower recruitment numbers in the United States, it has still far outpaced the equivalent rise in student enrolments over the same time period. For context, it reflected a 3% increase in students and a 13% increase in teachers. Not the same challenge as we see in the United Kingdom.

Is it the workload? Or pay?

So, perhaps the core issue here in the United Kingdom is the workload, or more specifically, the unexpected workload and volume. We will come back to it, but that does, in part, question the level of training and expectation setting that teachers are receiving before qualifying. Perhaps too much honesty at this stage would scare all of the candidates off mind you. That said, **Pepe Di'Iasio**, general secretary of the **Association of School and College Leaders (ASCL)** [11], said, *"Poor retention rates are chiefly the result of excessive workloads and uncompetitive pay compared with other professions,"* highlighting the link between workload and pay. That's another really important consideration, as we typically talk, or at least the media often does, about one singular salary level. A typical teacher gets paid X, and unsurprisingly, everyone has a view on the number and its appropriateness. In truth, for this specific topic, it's a combination of the amount of pay versus what you are expected to do to earn it. Just passing judgement on a number is pointless and always divisive.

So, we have desire to become a teacher, workload, expectations of the role for new teachers, and pay so far on our list. Our flow through the where we are now, may get quite meandering before we arrive at those main questions, but stick with me.

Let's touch on the financial landscape, remembering we can always find a number somewhere that suits our argument, but as I am looking for the facts, I'm hoping we can keep this on a very straightforward level. According to the **Institute for Fiscal Studies (IFS)** [12], between 2010 and 2019, total school spending in England rose by 1% in real terms. But since total pupil numbers grew by 11% over the same period, school spending per pupil fell by 9%, and I think all of us involved in education would concur that we saw and felt that.

The IFS also cited that since 2019, additional funding has allowed per-pupil funding to remain the same (in real terms) as the level in 2010. Now, just for context, we expect overall student numbers to fall by 4% by 2028, so there is a view that even if funding was frozen at its current level, the reducing roll would see per-pupil spending increase statistically by 1.5%. I have to say, I scratch my head somewhat here; as our roll falls, we get less student funding due to a smaller roll, but our costs remain largely the same, so we see more, not less, pressure.

For context, to help you understand the financial pressures on the system, between 2015 and 2022, the number of children with an education, health, and care plan (EHCP) increased 60% from 200,000 to 360,000. In simple terms, of the £7.6 billion of extra funding for education since 2015, £3.5 billion has been taken up by the growing high-needs budget.

So, back to the numbers that are most relevant to our teacher recruitment and retention discussion. The IFS, in their same report, shared: *"Average teacher pay across the UK in 2024 is expected to be over 6% lower in real terms than in 2010, and is at a similar level in real terms to that seen in 2001. The decline is concentrated among more experienced teachers, whose salaries have fallen 11% in real terms (new recruits have seen little real-terms change in pay). In contrast, average earnings are due to be about 6% higher in 2024 than in 2010, and about 18% higher than in 2001,"* also suggesting that *"these declines in teacher pay relative to average earnings may help to explain why teacher recruitment is significantly behind targets and why 1 in 10 teachers leave the state sector each year."*

Starting teaching

We can add a bit of extra context with the entry point for graduates into teaching. As of July 2024, the minimum starting salary for an ECT (early career teacher) was £31,650 (*slightly more inside London*) in the STPCD (school teachers' pay and conditions document) [13]. This is almost exactly in line with the median graduate salary of £32,000, as shared by the **Institute of Student Employers (ISE)** [14]. According to the **National Education Association (NEA),** the U.S. national average starting teacher salary in 2024 was $44,530 [15] (circa £35k), also indicating, in line with the United Kingdom, that teachers are making 5% less than they did 10 years ago when adjusted for inflation.

The problem with averages, of course, is that they often hide key details. In the United States, for example, teacher pay is significantly different by state, largely reflecting variability in the cost of living, so the average teacher salary in California is almost double that of Missouri [16]. In the United Kingdom, outside of London, there is no such consideration for regional variability in the cost of living, which I think significantly impacts recruitment in the south or in some cities.

In Australia, the New South Wales government shared on their **"Explore teaching as a Career"** [17] website that because of a government increase in salaries on 9 September 2023, a new graduate can now earn a salary package of $95,490 (circa £49k) straight out of university. They provided a comparison compared to other sectors for first-year earnings, as summarised in Table 7.1.

Unlike in the United Kingdom, where there is approximate parity between teaching and an average graduate pay, certainly in Australia, it seems to be tracking ahead of many other professions. Note that this includes an "attraction and retention" initiative of up to $17,000 [18].

There is a small caveat here, and one which often becomes a cause of discussion and challenge. In large part due to having a strong union voice and support in England, teachers, like many public sector workers, receive a significantly higher employer pension contribution compared to the private sector. At the time of writing, this had recently risen from 23.68% to 28.68% [19], and just to add to that, with more context, according to the IFS [20], average public sector pension contributions stood at 18% in 2021 and at just below 6% for private sector employees. To close the loop, employer contributions for teacher pensions in Australia are 11.5% and in the United States, approximately 11% [21] (*state variability*).

Table 7.1 First-Year Earnings Comparison

Teaching	Accounting	Engineering	Marketing	Law	Psychology
$95,490	$61,050	$66,600	$77,700	$77,700	$83,250

Source: https://education.nsw.gov.au/teach-nsw/explore-teaching/salary-of-a-teacher

I flag public versus private contribution rates. When we reference starting graduate teacher pay as being in line with average graduate pay as a whole in the United Kingdom, it is worth factoring in that there is actually a 20% differential on the overall package due to those contributions. Of course, starting out in a teaching career will not be much comfort in meeting your rent and food costs each month.

I am conscious, as I stated earlier, that a number is only relevant when we balance that with what we are asked to do in order to earn it, so we are going to tackle that in one of the key questions later in the chapter. However, based on copious reading and research, I am left concluding the entry point salary really can't be the main barrier; it's not significantly out of line with other graduate pathways and, as a package, could even be deemed attractive … albeit where you live may significantly influence that conclusion.

Opportunities for progression

Perhaps, then, the bigger issue is your ability to grow a competitive income as you progress. We will recognise that in England, we have a neatly marked-out progression based on the six main pay scales and three subsequent upper pay scales (UPSs), as set out in the STPCD. In most cases, teachers can progress automatically from M1 through to M6 on an annual basis, albeit they can apply for a two-point jump with supporting evidence of progress.

(*I am writing this book for anyone with an interest in education, so for some, I acknowledge I will be stating the obvious at times.*)

Anyway, assuming a natural pathway, after six years in the profession, a teacher most likely will arrive, after five incremental increases, at the main pay scale (MPS) 6. Based on the current scales [22], which would mean a salary of £43,606 or, having taken on additional responsibilities for a further three years (or sooner), £49,084 on UPS3.

Interestingly, the **Department for Education**'s 2023 **"School workforce in England"** [23] report published on June 24 highlighted that across our 468,693 teachers, the median pay was £43,801, almost exactly in line with the latest M6 pay scale. This might be a somewhat clumsy measure, but I will go with it for now and may contradict myself later, using a simple percentage calculation from a current starting salary of £31,650 against a median of £43,801 as an increase of 38% (*It's clumsy as those folks included in the average didn't start with an M1 pay level based on today's grade, so the uplift is understated.*) Anyway, I wanted a comparator number, so when looking at similar data for the United States, the average is $69,544 versus a starting salary of $44,530 [15] – or, with my new measure, a 56% differential. So, regardless of how simple my measure is, there is potentially a lower pay progression here.

Perhaps I should be bold here; in most jobs in the private sector, you get paid a salary to do it, and unless the role changes, you stay on that salary plus any annual cost of living increments. If you take on more responsibilities, you are given a different job description and pay to match that. The same approach applies in education, but for the first six years, we receive two increments, moving along the main pay scale plus any annual cost of living increment. That makes arriving at M6 feel like more of a blocking point than it would for others who are only used to one annual increment.

We probably shouldn't forget that most leadership roles will be based on a four- to five-point range and so again, many will have a few years of (performance permitting) automatic incrementation before arriving at their ceiling.

It certainly feels to me that, putting the opportunities for **TLRs (teaching and learning responsibilities)** pay increases to one side, a more motivating approach would be to extend the main pay scale much further to encourage and reward extended tenure. That sense of reaching a ceiling cannot be a positive one in the context of retention strategies. We can then perhaps factor in that knowing the most significant challenges teachers face include capacity and workload; that, for example, offering more income if you take on even more responsibilities (the pathway to the upper pay scale) will likely be less and less attractive.

So now we have set the scene, there are a few key questions I wanted to unpick.

THE IMAGE PROBLEM

Why is teaching often undervalued, unappealing, and how do we change the public perception?

Having spent far more time than I expected researching and engaging with system leaders, I expected to be able to conclude this question fairly rapidly as a global phenomenon. However, as with everything in education, there is nuance, and as a result of much broader societal challenges, regional differences in the perception of teachers and education as a whole.

I think we have two parallel topics here: the perception of the profession and how that feeds into recruiting, and secondly, society, and especially parents' perception of education and how it is more broadly valued.

In a 2024 article [24] for the **National Foundation for Educational Research (NFER)** [4], **Dawson Maclean** wrote: "*Teacher shortages are hardly a new phenomenon. However, the scale of the challenge has significantly worsened in recent years. This is indicative of a weakening attractiveness of teaching compared to other potential jobs, driven by a long-term deterioration in pay and working conditions.*" Now I have provided a snapshot on teacher pay as part of my introduction, but context is king so its worth reminding that using the NFER data, real terms pay in 2023 is 12% less than an equivalent in 2010. That's not uncommon across many sectors, though, so whilst something we should not dismiss, it is not "just" pay that is pushing those downward perceptions of teaching as a credible career pathway.

The **NFER** also highlights that high workloads drive teachers' decisions to leave the profession and, indirectly, join. During term time, teachers often work more hours than graduates with similar characteristics working in other sector jobs, and it's accepted that those extra hours worked during the school year tend to be offset by the extra holiday provision during the school holidays. Even with that in mind, most teachers reported that they were unhappy with their workload and that post-pandemic, teachers' working hours have increased significantly.

One of the considerations is that the challenges with pupil behaviour and their higher needs have also fed into additional staff workload. For any of us spending regular time in school, that is absolutely not a surprise and is one of the most significant drivers of workload.

The **Education Endowment Foundation** shared a detailed practice review in 2023 titled **"Supporting the recruitment and retention of teachers in schools with high proportions of disadvantaged pupils: understanding current practice around managing teacher workload"** [25], collecting data via a survey of 1,326 practising classroom teachers and school leaders from over 1,100 schools. They reflected that schools and trusts are already using multiple strategies to try and manage teacher workload, to the extent that there are few strategies that are not being widely adopted. Planning, preparation, and assessment (PPA) time was the most frequently reported strategy, followed by access to existing schemes of work/lesson plans (*and perhaps now think AI tools to support*), alongside collaborative lesson planning. On the other hand, the main barriers faced and enablers of workload reduction mirror one another.

Some of the main drivers of workload reported came from outside of the school gates, often from the government and Ofsted (imagine that), and also from parents and carers. Insufficient funding and staff capacity were reported as the main barriers to workload reduction, while increased support from other agencies and reducing the workload associated with behaviour management were the main priorities for future development.

We can all resonate with the feedback they captured and shared. The key for me is that some of the strategies needed to mitigate the workload and pressures on staff can be adopted by school leadership, but without national support, additional funding to facilitate more capacity in our school system, and a coordinated communication for parental understanding of the role of schools, we are always going to be in damage limitation mode.

Are we surprised right now that the profession is seen as overworked, under-heard, and in a capacity crisis? How might this feed into public perceptions that a career pathway into education will likely be turbulent?

A United Kingdom problem?

I always look to others who have worked across the sector for their insights, so I reached out to **Mark Steed**, who has spent 23 years in school principal and CEO roles and is now supporting schools at **Steed Education**. On the question of image and public perception, he indicated: *"This is a UK problem. International teachers* *are treated in much higher regard than in the UK."* Explaining that *"The teaching profession needs to be better remunerated. There has been quite a shift in wider working patterns post-Covid and whereas teaching was once seen as a very flexible career (long holidays, etc.), it is now one of the least flexible career paths for young graduates."*

We all accept that expectations change generationally, and whilst this isn't unique to education, he also shared, *"There is a generation of teachers who want quick promotions without gaining mastery at each stage of their career path."* That may be a broad view, and again, not unique to education, but the perception and possible expectation of rapid progress, no matter what, may also make the graduate pathway less attractive than others.

I asked **Matt Pitman**, head of secondary at **Global Village Learning** in Australia, similar questions. As you will have noticed throughout my book, I have tried to look at all topics through the widest possible international lens. Perhaps not surprisingly, he answered my question with his own question, asking: *"Is it undervalued or is the image problem directly related to the actual problems of a system that has far outstretched its best before date? Are we surprised that the general public do not value a system that may have very well failed them and now creates similar issues for their own children? The image of the teacher is directly linked to the system. If we want to and value our professionals, we need to address the shortcomings of the system they work within."*

That really helps, as there is certainly truth in that we can't separate the view of the teacher from our view of the education system. With pressures, failings, and, I might add, constant negativity at the governmental level, these often "false narratives" do persist. As I have shared before, it's easier to blame the system and those who work in it than it is to accept accountability for the funding failures and lack of system evolution.

Kat Cauchi, a former UK primary school teacher, echoed that view, explaining: *"I think there are a lot of misconceptions from the public about teaching such as the day-to-day tasks of teachers, responsibilities and accountability and working hours (the typical wow all that holiday and finish at 3pm assumption). Like with many incorrect perceptions in society, the press plays a role in this in what information they put out about teaching and how misinformed that can be. Additionally, a lot of what you see about teaching in the news is negative, the stories of what schools or teachers have done wrong far, far outweigh success stories or any positive write ups."* Kat's first point is an important one. We have high dropout rates with newly qualified teachers (now ECTs), and perhaps the perception of being a teacher really doesn't align with the pressures and reality of the role today.

I also managed to capture some perspectives from **Kai Vacher**, principal at the **British School Muscat**. He shared his perspective that teaching *"is undervalued because, as a professional graduate profession, it is relatively poorly paid. Working with young people is often perceived as a vocation: people don't do it for the money; but many teachers are attracted to international schools because they feel more* *valued than in the UK; and that starts with pay."* We are going to come on to pay in the next question, but it's a common "perception" that influences career pathways.

Kai also shared a broader international perspective, explaining: *"I lead two schools in Oman. In total we educate over 1300 students from more than 70 different countries. In many of these countries teachers and education is respected and valued in ways in which we can only dream of in the UK. For example, in many Asian countries, including China, teaching is regarded and respected as a noble profession. For example, many of my colleagues, including me, enjoy living in the catchment area of our schools; We are respected and cared for by our community. It is a joy to meet our students and their families in and around the town. How many teachers could say that in the UK?"* I think those reading this book will likely know the answer already: Respect for educators has sadly diminished in society and has been declining for some time.

Now I said this starts at the top, the government, using the sector as a suitable target for blame to deflect from lack of investment, and exactly on that point Kai said: *"The teaching profession has been persistently criticised and often ridiculed in the UK media and also by politicians for more than 50 years. OFSTED seems to have been designed around the needs of some parents rather than a system to support schools in improving. The same can not be said of accreditation systems such as COBIS [26], BSO [27], and CIS [28], which support and shape school improvement in the international schools sector."*

I can consolidate all the feedback and research data in this section into five key strands that impact perceptions, as follows:

1. **Perception and pay**: Clearly, teaching is often seen as undervalued due to relatively low pay compared to other graduate professions. While it's seen as a vocation, the lack of competitive remuneration, particularly in the United Kingdom, discourages many from entering or staying in the profession.

2. **Workload and systemic pressures**: Teachers face high workloads, long hours, and growing behavioural challenges in schools, which contribute to burnout and make the profession less appealing. These issues, compounded by external pressures from government and inspection bodies like Ofsted, deter prospective educators.

3. **Negative media and public misconceptions**: Misleading portrayals of teachers in the media, such as the idea of short working days and long holidays, foster misconceptions. The press often highlights failures in education, while successes and positive stories are rarely given attention, perpetuating negative perceptions of the profession.

4. **International respect for teachers**: In many countries, teaching is a highly respected profession, offering better pay and greater societal recognition than in the United Kingdom. Highlighting this difference can serve as a model for

how the United Kingdom can reposition teaching as a valued and respected career, or risk losing more educators overseas.

5. **Rebuilding the profession's image**: To improve the public perception of teaching, it's important to start with government-level support, including better funding, competitive pay, and positive messaging. The profession must be championed as central to our society, and there should be a focus on improving working conditions and addressing those systemic challenges that deter new teacher recruits.

So, how do we improve the image of education? Well, there's no magic wand, I'm afraid, but as I have shared in the list above, it starts at the top, signposting the profession and its impact on our society. It starts with suitable funding, competitive career pathways, competitive remuneration, and a change of language that reflects empathy and understanding of the challenges in the system and those shoulders that are currently having to bear the load.

That links quite conveniently onto the big topic of money, for which I have a question ready for us to dive into!

COMPENSATION AND RESPECT

Do salaries and working conditions reflect the immense challenges and importance of the job?

OK, now I know this is contentious, so I am intentionally treading lightly on this one. As I shared in my introduction to this chapter, there is merit in extending main pay scales in our UK system to enable a clearer and more sustainable route for progression. There is a somewhat "sector-specific" expectation that each year there is scale advancement in salary as well as the incremental cost of living increases; that's not the case outside the public sector. If you are in the same job and same role, your pay doesn't automatically progress until you change roles. While the UK government has taken steps in the right direction recently, education is still not a competitive graduate pathway in terms of earning potential, and dare I say it, student loan costs haven't helped when calculating the cost/benefit sums.

We normally work on simple economic principals, market forces, supply and demand, so with that in mind, **Kai Vacher** asked a very salient question in response to me asking if salaries and working conditions reflect the immense challenges and importance of the job. He answered: *"In some international schools, they do, but not in the UK state system. Why are 40,000 teachers leaving the UK state system each year? Why are so many teachers and leaders moving to the international sector? Why would many UK trained teachers and leaders never choose to return to a UK state school?"* Now, with 30 years under my belt, I have seen the growth of the international government pavilions at education conferences like BETT [29] grow year on year as they attempt to attract and recruit educators into the international school systems, and if like me, you visit conferences in the United Arab Emirates for example, including the GESS (Global Educational Supplies and Solutions) conference [30], you'll realise just how many expat educators from the United Kingdom and the USA are now based in these countries.

Apples with apples?

It's difficult to compare pay in state education with the offer from private international schools; it's never going to be equitable, and in some countries, tax is low (or non-existent), further amplifying the salary gap. But counter that with the loss of pension contributions and job security, and it's really quite nuanced. Let me contradict myself once again. Educators are voting with their feet, so it's not that nuanced; many are moving each year, so we have to respond if we want to slow the drain overseas.

I mention the P word, pension, because that's a huge plus in education; it's huge compared to almost anywhere else. It feels like a conveniently awkward question. It's really an elephant in the room because if you add the total pay package, that feels much more competitive sadly that's not helpful for an early career teacher, other than the knowledge that on retirement, they will have a better package than most. Nonetheless, the teacher package rarely gets used for comparisons, as it doesn't always suit the purpose of asking for more. Even the pension scheme mind you has had challenges with a ceiling or lifetime allowance (LTA) in place up until April 2024. That had proven to be a problem, too. In essence, if you were a school or trust leader and have reached your limit on pension contributions, we were almost accelerating your decision to step away or retire, knowing any more contributions would result in taxable deductions. I know this issue related to a very small slice at the top of our education establishments, but leadership recruitment is an equally huge challenge, and without those capable and experienced leaders at the top of the tree, frankly, the system would never excel.

Follow a delta strategy

The **National Foundation for Education** research suggests we should consider using a delta strategy for modelling teacher pay. The current scenario suggests that simply aligning teacher pay with general wage growth across the economy won't be enough to tackle teacher supply issues on its own. In fact, other factors could continue to put pressure on teacher recruitment and retention over time. To address this, closing the gap between average earnings and teacher salaries could be a step towards improving teacher supply. Increasing teacher pay at a faster rate than average wage growth would likely make teaching more competitive and attract more people to the profession.

Thinking of it like a delta strategy – in economics, delta represents a difference or change. In this context, it refers to the difference between teacher pay growth and the growth in average earnings. By adding a positive delta each year, teacher pay would gradually become more competitive compared to other sectors, helping to improve teacher supply over time. They modelled it by applying between 1 and 3 percentage points delta on top of the average earning rate [31].

A 3% delta uplift reflected an extra cost of £4bn to the treasury mind you, but did show in their modelling the following: *"The forecast shows that higher pay growth is associated with greater teacher supply across all phases/subjects. This is due to both higher pay making teaching more attractive to enter and improving retention of existing teachers, thereby reducing subjects' respective targets."* It is worth noting, though, that the scale of the impact varied noticeably by subject, depending mainly on their starting point.

If we want to mitigate in some small way, over a number of years, the inflow of educators and make the role more financially attractive, a commitment over 5 to 10 years of a delta uplift on teachers' pay would be a strong start. In parallel, there is clearly work to be done on teacher training to build realistic expectations of the role and pressures, which has to be a factor in the high early dropouts in the first few years of teaching.

Will that fix the issue of retention? Nope. It will hopefully provide marginal gains, but as **Matt Pittman** explained: *"It is a complicated issue. Do I believe educators should be paid more for the work they are currently doing? Yes. But truly, is the answer more pay or more support and genuine system reform that would create the space for a greater work-life balance for all in school communities? If we are to persist with the demands of the job as they are now, without any consideration for change, more compensation is absolutely required, not only for the brilliant people within the profession currently but to attract future educators to the sector."* Matt recognised when sharing with me, that it is widely known that the job is one of immense challenges, and without significant pay or significant change, it's fair to ask why anyone would sign up for it.

I wear quite a few hats, so I need to be mindful of being accused of hypocrisy, but this is a time when we need to give educators a louder voice and act on their perspectives. Far too many system leaders are from other sectors outside of education, and the changes being made are not always in the best interests or aligned with the needs of those actually on the ground in schools. We absolutely need to ensure we give educators the chance to lead their profession. Can I go a step further and say "different" educators and voices in the sector? It does always seem like it's the same faces at the table and the last thing any of us need right now is an "Edu Clique."

A growing job description

Assuming you have read my book in order, which isn't a given as I have tried to write each chapter as a stand-alone topic, but assuming you have, you'll have followed the discussions of good schools, the shifting curriculum agenda, the growth in SEMH challenges with our students, challenges with school attendance, and technology and AI refining the role of the teacher, and have seen that not only is the real job description for an educator far larger than the one they signed when recruited but that it is undergoing rapid change. Given the breadth of skills we require of our teachers, the extent of independent work and accountability they carry, and the requirements for social and family welfare, nobody can honestly look at the brief and say the role is adequately and fairly valued.

Our whole country and its social fabric are funded by the expectation of, and output from, economic growth, and yet rarely do we connect the dots in a tangible way to see that the nurture and support of our education system will result in the biggest gain or loss on that system in the years ahead. We neglect our future workforce, underfund their development, and expect economic growth from companies desperate to recruit skilled workers; worse still, find them online or overseas. We have to close the loop and re-prioritise our future workforce as the primary and priority investment.

A suggestion

Al's very simple solution is increase funding for our school systems with a system restart 15% uplift on all GAG (General Annual Grant) funding. Agree on a subsequent five-year funding formula rather than have an annual wait and see. Effective planning and budgeting require stability and a clear and secure multi-year plan. Then, track teacher pay awards based on a 3% delta above-average pay growth. Again, lock it in for five years so the budgetary implications can be planned. **Sir Kevan Collins** made a recommendation for a £15bn [32] package to kick-start and support students post-pandemic, and the government responded with a £1.4bn package, so I appreciate that my thoughts may fall (if even heard) on deaf ears.

Someone needs to be bold and see that in the long term, the costs of not acting will be so much more significant.

RESPECT FOR THE PROFESSION

The challenges we face and possible solutions

I have the perfect audience with this book, so I know we can all agree that teaching is one of the most important jobs out there, but as we know the role doesn't always get the respect it deserves. There are a few obvious reasons why, some we have already covered as well as some sound approaches to help address perceptions.

Here are the main challenges as I see it.

How Society Sees Teaching: In a lot of countries, teaching isn't seen as prestigious or respected as jobs in law, medicine, or finance. Ironically, the 2018 **OECD TALIS (The Organization for Economic Cooperation and Development, Teachers**

and School Leaders as Valued Professionals) survey [33] shows that countries like Finland and Singapore, where teachers are highly respected, tend to have better educational outcomes.

The Pay Doesn't Match the Work: I think we have covered that fairly fully already.

Burnout Is Real: Schools and teachers are stretched thin with heavy workloads, long hours, and a lot of "social" work that is on top of their core roles. The **National Foundation for Educational Research** [4] reports that teacher workload is a key factor in dissatisfaction and high staff turnover rates.

Lack of Ongoing Development: In many places, teachers don't get enough opportunities to keep learning and growing professionally. This limits their ability to stay on top of new teaching techniques and reduces the perceived value of their expertise. The **Education Endowment Foundation** [34] highlights that continuous professional development improves teaching quality and boosts job satisfaction.

So, what can we do?

Sometimes my strategy of keeping it simple, stupid works for me. Perhaps those reading will think I am doing an injustice to the challenges by trying to simplify things into neat little boxes, but sometimes we fail to consume the steps needed. We fail to focus on the priorities because they are just too big to grasp or because they are wrapped up in a 150-page policy recommendation.

So, as a rule, if you reappraise and set pay for a profession at the appropriate level, not only do you attract and retain people, but you also set a perspective on the value of that role. In other words, for example: "Nationally, we choose to pay teachers X because it's such an important job."

Then, fund the system better to help improve working conditions, perhaps have more support staff or a greater investment in appropriate, evidence-informed technology that reduces the admin and non-teaching tasks teachers have to do. Create time and capacity for staff to focus on the pedagogy.

Invest in professional development, and not just when they start their careers but throughout. Most schools will say they do, but it's rarely sufficient or suitably invested in. I'm not proposing we go quite this far, but linked to professional development, Finland requires teachers to have a master's degree, and the government supports their ongoing training. Perhaps that links to public perceptions and respect?

Change the national narrative and start telling the world how important teachers are. Imagine that. Changing public perception starts with highlighting teachers as the skilled professionals they are, reflecting empathy for the challenges they face and signposting the huge impacts of education. In South Korea, teachers are referred to as **nation builders**, which I think is brilliant and spot on.

Trust educators and the system more and build more flexibility and autonomy into our systems to allow innovation and adaptation to suit children's needs. Like anyone, when we have more control over our role, we feel more valued and can be more innovative in our work.

Respect for teachers doesn't happen overnight, but if we want better student outcomes and a more robust education system, we need to start sometime, so how about now? Raising salaries, improving working conditions, investing in professional development, and changing how society views educators are all key.

References

1. E. Peirson-Hagger, "The Scale of the Teacher Retention Crisis Revealed," TES Magazine, 21 06 2024. [Online]. Available: https://www.tes.com/magazine/analysis/general/teacher-retention-scale-crisis-revealed-dfe-data
2. "The National Association of School-Based Teacher Trainers," NASBTT, [Online]. Available: https://www.nasbtt.org.uk/
3. I. Najarro, "Here's How Many Hours a Week Teachers Work," EducationWeek, 14 04 2022. [Online]. Available: https://www.edweek.org/teaching-learning/heres-how-many-hours-a-week-teachers-work/2022/04
4. "National Foundation for Educational Research," NFER, [Online]. Available: https://www.nfer.ac.uk/
5. "Shifting Career Motivations are not to Blame for Worsening Teacher Shortages," NFER, 18 07 2024. [Online]. Available: https://www.nfer.ac.uk/blogs/shifting-career-motivations-are-not-to-blame-for-worsening-teacher-shortages/
6. P. J. Jerrim and S. Sims, "The Teaching and Learning International Survey (TALIS)," Department for Education, 06 2019. [Online]. Available: https://assets.publishing.service.gov.uk/media/5f6484c2e90e075a01d2f4ce/TALIS_2018_research.pdf
7. OECD, "Organisation for Economic Co-operation and Development (OECD)," [Online]. Available: https://www.oecd.org/
8. B. Bartanen and A. Kwok, "From Interest to Entry: The Teacher Pipeline From College Application to Initial Employment," *American Education Research Association*, vol. 60, no. 5, pp. 941–985, 2023.
9. K. Pennington McVey and J. Trinidad, "Nuance in the Noise: The Complex Reality of Teacher Shortages," Bellwether Education Partners, 2019.
10. L. Loewus, "Teaching Force Growing Faster Than Student Enrollment Once Again," Education Week, 17 08 2017. [Online]. Available: https://www.edweek.org/leadership/teaching-force-growing-faster-than-student-enrollment-once-again/2017/08
11. "Association of School and College Leaders (ASCL)," [Online]. Available: https://www.ascl.org.uk/
12. L. Sibieta, "School spending in England: A Guide to the Debate during the 2024 General Election," Institute for Fiscal Studies, 06 2024. [Online].
13. "School Teachers' Pay and Conditions," Department for Education, 2024. [Online]. Available: https://www.gov.uk/government/publications/school-teachers-pay-and-conditions
14. "What is the Average Graduate Salary?," Institute of Student Employers (ISE), 10 11 2023. [Online]. Available: https://insights.ise.org.uk/attraction-and-marketing/blog-what-is-the-average-graduate-salary/
15. "Educator Pay in America," National Education Association (NEA), 18 04 2024. [Online]. Available: https://www.nea.org/resource-library/educator-pay-and-student-spending-how-does-your-state-rank
16. M. Ziegler, "Maps of School Teacher Salary Averages for 2024," Fox News, 26 05 2024. [Online]. Available: https://www.livenowfox.com/news/school-teacher-salary-average-map-2024-how-much-paid-state

17 "Explore Teaching as a Career," News South Wales Government, Australia, 2024. [Online]. Available: https://education.nsw.gov.au/teach-nsw/explore-teaching/salary-of-a-teacher
18 "Teacher Salaries 2024," Department of Education, Western Australia, 2024. [Online]. Available: https://www.education.wa.edu.au/teacher-salaries
19 "Updates to Contribution Rates," Teachers Pensions, 09 04 2024. [Online]. Available: https://www.teacherspensions.co.uk/news/employers/2024/02/updates-to-contribution-rates.aspx
20 B. Boileau, L. O'Brien and B. Zaranko, "Public Spending, Pay and Pensions Green Budget 2022 - Chapter 4," Institute for Fiscal Studies (IFS), 08 10 2022. [Online]. Available: https://ifs.org.uk/publications/public-spending-pay-and-pensions
21 "Contribution rates - Teachers Retirement System (TRS)," TRS Illinois, 2024. [Online]. Available: https://www.trsil.org/employers/payments/contribution-rates_earnings-limitations
22 "Teacher Pay Scales 2024-25: What will Your Salary Look Like?," TES Magazine, 29 07 2024. [Online]. Available: https://www.tes.com/magazine/analysis/general/teacher-pay-scales-how-much-are-teachers-paid-england#Main%20UK
23 "School Workforce in England - Reporting Year 2023," Department for Education, 06 06 2024. [Online]. Available: https://explore-education-statistics.service.gov.uk/find-statistics/school-workforce-in-england
24 D. McLean, "An Image Problem," National Foundation for Educational Research, 05 06 2024. [Online]. Available: www.nfer.ac.uk/blogs/an-image-problem
25 K. Martin, R. Classick, C. Sharp and H. Faulkner-Ellis, "Supporting the Recruitment and Retention of Teachers in Schools with High Proportions of Disadvantaged Pupils: Understanding Current Practice Around Managing Teacher Workload," Education Endowment Foundation, 2023.
26 "Council of British International Schools (COBIS)," [Online]. Available:/www.cobis.org.uk
27 "The Association of British Schools Overseas (AoBSO)," [Online]. Available: www.aobso.uk
28 "Council of International Schools," [Online]. Available: www.cois.org
29 "Bett UK (conference)," [Online]. Available: www.bettshow.com
30 "GESS Dubai (Conference)," [Online]. Available: www.gessdubai.com
31 J. Worth and S. Tang, "Next Government Needs Long-Term Pay Strategy that will Help Teacher Supply Challenge," National Foundation for Educational Research, 14 05 2024. [Online]. Available: https://www.nfer.ac.uk/blogs/next-government-needs-long-term-pay-strategy-that-will-help-teacher-supply-challenge/
32 S. Sandhu, "Sir Kevan Collins: What the Education tsar Wanted for the School Catch-up Plan versus What Children will Get," The I Newspaper, 03 06 2021. [Online]. Available: https://inews.co.uk/news/education/sir-kevan-collins-education-tsar-wanted-school-catch-up-plan-versus-children-get-1033137
33 OECD, "TALIS 2018 Results (Volume II): Teachers and School Leaders as Valued Professionals," Paris, 2020.
34 J. Collin and E. Smith, "Effective Professional Development: Guidance Report," Education Endowment Foundation, 2021.

8 Why can't we have a long-term plan for education?

First and foremost, I am by no means the first to be asking this question, many far wiser than me have been collaborating around the world to look to the future of our education system and create both a plan and the evidence to help support change. Sadly though, that change has been slow in coming, and we seem rigidly anchored to the safety net of the past.

A few years ago, I came across an article referencing **John Gatto** [1], a teacher from New York State, who made a now-famous speech [2] in 1992 denouncing the American school system, questioning its "hidden" curriculum and its impact on our future learners, leaving school as he described it as "a generation of helpless, powerless people."

Whilst in the middle of writing this book, I saw a video posted by **Dan Fitzpatrick**, typically known as "the AI educator," who had already shared some insights with me for Chapter 4 of this book. He referenced this speech by John Gatto in the context of a changing artificial intelligence (AI) world, and suffice to say, it really resonated with me [3], and perhaps highlighted I really hadn't paid enough attention before.

A 2012 blog on the *Huffington Post* [4], titled **"Seven Lessons I Teach"** [5], summarised the following: *"In the 'Seven Lesson Schoolteacher,' Gatto talked about being paid to teach confusion, class position, indifference, emotional dependency, intellectual dependency, provisional self esteem and the notion that one can't hide from the system. Britain's school system, like America's, has not deviated much from those seven lessons in the last 21 years. A few hours spent in a school, in the company of schooled children, or even hanging around on education forums will amply prove that."* I'll come back to this article in a few paragraphs, but firstly, I wanted to share because I loved the way that Dan encapsulated Gatto's seven lessons within the context of our rapidly changing and AI-driven world, and I have tried to summarise them as this:

The education system remains stuck in the past, and this is not merely a concern; it is a crisis. In his essay, Gatto exposed what he saw as the hidden curriculum, one that continues to shape the futures of young people. With the onset of the AI revolution, Dan (and I agree wholeheartedly) feels that Gatto's insights are more relevant now than ever before.

The seven insights were articulated with an eye to the advent of AI in this way.

1. **Confusion**

    Gatto identified the disarray in school timetables—maths, then history, then art—each taught in isolation, with no continuity or connection. In a world where success comes from linking disparate pieces of knowledge, schools are doing the opposite, encouraging children to view everything in isolation.

2. **Class Position**

    Schools often categorise and label students, much like products on an assembly line. Through testing, social hierarchies are reinforced, sending a clear message: know your place. Yet, with AI's potential to democratise learning, anyone with access to the internet can learn anything, positioning themselves however they choose.

3. **Indifference**

    The constant ringing of bells, signalling the end of one subject and the start of another, teaches students not to invest deeply in anything. This repetitive cycle turns them into mere task-switchers. However, as AI takes over routine tasks, future success will increasingly rely on passion and the ability to focus deeply on meaningful pursuits.

4. **Emotional Dependence**

    Children are conditioned to seek gold stars and fear red marks, fostering a dependence on external validation. As AI becomes more prevalent, the need for individuals with strong internal values—those who are not easily swayed by the opinions of others—will be essential.

5. **Intellectual Dependence**

    The traditional "sage on the stage" model, where teachers lecture and students passively absorb information, remains prevalent in most classrooms. This form of learning produces minds that wait to be told what to think, a dangerous trait in an AI-driven world. Critical thinking, not passive absorption, is now imperative.

6. **Provisional Self-Esteem**

    In school, self-worth is often tied to grades. However, outside the confines of the classroom, those numbers hold little meaning. As AI reshapes careers, individuals must learn to build self-esteem not on grades but on resilience and adaptability.

7. **Surveillance**

    Schools are increasingly normalising surveillance, with children subjected to constant monitoring. This raises a generation unprepared to protect their digital rights, unable to set boundaries in a world where AI-powered surveillance is pervasive.

I have paraphrased the spirit of Dan's summary, and that of Gatto, which is expanded in his 2002 book, ***Dumbing Us Down: The Hidden Curriculum of Compulsory Schooling*** [6], and from both, the conversation concludes with the question, where does this leave the education system?

The argument is that it continues to produce compliant, confused workers for a world that no longer exists. As Dan said, "*The AI era calls for creative problem-solvers, lifelong learners, and independent thinkers.*" Now is the time to rebuild the education system, shaping one that equips every child to flourish alongside intelligent machines. Our children's future is digital, which is why reform cannot wait.

As with all things, the pathway and experiences of learners are hugely variable based on the school they attend, the broader educational system, the teachers they encounter, and many other variables. So, whilst the critique stands up, many schools and educators have managed to mitigate the impact of a restrictive system better than others.

Coming back to the **Huffington Post** article, the author, **Nikki Harper** reflected on Gatto's seven lessons and felt these needed adapting, to reflect from the position of a home educator, I was keen to unpick, as a successful education "system" is one that provides the right environment for all, one that currently, perhaps, accelerates perceptions that home education is preferable or more suitable for some children.

She identified her seven pillars as:

1. **Intellectual Freedom**: Children should be empowered to follow their own interests and passions in learning, rather than being confined to a rigid curriculum, as true intellectual freedom fosters a deeper engagement with education.

2. **Passion**: Allowing children to pursue subjects they are passionate about without interruptions helps them fully engage and excel, in contrast to the regimented, time-bound nature of traditional schooling.

3. **Context**: Learning should encompass the broader context of a subject to promote real understanding, rather than isolating facts from their historical or thematic connections, as often happens in conventional education.

4. **Self-Respect**: A child's self-worth should be independent of external validation from teachers or grades, fostering healthy self-esteem that is based on their own effort and standards.

5. **Reality**: Home education takes place in the real world, allowing children to engage with a broader spectrum of people and experiences, unlike the artificial environment of schools, which often do not prepare them for real-life situations.

6. **Individuality**: Schools often stifle individuality through conformity, but home education allows children to express and embrace their unique identity without the pressure to fit in.

7. **Insubordination**: Questioning authority and developing a healthy sense of scepticism is crucial for children to understand when to follow rules and when to challenge them, promoting independent thought and resistance to unjust systems.

I struggle to see any of those perspectives that I would disagree with, other than perhaps reality, but I respect that this one is contentious and highly variable in experience. In fact, what we see increasingly is a strong consensus on what we need but a barrier to how that translates into policy, planning, and implementation.

It's certainly not up for debate; the demands and needs of modern life now are hugely different to those of 10, let alone 25 or 50 years ago. The more our world infuses digital technology the more we amplify the need for those most human of qualities. In the 2014 **"OECD Yearbook," Andreas Schleicher**, special advisor on education policy to the secretary-general of the **OECD Directorate for Education and Skills,** said [7]: *"Jobs, wealth and individual well-being depend on what people can do with what they know. There is no shortcut to equipping people with the right skills and to providing them with opportunities to use their skills effectively. If there's one lesson the global economy has taught us, it is that governments cannot simply spend their way out of a crisis."*

The pace of change

Perhaps we need to be bolder, reflecting on the pace of change in society and the onward march of AI and digital connectivity. I have a lot of time and respect for the work and research undertaken by **Professor Sugata Mitra**, visiting professor at the Massachusetts Institute of Technology (MIT) Media Lab and professor of educational technology at Newcastle University. He is best known for the **"Hole in the Wall"** [8] computer learning research he undertook in India, based on the theory that "kids can teach themselves," where young children figured out how to use a PC left in a hole in a wall, entirely on their own – and then taught other peers how to use it too, saying, *"In 9 months, these children taught themselves to use the computer to a similar level as the average secretary."* I thoroughly recommend his 2007 TED Talk [9] on the subject. He is an excellent and engaging speaker too.

I've digressed slightly with a small introduction on Mitra's work, but I wanted to reference his presentation in 2012 from MIT titled **"Is Education Obsolete?"** [10], where Mitra asked: *"Is education obsolete? Might the connections we get from the cloud make education as obsolete as horsemanship and swordplay? In 300 years, might people say, "there was a time that people used to believe that education was very important."*

Mitra also shares a conversation he had with Arthur C. Clarke about the film ***2001: A Space Odyssey***. In the film, humanity discovers a large black monolith and tries to understand what it means. People became obsessed with understanding the object. Mitra compares the Hole in the Wall project to Clarke's monolith. When the two met, Clarke shared two ideas that have stuck with Mitra: a teacher that can be replaced by a machine, should be, and when learners have interest, education happens.

I don't personally believe a *good* teacher can ever be replaced by a machine, but the concept of learning directly linked to interest is key. That's all about relevance to the world the learner exists in; it has changed hugely, but fundamentally, the curriculum hasn't. Well, I wasn't expecting to have a space odyssey in my book, but I hope you get the gist of the message.

The 2 sigma context

At the same time as we reflect on an education system that offers the right exposure and learning for the future skills our children need, we attempt to create the places and spaces that support their emotional and interpersonal needs, and we also continue to reflect on the effectiveness of teaching and most importantly learning. How do we optimise the learning opportunities for our children? You will of course, know from my bio that I am not an expert on pedagogy, but whilst writing this, the well-known **Benjamin Bloom's "2 Sigma Problem"** [11] popped back into my head. My best paraphrase would be: How do we make teaching the "group" as effective as teaching "one to one," from his research in 1984 [12], which evidenced that the average student tutored one to one performed two standard deviations better than students taught in a classroom environment.

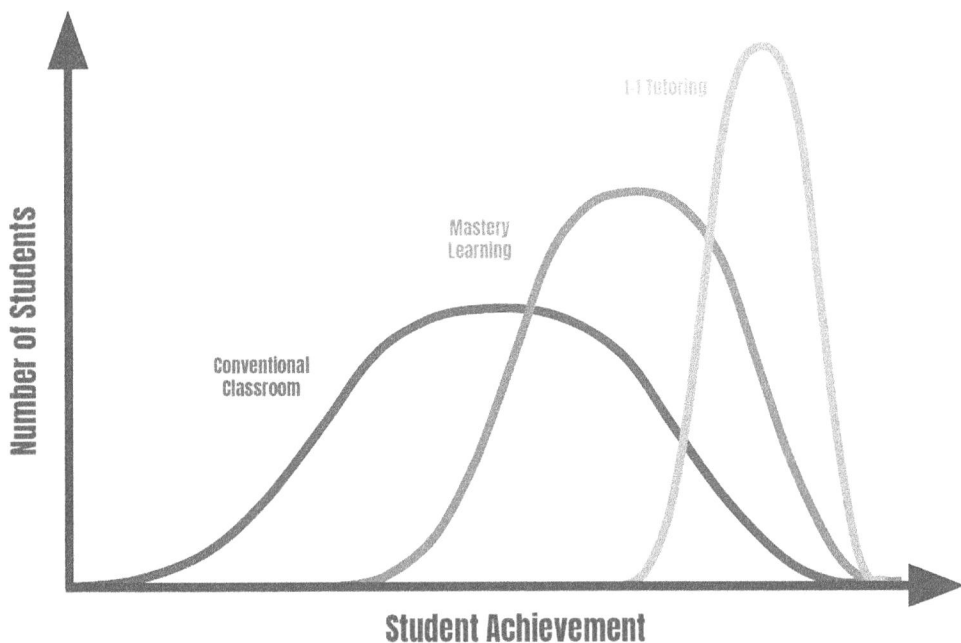

Figure 8.1 Highlighting student achievement with Bloom's 2 Sigma problem

I'd suggest that for the first time, perhaps the AI-powered personalised learning platforms mentioned in Chapter 4 start to bridge that gap, aligning with Bloom's goal of achieving the benefits of one-on-one tutoring in broader educational settings. I do want to note that there has been recent challenge to the efficacy of Bloom's model and the very narrow group used in his research, but I'd argue the concepts and aspirations are still highly relevant (Figure 8.1).

Anyway, alongside the personalised learning "tutoring" opportunities, it also seems relevant with current challenges around teacher numbers internationally, creating pressures on teachers: cohort ratios and an ever-growing diversity of physical and online learning experiences catering to learners with diverse needs. Updating our educational offer to be current, reflective, skills based, and more would be a step, but not if we cannot also find the right ways to best deliver an engaging and impactful personalised learning journey ... at scale.

So now that we have set the scene, here are a few questions I wanted to unpick specifically.

THE CURSE OF POLITICS

How does frequent political change derail well-intended educational reforms?

This section naturally focuses on my own experiences, and I want to keep the topic relatively light, as we could go down a million rabbit holes on this one. It's quite fascinating – and a bit frustrating – how often well-meaning educational reforms get tossed about like a ship in a storm whenever there's a change in the political winds, no matter which international ocean we are traversing. If you've ever wondered why plenty of well reasoned and evidenced ideas in education never seem to stick around long enough to make a real difference, frequent political change is often the culprit.

We can probably all align with this example cycle, a new government comes into power with a fresh set of ideas on how to revolutionise education. They plan to roll out ambitious programmes, revamp curriculums, and perhaps even invest in new technologies for schools (briefly). Teachers start adapting, students begin adjusting, and just as things are starting to settle, there's another election. A different party wins, or a new minister is appointed and suddenly, it's all change again. The new leaders have their own vision, which might not align with the previous one, and so the cycle begins anew.

This constant chopping and changing can be quite disruptive. It creates a sense of instability within the education system. Those on the front lines of implementing these reforms often find themselves in a perpetual state of adaptation. Just when they've got the hang of one set of policies, they're expected to pivot to another. It's a bit like being asked to change direction midway through a marathon – not exactly conducive to reaching the finish line on time! Apologies, analogies are not my strong point. **Michael Fullen** does a much better job in his book ***The New Meaning of Educational Change*** [13], where he reflects on the dilemmas and consistent barriers to delivering large-scale system reform and highlights that integrating individual and systemic success, in the context of constant change, has proven to be a rare feat in current school reform efforts.

Let's not forget about the resources involved with change. Implementing new reforms isn't cheap. It often requires significant investment in training, materials, and infrastructure. When reforms are abandoned prematurely due to political shifts, it's not just the wasted money that's concerning but the lost opportunity to make a lasting positive impact.

Students aren't immune to these shifts either. Inconsistent curriculums or teaching methods can affect their learning experience and outcomes. One year, they might be focusing on project-based learning, and the next, they're back to traditional rote memorisation. It's no wonder that educational outcomes can become erratic under shifting conditions. Parents and the wider community also feel the impact. Trust in the education system can wane when there's a perception that schools are at the mercy of political whims or that they simply don't "get" the changes. Now more than ever, we have a disconnect with public perceptions of our education system and its core purpose and value.

Playing the long game

Education is a long game. It requires consistency and a stable environment to nurture growth and improvement. We need long-term plans that have time to evolve, embed, and then evidence impact.

What we have historically lacked are brave politicians. I'll be more specific, those willing to fight for and support change, but not expect to take the credit at the end. Most education systems within democracies are locked in a cycle of never gripping the big decisions but rather the ones they can implement and show success from all within one election cycle. Sadly, it often feels that the positive impact on political careers trumps the actual needs of the system. I have referred to it before: we tinker at the edges, causing disruption and pressure on our teachers, and skip any more significant changes. That's why many of our systems are still based on dated educational foundations from decades (or centuries) ago.

Just pause and reflect on the UK curriculum over the last 15 years: Have we adapted, have we evolved, or have we doubled down on interventions that solidify the "traditional" legacy view of our curriculum? I'll massively simplify for effect, but it's as if, as long as our children can read and write, and we throw in a bit of STEM (science, technology, engineering and mathematics) to show we are modern thinking, all will be OK.

Reading the 2006 research article **"Educational Change Over Time? The Sustainability and Non-Sustainability of Three Decades of Secondary School Change and Continuity"** [14], I was reminded that they, too, concluded that *"most mainstream educational change theory and practice in the field of educational administration neglects the political, historical, and longitudinal aspects of change to their detriment."* And: *"These forces and their convergence have ultimately reaffirmed the traditional identities and practices of conventional high schools and pulled innovative ones back toward the traditional norm in an age of standardisation."*

Research undertaken in the ***Journal of Educational Change*** [15] cited when it comes to intent: *"It is important to note that whilst the general intentions of school reform are almost always to improve standards of teaching, learning and achievement in increasingly unstable and turbulent economic and socially fragmented environments, their singular and cumulative effects are not always perceived to be efficacious or beneficial by those whose responsibility it is to enact them."* In other words, reform may not always lead to renewal.

Take, as a different example, the frequent policy changes in the United States, where shifts between administrations have led to swings from **"No Child Left Behind"** [16] to **"Every Student Succeeds Act"** [17], each with different accountability measures and educational priorities. These shifts require states and schools to constantly adjust, which can be both costly and confusing, but with little meaningful or directly tangible change in outcomes.

Closer to home, we've seen similar patterns. We have a transition of the accountability and organisation of our schools from Local Authority (LA) control to the academy system. I do see it building resilience in our system, and in some cases, with scale comes capacity and sustainability, but for all the change, have we seen a fundamental shift in our educational outcomes?... It's debatable. I err on the side of some improvement, and something I discussed earlier in the book so we won't disappear down that topic right here.

Throughout this book I try and tackle those difficult questions that hopefully prompt discussion, challenge, and with both fingers firmly crossed, an opportunity for change. There are lots of changes except the fundamentals of our curriculum and offer, lots of changes but nothing that actually frees up the capacity to deliver significant and sustained change. They all individually make good press and media opportunities and soundbites at the government level, but mostly add workload and a shuffling of priorities for the staff on the ground.

So, what's the way forward? How do we ensure that educational reforms have the staying power they need to make a real difference? One idea is to foster greater collaboration across the political spectrum when it comes to education policy. If there's a shared vision that transcends party lines, reforms are more likely to endure beyond individual administrations. Imagine that all political leaders acknowledge that this isn't a topic where they look for a personal win, but genuinely one for the greater good and future generations.

Another approach is to actually involve educators, parents, and students more deeply in the decision-making process, genuine co-production. As a rule, when reforms are built on a foundation of broad consensus and stakeholder engagement, they're less likely to be discarded at the next election.

Ultimately, education should be above politics. To do that effectively, we need to find ways to insulate educational policy from the ebbs and flows of political change.

Is any of this easy? No, is any of it likely? Well, that depends largely on the political climate and how "wins" can be given in return for support of a longer-term plan. Mostly, governments start with a clear focus on the economy; more economic output; and more gross value add (GVA), which is a typical measure of the contribution from each company, industry, or sector to the national economy. If we accelerate economic growth, we will have more inflow of revenues into the public purse to tackle all of the other considerations, health, education, and so on. Ideally, we pull a magic lever, and it can happen quickly, but in practice, the influence of global economies is a much stronger factor. For the bits within our control, economic growth typically means creating more jobs, having a skilled workforce to fill those jobs, and supporting the aforementioned growth.

So, as the economy dominates more, there is a handy link that education and skills are elevated on the priority list as being the fuel for future growth. The first focus tends to be adult skills, but the bigger strategic thinkers recognise we prime the pump decades in advance and that for UK or US PLC to be competitive in 2040, change has to come now in our foundational education systems.

I've always been convinced that asking for one big ask with a 20-year impact date is never going to fly politically. There just have to be wins along the way, unless, of course, you are a society where the ruling government is stable and never changes. Think of **Vision 2030** [18] and the transformation of education in Saudi Arabia as an example where the Saudi government allocated the equivalent of £37.5bn to education – more than any other sector in the country. Sadly, we don't see such decisive planning in Western countries, and so we have to break down the ambition into clear stepping stones, allowing a strategic plan to be agreed by all, but opportunities for wins along the way, no matter who is the government of the day. It's the only realistic way to shift the dial, and could and should provide all those previously mentioned opportunities for true stakeholder engagement.

Work is already underway

The best example of work towards this is by the **Foundation for Education Development** (FED) [19], who is fully invested in the belief that long-term strategic education planning is vital to the success of countries and their people. They have actually taken that belief and converted it into action, shaping over some years now a long-term plan for education, built on that core coproduction from voices across the educational landscape.

As always, this work and progress is coming from within the sector, not from the government sadly; the civil servants within education departments are still focused on the "whack a mole" mindset of responding to immediate pressures, so at the time of writing in 2024, the **Biden-Harris Administration** focused on their **"Improving Student Achievement Agenda"** [20], which in parts, mirrored the similarly timed UK government focus on **"Working together to improve school attendance"** [21], where they respond to target the problem and not the root causes.

Let's explore some (hopefully) common ground everyone can align with and then conclude this chapter with a few considerations of what we could do, if we could align all of our political and system leaders.

FINDING COMMON GROUND

Can we build a broader societal consensus around the goals of education?

I think so. In fact, there are plenty of folks way better informed that have come together to try and help shape a road map. I always try and take a view from a wider lens, recognising the interconnected nature of our education ecosystem, and I think if we are measured, and don't try and undo all the good we already have within our system, then there are clear areas of focus that could shape a longer-term plan or, better still, a strategy. As Dan Fitzpatrick said, *"Plans keep the lights on. Strategy ensures there's a future worth illuminating."*

John Mikton, the technology for learning coordinator at **Ecole Internationale de Genève**, shared: *"Yes, but this ultimately requires a shared framework—a common moral compass, cultural empathy, and a unified understanding. As a society, we must agree on core beliefs, attitudes, and perspectives, supported by research, that form the backbone of education. Regardless of race, religion, culture, or geography,* *we all face common challenges such as climate change and rapid technological advancement, often with little say or input. It's crucial that education reflects this shared understanding to prepare us for these global challenges."*

Let's start with a very narrow, primary focused definition provided by the **Department for Education:** *"The major goals of primary education are achieving basic literacy and numeracy amongst all pupils, as well as establishing foundations in science, mathematics and other subjects"* [22]. Erm, well, that's one way of saying it, but certainly not how I would want to kick the conversation off.

Nick Gibb shared in his 2015 speech on **"The Purpose of Education"** [23]: *"Education is the engine of our economy, it is the foundation of our culture, and it's an essential preparation for adult life. Delivering on our commitment to social justice requires us to place these 3 objectives at the heart of our education system. We all have a responsibility to educate the next generation of informed citizens, introducing them to the best that has been thought and said, and instilling in them a love of knowledge and culture for their own sake. But education is also about the practical business of ensuring that young people receive the preparation they need to secure a good job and a fulfilling career, and have the resilience and moral character to overcome challenges and succeed."*

It's not a frequent event where I concur with Mr. Gibb, but if we take the sentiment, as clearly, the actions subsequently on our curriculum didn't follow a path that was fair for all, those key points of **instilling a love of knowledge and learning, preparation for a future career,** and **moral character** are certainly good umbrella topics. I'm not sure we have excelled at any of these, sadly, but we can expand a little to help focus our perspectives.

Instilling a love of learning

Let me start at a high level, our learning journey, our curriculum, and the spaces we learn in have to feel safe spaces that encourage us to learn, be curious, innovate, and also need to feel relevant. Understanding the props of learning as children get older is key for the agency. We also need to feel like we have an equal and fair opportunity to achieve. If you have asthma and can't run very far, you won't be motivated if you know at the end of your journey, you have to take a test running a marathon. It's a clumsy analogy, but that's how many children feel with required academic subjects, and more flexible and varied pathways that play to all of our strengths would add a real sense of possibility for many.

If I break it down further and try to include all the key elements that I consistently hear or see, I would encapsulate this as follows in the next few pages.

First up, and as we all know, instilling a love of learning in children is a multi-faceted process rooted in psychological understanding and educational best practices. At its core, our goal is to help children develop a core motivation or love of learning, which requires that nuanced balance of encouragement, autonomy, achievability, and engagement. The best approaches focus on nurturing the whole child, respecting their individuality, and providing an environment that fosters that curiosity I mentioned earlier alongside personal growth.

Our core starting point is in creating a nurturing and safe environment, feeling secure, both emotionally and intellectually so that they can explore freely, ask questions, and, just as importantly, make mistakes (I have a Ph.D. in this ☺). Fear of failure, or resulting judgement, is a real barrier to curiosity, and an environment that reduces this fear allows children to take the kinds of intellectual risks that help support better understanding and innovation.

Encouraging curiosity and inquiry is another key element in this process. Children are naturally inquisitive, and tapping into this innate curiosity can lead to a genuine love of learning. One effective way to do this is through enquiry-based learning, where students are encouraged to explore topics by asking their own questions and then follow where that curiosity leads. This approach makes learning more meaningful and personal, as it aligns with the child's natural inclinations. I'd argue this helps grow that important link with a sense of relevance to our learning.

Something I am very keen on, and see in many outstanding schools, is that in addition to nurturing that core curiosity, children are also provided with hands-on, experiential learning opportunities. Real-world experiences, whether they come in the form of projects, experiments, or field trips, an XR (Extended Reality)-enabled converted school bus in our case, all engage children in active learning. This type of learning is more memorable because it involves direct engagement.

Central to all of these approaches is promoting autonomy and a sense of choice in learning. When children have a say in what they learn or how they approach a task, they naturally develop a sense of ownership over their learning. Autonomy encourages engagement and fosters a deeper investment in the subject or topic. The argument is that by allowing children to take control over at least some aspects of their learning, we are in effect, supporting them in developing self-regulation and independent skills, all pretty key to a pathway into lifelong learning.

I am mindful that I am preaching to the converted in this book, or indeed to many reading, but a common reminder in many ways is that children are much more likely to develop a love of learning when they are motivated by internal satisfaction rather than by external rewards. Praising effort and persistence, rather than intelligence or final outcomes, helps instil a growth mindset. This neatly links back to my stumbling butterfly proverb from an earlier chapter, too.

Another key strategy is to make learning relevant to the child's life and experiences. Children are typically much more motivated when they can see how their learning actually links to their world (relevance), whether it's linking a maths problem to a real-life situation or demonstrating how a historical event relates to present-day issues. In this interconnected topic, you'll hopefully align this with my previous discussions on the value of project-based learning, too.

Fostering a growth mindset is really important, too. I talk about this a lot at any age and stage, but when children view intelligence as something that can grow with effort, they are more likely to stick at it when their learning becomes difficult. This approach becomes more about the journey than the destination, and they learn to see challenges as opportunities for development. It would be best if you had a level playing field of pathways, of course, to make this equitable and frankly sustainable. Children won't always get things right, but by framing mistakes as part of the learning process, we help develop resilience and persistence, which are some of the foundations for personal growth.

Mistakes are simply stepping stones to success.

Developing a love of reading is another foundational pillar in developing a lifelong learner. Reading opens the door to limitless worlds and ideas, and fostering the habit of reading for pleasure is one of the most effective ways to promote a love of learning. I think we all agree that children should have access to a wide variety of books that cater to their interests, and reading should be presented not as a chore, but as a gateway to discovery. Storytelling further ignites the imagination and sometimes critical thinking, which nurtures an appreciation for learning in any setting.

Play and creativity also have an important place in this equation. Learning should not be all structured or formal; there must be room for play, exploration, and creativity. We always see it in a good early years and foundation stage and year 1 setting. Play-based learning, particularly for younger children, is known to encourage exploration and a child's cognitive development in many ways. Creativity, that key ingredient, whether through art, games, or unstructured play, helps children develop problem-solving skills and to think outside the box, both of which are essential for academic and personal growth. This ties in nicely with problem- or project-based learning, as it develops through the stages of the curriculum.

Finally, social learning and collaboration are critical components of fostering a love of learning. I've talked about this in the context of the recent growth in online and hybrid school settings in an earlier chapter. Children often learn best in social contexts, where they can share ideas, collaborate, and learn from their peers. I think that holds true for adults, too, mind you. Collaborative projects not only build academic skills but also develop teamwork, empathy, and communication; skills that we all acknowledge are vital for success both inside and outside of the classroom.

So, no rocket science, nothing shared as a revelation, just a refocus on the core building blocks that, for me, create an environment to foster a love of learning. Creating an environment where children develop a love of learning really does require a holistic approach: nurturing curiosity, providing meaningful and relevant experiences, promoting autonomy, fostering a growth mindset, and modelling the pleasure and impact of discovery.

I hope you are nodding along at this stage. While I am sure there is more that I could have added, hopefully, it's a fair summation.

Preparation for a future career

Preparing our children for their future careers requires what I believe is a transformative shift in our approach to education. Note, not a replace and rebuild, but a shift. Our current model, emphasising memorisation and plenty of standardised testing, is increasingly out of step with the rapidly changing demands of our new global workforce. As technological advancements, globalisation, and shifting workplace structures reshape business, it becomes ever more important to reconsider what and how we teach our children. I've covered much of this in earlier chapters, based on the voices of many much wiser than me, but as with all reflections, we can distil it into a few primary building blocks.

I am going to argue that perhaps the most essential skill set for future careers is the ability to think critically and solve complex problems. As automation continues to replace those routine tasks, the value of human workers will lie in our capacity to handle ambiguity and complexity—skills that machines (currently) cannot easily replicate. I know, sorry, I'm back on my soft skills = power skills messaging here. Sadly, many education systems today often prioritise factual recall but do less to foster the type of higher-order thinking needed to navigate these challenges. Instead, schools and curriculums really need to place greater emphasis on analysis, evaluation, and creativity.

As we have discussed, project-based learning and enquiry-based approaches are particularly effective in developing these skills. It's not a leap to recognise that by encouraging our students to engage with real-world problems and think creatively to find solutions, we prepare them for the kinds of challenges they will more likely face in the workplace.

Prioritising digital literacy and technological competence

In this ever-digital age, technological competence is fundamental. Digital literacy is no longer optional; it is just as important as reading and writing. So, we have to go way beyond simply teaching basic computer skills and ensure that children develop a deep understanding of how technology works. Coding, data literacy, digital citizenship, and familiarity (developing confidence) with emerging technologies such as AI, cybersecurity, and data manipulation are no longer niche skills but the essential tools for navigating the future workforce.

The **World Economic Forum** has already identified technological literacy as a critical skill for 21st-century jobs. We should be looking to embed these skills much more consistently into the curriculum, ensuring that all children are comfortable using technology and can innovate and adapt as new tools and platforms emerge. This includes teaching children to be responsible digital citizens (DigCits), so they can navigate the digital world safely and ethically.

The importance of understanding issues such as online privacy, cyber bullying, and spreading misinformation cannot be underestimated in an increasingly interconnected digital world. I know you will agree, but for many, the nod of agreement does not translate into the actions of how we embed this. Over the last few years, we have seen more and more fake content being shared that children take as fact when lacking the skills to question, research, and challenge the authenticity and validity of content and views.

Fostering adaptability and a commitment to lifelong learning

As career paths become more fluid and unpredictable, and boy, is that an understatement right now, adaptability and a commitment to lifelong learning are essential. In the future, it is increasingly likely that as adults we will change careers multiple times, requiring us to update our skill sets continuously. The ability to learn independently and adapt to new roles will be a defining characteristic of future success. Our schools, therefore, I would argue, need to instil in students not only the skills they need now but also a mindset of growth and curiosity that will sustain them throughout their working lives. I know, easier said than done.

The focus on adaptability is supported by research [24, 25], which shows that workers will need to be flexible and open to acquiring new skills as industries evolve. This requires moving away from the rigid model of education that prioritises the acquisition of fixed knowledge and towards one that values curiosity, innovation, and the child's ability to learn how to learn. Developing a growth mindset – where students believe that their abilities can improve through effort, will be vital in helping them embrace challenges in life and be resilient when they face difficulties. Does anyone hear the flapping wings of a stumbling butterfly?

Cultivating those social and emotional skills

Alongside acquiring technical expertise, social and emotional skills will be increasingly important in future careers. I know this is very much at the forefront of our schools today, when supporting learners with a variety of complex needs. Appreciating that the changing dynamic and complexity of modern workplaces, which are often highly collaborative, emphasises the need for a breadth of strong interpersonal skills. Empathy, teamwork, leadership, and effective communication will help people to thrive in diverse and often remote teams.

Daniel Goleman, the author of *Emotional Intelligence: Why it can matter more than IQ* [26], shared in his research into emotional intelligence (EQ) that people with high EQ tend to perform better in collaborative environments, manage stress more effectively, and demonstrate greater leadership potential – all the things we know are qualities vital for success in the modern workplace.

We can all see that education must place a strong emphasis on these social and emotional skills. Group projects, collaborative learning, and extracurricular activities such as sports, drama, and the arts are all good ways to develop teamwork and communication skills; ironically, those same subjects are being squeezed of curriculum time in favour of a narrow offer. Schools could also expand or develop social and emotional learning (SEL) programmes, where students learn to regulate their emotions, empathise with others, and develop resilience – attributes that are acknowledged as being indispensable for both our personal and professional success.

Building global awareness and cross-cultural understanding

In a globalised world, "cultural competence" or understanding is increasingly a critical or powerful skill. The future workforce will likely operate in international teams or engage with clients, colleagues, and partners from diverse backgrounds. So, with that in mind, I'd remind us that students need to develop the ability to communicate and collaborate effectively across cultures. Preparing children for this globalised context requires a focus on global awareness and intercultural communication skills. We tend to focus more on knowing our own cultures than looking outside. This has a different weighting in countries and education systems around the world, mind you, and is often based on historical links.

It can be fostered and developed, though; international exchange programmes, bilingual education, and lessons in global citizenship all contribute to a broader understanding of the world beyond our borders. Exposing students to different perspectives and encouraging them to think critically about global issues prepares them to engage meaningfully and more purposefully in an interconnected world. Studies [27] indicate that individuals with cross-cultural competence have a competitive advantage in the job market; that alone should be enough to reinforce the importance of these skills for future careers.

Balancing specialisation with broad-based skills

Having hopefully read Chapter 2, you will already be familiar with my argument that a critical consideration in preparing children for their future careers is finding the right balance between specialised "content" knowledge and the acquisition of a broad base of skills. While we all accept that deep technical expertise will remain important in certain fields, the pace of change in today's job market means that broad, transferable skills are increasingly valued. Creativity, adaptability, critical thinking, and communication are skills that cut across all sectors, industries, and roles, empowering us with the flexibility to navigate career changes and hopefully, seize new opportunities.

So, education systems fundamentally have to aim to provide both; but with the balances shifted from our current, historical bias, ensuring that students acquire the technical competencies required for specific roles while also equipping them with the soft (power) skills that will enable them to adapt as the world of work, continues to evolve. Striking this balance is probably the biggest challenge facing our education frameworks right now. It simply has to shift.

Preparing children for future careers requires a comprehensive rethink of our educational priorities. Critical thinking, digital literacy, and adaptability must be at the heart of our teaching, but we must also recognise the importance of emotional intelligence, global awareness, and broad-based skills. The future will belong to those who can think critically, adapt to new challenges, and work effectively in an increasingly interconnected and complex global environment

Moral character

Fostering and developing moral character in students is accepted as a fundamental objective of education. I agree with this third and final "pillar" Nick Gibb referenced. Moral character is often seen as integral to both personal and societal wellbeing. In today's world, where children are exposed to diverse and sometimes conflicting value systems, education plays a critical role in helping them develop the moral compass necessary for ethical decision-making and becoming responsible citizens. A few different strands flow from this, which I have tried to summarise under the umbrella of expanding "moral" education within the curriculum.

Sticking to a high level, on this one, it involves teaching students about concepts such as honesty, fairness, empathy, and respect. While some subjects naturally lend themselves to moral discussions (such as literature or history), it is really important that these themes are embedded across the curriculum. That's naturally not always possible, but I could, for example, be a teacher in a science lesson encouraging discussions about the ethics of technological advancements, environmental responsibility, or medical research. I should add that this does happen, but with all the other expectations on what to cover, it could have more focus.

I guess as a natural follow-on from my thoughts on what makes a good school, it's not going to be a surprise to read that another core strand here is around creating a values-driven (not just values-based) school culture. Beyond that formal curriculum, the school environment plays a pivotal role in shaping moral character. A school culture that prioritises respect, fairness, and kindness fosters an environment where moral development can thrive. This involves setting clear expectations on behaviour, recognising and rewarding acts of kindness, and addressing incidents of bullying or disrespect decisively. Teachers and support staff should model the values they expect from students. I have no doubt that reading this you will be ticking these off the list as a given in any good school.

The **National Center for Education Statistics** highlighted in their 2020 report, **"The Condition of Education 2020"** [28], the importance of the school "climate" in fostering moral development, noting that students are more likely to internalise moral values when they are part of a supportive and respectful school environment. Schools that create strong, positive relationships between students and teachers contribute significantly to the moral and emotional development of their students.

Throughout our lives, empathy, that ability to understand and share the feelings of others, is foundational to moral character. Education, certainly in the formative years, fosters empathy by simply encouraging children to consider the perspectives of those who are different from themselves and through classroom discussions, books that reflect diverse viewpoints, and encouraging children to "step into the shoes" of others. In his book, **Altruism in Humans** [29], **Daniel Batson** highlights that empathy is closely linked to more prosocial behaviour, such as helping and cooperating with others. Children who are able to empathise with others are more likely to engage in moral actions and make ethical decisions. Encouraging empathy in the classroom also has the potential to reduce the incidences of bullying, as students become more attuned to the emotional impact of their actions on others.

I probably need to move on to reflecting on our moral dilemmas, fostering that moral character is not only about teaching students what is right or wrong, but naturally interlinks with developing those critical thinking skills necessary to navigate challenging moral dilemmas. This is often initiated by creating opportunities for children to reflect on and discuss moral challenges they might encounter in life. I discovered during my research, rather than knew about the philosopher **John Dewey** [30], and he argued that moral development requires active engagement with moral problems, where students reflect on their own values and consider the consequences of their actions. Dewey's philosophy underlines the importance of reflection and dialogue in the moral growth of children, and where we, of course, proactively encourage debate and reflective thinking.

Moral character is not developed in isolation; it flourishes through interaction with others and active participation in community life. Many schools foster moral development by encouraging students to engage in community service and social justice initiatives. Projects that involve helping others, whether through volunteering, fundraising, or advocacy, help students understand the importance of contributing to the wellbeing of others and the broader society. In the same light, service learning, which combines academic instruction with community service, has been shown to nurture moral development. Research published by the **Michigan Journal of Community Service-Learning** [31] shows that students who participate in service learning experience greater growth in their moral reasoning and social responsibility than those who do not.

To wrap up, this last factor is probably the one that gets mentioned the most and, rightly so, probably the most powerful influence on a child's moral development is the behaviour of adults around them. We see the implications on a societal basis right now. Teachers, parents, and other figures of authority can absolutely serve as role models for moral behaviour. Children learn about ethical behaviour not only through direct instruction but also by observing how adults handle moral challenges, interact with others, and navigate conflicts.

Albert Bandura, a professor of social science in psychology at **Stanford University**, shared a social learning theory [32] that reinforced the idea that children learn behaviours and values through observation and imitation. When teachers model that ethical behaviour, perhaps in simple things like demonstrating fairness in marking, showing kindness to students, or addressing unethical behaviour immediately, they send an important message to students about the importance of moral integrity.

If we accept that fostering and developing moral character requires a multi-faceted approach that integrates both formal teaching and learning and the nurture of a values-driven school culture, one where empathy, reflection, social responsibility, and role modelling are all essential components in helping develop a strong moral compass, then we have to have a curriculum that allows time and capacity for that nurture to receive greater priority and, perhaps key, opportunity than it does today. Sometimes the most significant changes we can make are to influence capacity; a less curated curriculum means more time for nurture and personal growth. Ten years from now, as the traits and human qualities will largely shape working adults' standing and success in the workplace, we continue to marginalise them within our formal education frameworks.

So what's our recipe for change? From all the insights and research, I have captured a fair distillation feel to me of some key areas:

1. **A shared framework for education:** Achieving a consensus on this requires a unified understanding of core educational goals that transcend all other factors. Much of this coproduction has been undertaken, but a consistent application of a long-term plan would allow for strategic and sustained change to be delivered with confidence.

2. **Instilling a love of learning:** Education needs to create safe, supportive environments that encourage curiosity and intellectual risks, while providing hands-on, experiential learning opportunities. A flexible curriculum that values varied learning pathways can help foster a love of learning and ensure equal opportunities for success.

3. **Preparing for future careers**: Education needs to shift the balance from memorisation and testing towards key skills like critical thinking, digital literacy, and adaptability. Schools should prioritise lifelong learning, equipping students to navigate the complexities of a globalised, rapidly changing workforce.

4. **Prioritising social and emotional skills**: The development of emotional intelligence, collaboration, and empathy is essential for success in both personal and professional life. Schools should further embed social-emotional learning into the curriculum and provide opportunities for students to develop teamwork and leadership skills.

5. **Fostering moral character:** Education plays a critical role in teaching students' values like honesty, empathy, and fairness. By promoting ethical decision-making and encouraging community service, schools can help shape responsible citizens who contribute to society's wellbeing.

CONCLUSION: IS THERE A WAY FORWARD?

How could we support and drive change within the limitations of political cycles?

I have covered a fair bit in this chapter already, and what's clear is that the "secret sauce" to progress is always going to be political will; without that, all we have within education at a strategic level is a well-intentioned and supportive talking shop. Many far wiser than me have recognised this and ensured to be as inclusive with politicians and civil servants to try and build bridges of goodwill should the opportunity to support arise.

Suppose we all accept, albeit in varying degrees by country, that we have these barriers because of policy discontinuity, with those shifting priorities for each new administration amplifying electorally created barriers to long-term planning. In that case, clearly, we have to extract education policy and planning outside of the day-to-day department for education, or equivalent body, in your country.

If we recognise a history of implementation challenges, where ongoing programs can be halted and redirected at a moment's notice, resulting in lost time, resources, and a huge instability in the system (Can I add frustration in here, too?), then we have to have education policy locked in and baked into our actions for an agreed (fixed) term. Confidence in any sector comes from consistency and long-term stability.

If we know the main pressures on our systems are linked to lack of resources, funding, and an inability to plan for the long term, while we have to operate with an annual begging bowl, then school funding and budgets, no matter how generous or restricted they might be, need to be set in sensible five-year settlements to allow for better planning and resource allocation.

What would these look like?

What we need is for education to have a separate independent education body that is non-partisan and has authority over educational policy and its continuity. We have to enact legislation that supports (and protects) long-term educational plans, changes, and funding to deliver that certainty and to insulate the system from well-intentioned tinkering. We have to ensure within that overarching body that there are conduits for regular and broad engagement with educators, students, and parents alongside specialists to build consensus that goes far beyond a single electoral cycle.

Finally, it has to be phased: The stepping stones need to be clearly defined within the long-term plan, from which we build confidence, can measure impact, and can provide the politicians with the intermediate "wins" they need in return for keeping hands off the longer-term plan. Education and politics don't mix; it is the one and only sector where our actions now influence measures. A decade later, many, including the FED, see this and are pushing (and waiting) for a strong government to be bold and do the right thing.

That is as simple and concise as I can be. The only way to move forward with real purpose is to break the link, enable independent oversight, and commit to thinking long term. The nuance of the details will change year to year as we adapt to the changing needs of our learners and the workplace, but the fundamental need for a long-term commitment to funding, curriculum redesign, fostering skills, providing an inclusive place and space for every child, and reigniting that love of learning for all children must be at the core.

References

1. "John Taylor Gatto," 2004. [Online]. Available: https://en.wikipedia.org/wiki/John_Taylor_Gatto
2. J. T. Gatto, "The 7-Lesson Schoolteacher," New Society Publishers, [Online]. Available: https://www.newciv.org/whole/schoolteacher.txt
3. D. Fitzpatrick, "7 Reasons Why We are Failing to Prepare our Kids for the AI World," Linkedin, 15 08 2024. [Online]. Available: https://www.linkedin.com/posts/theaieducator_7-reasons-why-we-are-failing-to-prepare-our-activity-7229788943276265472-7iM4
4. "The Huffington Post," [Online]. Available: https://www.huffingtonpost.co.uk/
5. N. Harper, "Seven Lessons I Teach," Huffington Post, 24 06 2012. [Online]. Available: https://www.huffingtonpost.co.uk/nikki-harper/7-lessons-i-teach_b_1622031.html
6. J. T. Gatto, *Dumbing Us Down: The Hidden Curriculum of Compulsory Schooling*, 10th Anniversary Edition, 2 ed., New Society Publishers, 2002.
7. OECD, "OECD Yearbook 2014: Better Policies for Better Lives," 2014.
8. S. Mitra, "Hole in the Wall Education Project," 2016. [Online]. Available: https://www.hole-in-the-wall.com/
9. S. Mitra, "Kids can Teach Themselves," TED Talks, 02 2007. [Online]. Available: https://www.ted.com/talks/sugata_mitra_kids_can_teach_themselves?subtitle=en
10. N. Matias, "Is Education Obsolete? Sugata Mitra at the MIT Media Lab," Civic Media, 16 05 2012. [Online]. Available: https://civic.mit.edu/index.html%3Fp=804.html
11. "Bloom's 2 Sigma Problem," Wikipedia, [Online]. Available: https://en.wikipedia.org/wiki/Bloom%27s_2_sigma_problem
12. B. S. Bloom, "The 2 Sigma Problem: The Search for Methods of Group Instruction as Effective as One-to-One Tutoring," *American Educational Research Association*, vol. 13, no. 6, pp. 4–16, 06 1984.
13. M. Fullan, *The New Meaning of Educational Change*, Teachers College Press, 2015.
14. A. Hargreaves and I. Goodson, "Educational Change Over Time? The Sustainability and Non-Sustainability of Three Decades of Secondary School Change and Continuity," *Educational Administration Quarterly*, vol. 1, no. 42, pp. 3–41, 2006.
15. C. Day and L. Smethem, "The Effects of Reform: Have Teachers Really Lost their Sense of Professionalism?," *Journal of Educational Change*, vol. 10, pp. 141–157, 2009.
16. "No Child Left Behind Act," Wikipedia, 2001. [Online]. Available: https://en.wikipedia.org/wiki/No_Child_Left_Behind_Act
17. "Every Student Succeeds Act," Wikipedia, 2015. [Online]. Available: https://en.wikipedia.org/wiki/Every_Student_Succeeds_Act
18. C. Woodward, "Vision 2030 – Education in Saudi Arabia," HMC, 29 03 2022. [Online]. Available: https://www.hmc.org.uk/blog-posts/vision-2030-education-in-saudi-arabia/
19. "The Foundation for Education Development (FED)," [Online]. Available: https://fed.education/

20. "FACT SHEET: Biden-Harris Administration Announces Improving Student Achievement Agenda in 2024," The White House, 17 01 2024. [Online]. Available: https://www.whitehouse.gov/briefing-room/statements-releases/2024/01/17/fact-sheet-biden-harris-administration-announces-improving-student-achievement-agenda-in-2024/
21. "Working Together to Improve School Attendance," Department for Education, 07 03 2024. [Online]. Available: https://www.gov.uk/government/publications/working-together-to-improve-school-attendance
22. "Education System in the UK," 2012. [Online]. Available: https://assets.publishing.service.gov.uk/government/uploads/system/uploads/attachment_data/file/219167/v01-2012ukes.pdf
23. N. Gibb, "The Purpose of Education," Department for Education, 09 07 2015. [Online]. Available: https://www.gov.uk/government/speeches/the-purpose-of-education
24. "The Future of Jobs Report 2020," World Economic Forum, 20 10 2020. [Online]. Available: https://www.weforum.org/publications/the-future-of-jobs-report-2020/
25. J. Manyika, S. Lund, M. Chui, J. Bughin, J. Woetzel, P. Batra, R. Ko and S. Sanghvi, "Jobs Lost, Jobs Gained: Workforce Transitions in a Time of Automation," *McKinsey Global Institute*, vol. 150, pp. 1–28, 2017. https://www.mckinsey.com/~/media/mckinsey/industries/public%20and%20social%20sector/our%20insights/what%20the%20future%20of%20work%20will%20mean%20for%20jobs%20skills%20and%20wages/mgi-jobs-lost-jobs-gained-executive-summary-december-6-2017.PDF
26. D. Goleman, *Emotional Intelligence: Why It Can Matter More Than IQ*, Bloomsbury Publishing, 2020, p. 352.
27. J. P. Johnson, T. Lenartowicz and S. Apud, "Cross-Cultural Competence in International Business: Toward a Definition and a Model," *Journal of International Business Studies*, vol. 37, pp. 525–543, 2006.
28. B. Hussar, J. Zhang, S. Hein, K. Wang, A. Roberts, J. Cui, M. Smith, A. Bullock, A. Barmer and R. Dilig, *The Condition of Education 2020*, Institute of Education Sciences, 2020.
29. C. D. Batson, *Altruism in Humans*, Oxford University Press, 2011.
30. J. Dewey, *Moral Principles in Education*, CreateSpace Independent Publishing, 2017.
31. M. L. Bernacki and E. Jaeger, "Exploring the Impact of Service-Learning on Moral Development and Moral Orientation," *Michigan Journal of Community Service Learning*, no. Spring, pp. 5–15, 2008. https://digitalscholarship.unlv.edu/edpsych_fac_articles/8/
32. P. Main, "Social Learning Theory - Bandura," Structural Learning, 24 10 2022. [Online]. Available: https://www.structural-learning.com/post/social-learning-theory-bandura

The barriers to growth in our education systems (are they within)?

Ok folks, I am well aware that, as a chapter topic, this is a very open question. In many ways, I could have chosen to use the word *change* rather than *growth*. However, I am intentionally leading our conversation towards a discussion around an evolving system rather than one that requires a completely different alternative. In terms of mitigating the normal anxieties that tend to arrive as soon as the word change appears within any organisation, no matter its size and scale, I think maintaining a growth mindset is probably a softer entry point to the conversation.

This chapter hopefully follows nicely from the previous chapter, which focused on the political challenges to change. So, now it's only right to look a bit closer to home, too.

Ironically, within education (and elsewhere), we often talk about the importance of a "growth mindset" when reflecting on our journeys. For those less familiar, a growth mindset is a belief that a person's abilities can always be improved through effort, learning, and, probably most importantly, persistence. It's about how someone approaches challenges, learns from failures, and adapts and evolves as a result. As a rule, the resulting impact is that people with a growth mindset are more likely to achieve their goals and reach their full potential.

The term "growth mindset" was coined by Carol Dweck, professor of psychology at Columbia University and Stanford University, in her 1988 research paper, **"A social-cognitive approach to motivation and personality"** [1] and her subsequent 2007 book ***Mindset: The New Psychology of Success*** [2].

There is a real irony here because when we reflect on the pathway (below) to a growth mindset, it almost universally resonates with the traits we see daily in our educator cohort, yet the ability to translate that into coordinated system change seems wholly disconnected. As a result, I can only conclude that the lack of a growth mindset at system levels falls squarely on the shoulders of others further up the food chain, with, how do we say, "less skin in the game" and certainly less continuity of leadership.

Just imagine if our education system had a growth mindset similar to many educators, but as a collective and self-reflective ecosystem (Figure 9.1).

Now, I've set the scene with a reflection in the context of our own individual approaches to managing personal growth, but as I have said, there is a disconnect to how that translates into the broader systemwide change we need. If you have chosen to read my book in sequence, arriving at this chapter, you will be all too aware of the collective acknowledgement that the education systems, globally, need to adapt. The priority may be inclusivity and accessibility of our education systems; a need to reflect and support the changing skills expectations of employers; to find better ways to assess learning and attainment; to make our schools the right place for every child to excel with their social, emotional, and mental health needs; the list goes on and on.

In the last chapter, I touched on the challenges at the very top, the political desire to "tinker" and "win" within an electoral cycle; I discussed finding common ground on what a good education system looks like and how we make better decisions. However, *growth* is a much wider term, especially in this context.

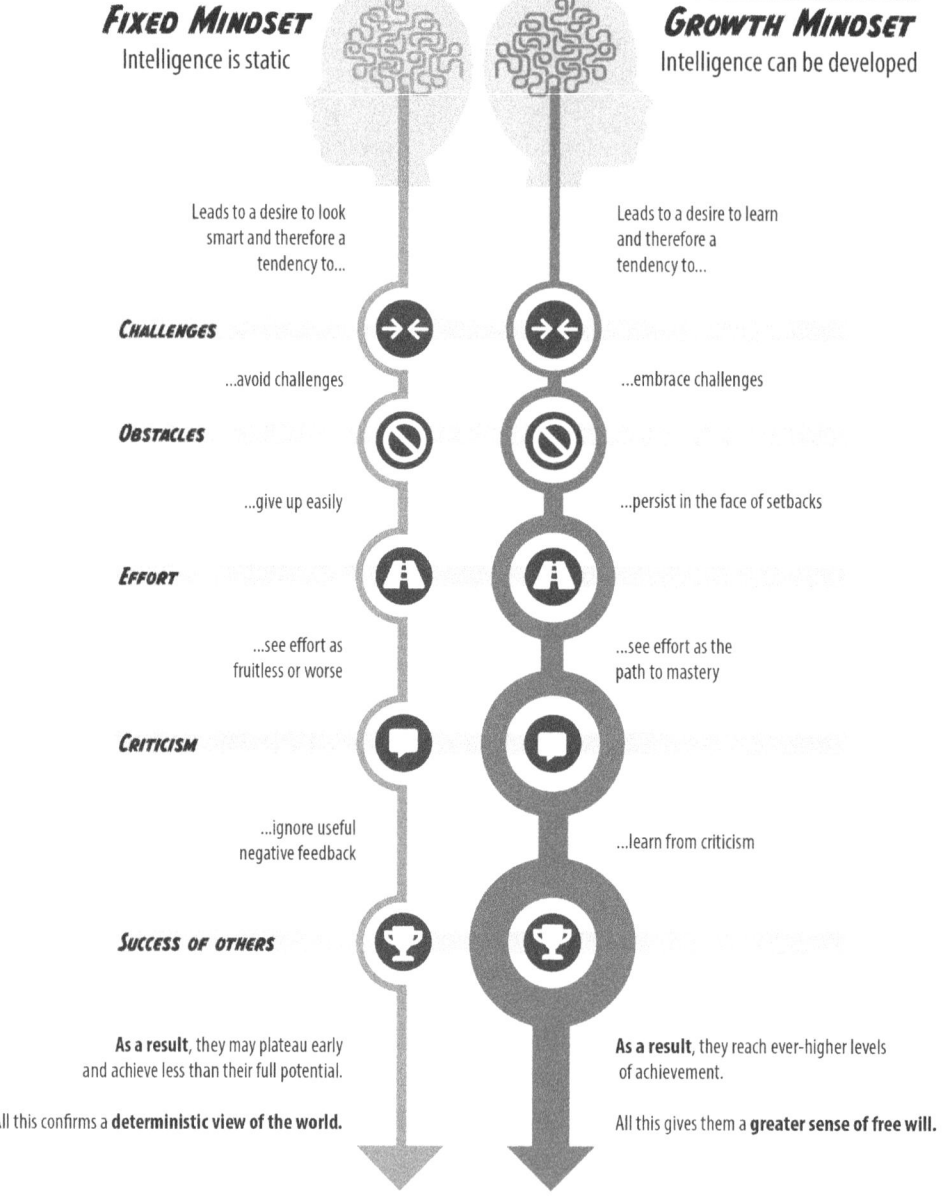

Figure 9.1 Comparing a Fixed and Growth Mindset.

More school places

We need physical growth in our education system; we need more places for children (in some areas), and due to population changes, we have a surplus in others. Within England at the time of writing (2024), after many years of population growth, we are currently seeing a huge "bulge" pressure on year 7 places in our secondary schools and undersubscribed in many of our Early Years Foundation Stage (EYFS) cohorts at primary.

As the **National Association of Head Teachers** shared in a 2023 press release, **"National strategy needed to end the anxiety of school admissions scramble"** [3], responding to this population bulge that has been moving through primary schools and is now leaving many secondary schools over-subscribed, *"there remains a problem that in an increasingly fragmented school system, we lack a coordinated approach to place planning. Local authorities are responsible for ensuring sufficient school places, but they still lack the power and resources necessary to do so. Until the government creates a national strategy to guarantee there are enough school places for every child in England, the annual anxious wait for families will continue."*

So, in this context, we need a coordinated strategy on school places (capacity) within our system. If you suddenly see greater pressure on secondary places, then you should expect a similar pressure on teacher recruitment to deliver the education provision for those children. We have covered recruitment and retention in an earlier chapter, so I won't head off into the details, other than to say that the government urgently needs to do more to address the recruitment and retention crisis schools are facing, so that there are enough suitably qualified, specialist teachers to support the growing numbers of children moving through the system. Please also note that you can just add your country of choice here (   ); you will generally find the same challenges and needs within your system at the mainstream level.

That shift in number moving as a "bulge" through our system in England has resulted in the opposite, a shortfall at the primary level in many regions. A June 2023 House of Commons debate titled **"Falling pupil rolls in England and school closures in London"** [4], which highlighted that in May 2022, 7.94 million children were on roll in mainstream state-funded schools in England; this was a 1% increase compared with the previous year, and the roll has been increasing every year since 2010 [5]. However, the number of primary children on roll declined from 4.44 million in 2019 to 4.40 million in 2022 (a 1% decline). This doesn't sound huge until you consider that the number of secondary children increased by 7% over the same period.

Those 40,000 fewer primary children also translate into a school primary, perhaps having 10 or 20 fewer children entering the school, and as a result, £45,000–£90,000 less funding for the year (Table 9.1).

Again, this isn't an England or UK specific demographic journey, the US-based **National Center for Education Statistics (NCES)** shared in their 2024 **"Projections of Education Statistics"** report [6] that between 2010 and 2019, they saw a 3% increase in children enrolled in elementary and secondary education (54.9 million rising to 56.3 million) and a projected 8% decrease between 2019 and 2030, falling to 52.1 million as a total cohort. That's a much larger swing than we are seeing in England.

Table 9.1 Local authority estimated number of pupils

	Primary children		Secondary children	
	Number (millions)	Annual % change	Number (millions)	Annual % change
2021/22 (actual)	4.46		3.47	
Forecasts				
2022/23	4.45	−0.4%	3.56	+2.7%
2023/24	4.41	−0.8%	3.64	+2.1%
2024/25	4.37	−0.9%	3.68	+1.1%
2025/26	4.33	−0.9%	3.70	+0.6%
2026/27	4.28	−1.0%	3.71	+0.2%
2027/28	n/a	n/a	3.70	−0.1%
2028/29	n/a	n/a	3.68	−0.6%

Source: Department for Education, School capacity: 24 March 2023 [5].

In Australia to date, they are seeing a 1.4% growth rate in overall student population since 2019, but research by **Independent Schools Australia (ISA)** [7] cited in their 2021 Research Report [8], that *"While population growth in secondary grade levels remains steady, growth is slowing considerably in primary grade levels within Australia, particularly at years 0–1 where negative population growth occurred in 2020,"* so there is a similar short-term challenge.

So now our poor planning for growth within the context of physical capacity exasperates our already-stretched financial budgets in our schools, too. We are suddenly short of income to pay our full teacher and assistant cohort at one end, and have an inability to find, let alone pay for, additional teaching capacity at the other. Ironically, where a system should be able to build on marginal gains, we find ourselves with a domino effect of marginal pains.

Ironically, where a system should be able to build on marginal gains, we find ourselves with a domino effect of marginal pains.

Stick with me for this introduction, I am trying to pull together a number of different threads that will help resolve our core questions in the chapter. So, knowing that we have to adapt and flex our education systems in order to respond to changing population growth, and knowing those changes in student numbers can create more pressure on budget reductions or increased teacher demand, we also have to factor our growth linked to policy-based system change.

System growth

Let's just remember, as I discussed in Chapter 3, we have an ambition to grow our academy system in England to cover the entirety of our school estate, with a phased migration from locally controlled schools to a full academy-led system. Not only do we have the aspiration to re-factor all of our school's status (those yet to convert), but we also have a multi-academy trust (MAT) growth ambition, looking to consolidate many of our stand-alone and smaller trusts into ones of sufficient size to be strong and sustainable [9].

As of January 2024, **Department for Education** data [10] shows that 42.7% of primary schools are now academies, accounting for 44.2% of primary school children and that 81.9% of secondary schools are academies, accounting for an almost matching 81.7% of secondary school children. In terms of system change, that's still more than half of all primaries potentially changing status in the years ahead and, collectively, a significant window of growth for the academy system. So, we have significant growth of the academy cohort ahead, alongside a period of consolidation, with larger individual MATs, but fewer of them. As of June 2024, the average number of schools in a MAT was 8, but geography plays a part, and some regions, such as the southwest, have an average of nearer 14 [11].

We have many different themes of growth at the same time, and at some point, we have to pause and say what (or who) is preventing us from achieving the growth or change, if not scary, that's needed. It's not unique to our region; it is most definitely nuanced, but the big picture items are a global commonality.

Overseas

Let's jump on a virtual plane and head to sub-Saharan Africa. Research [12] was undertaken there to identify the **"Barriers and Challenges Affecting Quality Education"** linked to the **United Nation**'s Sustainability Goal (SDG) number 4, namely, *"Ensuring Inclusive, Equitable, and Quality Education and the Promotion of Lifelong Learning Opportunities for All"* [13]. This might seem a bit left field from our current topic, but thematically, it aligns with our own growth plans of an inclusive system that is appropriate and accessible for all learners (remembering the increasing challenge with disengaged or absent students). Three barriers were identified: (1) funding constraints; (2) access and inclusion; and (3) teacher education, in particular, a lack of training and resources to equip teachers with high-quality, learner-centred pedagogy.

Ok, it's a few thousand miles away, and the detailed nature of the challenges is different, but at a high level, funding is a key limiting factor in our education system, providing the right offer and support with sufficient capacity to make our schools fully inclusive is an ongoing challenge and teacher training, is a never-ending cycle. Consider now, with the advent of artificial intelligence (AI) and other digital skills, there is certainly an additional set of skills and training our educator workforce needs. It's easy to get stuck in the mud because our problem is unique, but recognising it's not as unique as you think provides the option to start looking beyond for answers or simply ideas.

I have no desire to suggest that around the world we all have the same barriers to education; that's absolutely not the case. The elements I have included are focused on key levers of system growth. I do want to flag at a foundational level, the core barriers identified to accessing education are conflict and violence, climate change, lack of qualified teachers, the cost of attending school, being female, being an older child, as well as language and literacy barriers. **Concern Worldwide** shared a summary of this in much more detail in August 2024, titled **"10 of the biggest problems facing education"** [14].

So now that we have set the scene on our changing landscape, let's dive into a few key questions I wanted to unpick.

FEAR OF CHANGE

How does resistance to innovation and risk-taking hold us back?

I have been mulling this question over for some time, not least because the natural response is often to focus on denial. We are just as good as everyone else in any other sector when it comes to change. In fact, over the last decade, education has had to deal with lots of small changes, so in truth, we are pretty good, right? It's another awkward question, but actually no, I really do not think education is good at change. The landscape of where we are right now, and the topics covered in this book give us a pretty good evidence base to know we have not adapted quickly or always embraced change. Let's be clear, though, that many of the big changes in education have not been down to educators; that's at a much higher level. Nevertheless, some certainly are.

I have spent the last 30+ years in the sector, albeit typically one or two steps removed from the classroom, so my perspectives come with a caveat. Nevertheless, as we move to the closing part of this book, let me be completely honest. I spend time every week speaking and supporting teachers who want to step out of the classroom, partially or fully, and they have a huge challenge with imposter syndrome moving to say, an educational technology vendor, or a consulting role. They have no need to feel like an imposter, and I support them by highlighting the unique, transferable, and valuable experience they bring to the table. Many suffer unfairly with this mindset. My point is that when the shoe is on the other foot, educators can, at times, be really quick to dismiss the perspectives of anyone else and invoke the imposter syndrome on others.

There has been a long challenge to ensure teachers are respected and elevated in their roles, and rightly so; after all, we see the societal challenges and lacking respect for education right now, but within that bubble, there is often a lack of empathy and respect for those that feed into the system, from support staff to IT technicians in the school through to external advisors.

I often use the analogy (remember I am bad at these), of an F1 team, it is a fusion between the skills of the driver and the skills of the engineers and strategists. Nobody would suggest that to improve and start a new team, we should only have the new model race car designed by drivers. It would look amazing, handle and feel great from a driver's perspective, but it probably wouldn't go very fast. Conversely, leaving it exclusively to the engineers would make it blindingly fast, but impossible to steer, and there would be no space in the cockpit for the driver. My clumsy analogy is that you need both skills to make a successful race car.

So, let's set up the school's digital strategy. Educators will lead, educators will decide, IT will install, and even though they were not invited to the initial Continuous Professional Development (CPD), if we have any issues, we will call them to resolve them. I have exaggerated for effect, but I see it far too regularly. So, how does this feed into a question around fear of change? Much like in my AI chapter, we tend to want to lead and change things we know best; when change requires embracing something outside your comfort zone or requires relinquishing control to someone better easily, it is easy to want to resist, delay, defer or ignore to avoid the change.

Suppose we suggest that we revise teaching and learning to reflect the new requirements of employers and society. In that case, it's easy to see that as a direct critique of what has been done to date, almost a negative towards the profession. I see that, and I can understand why, but if everyone is cautious of change, the system slows, stays where it is, and the underlying problems grow.

Let's sprinkle in some balance here; children are our most valuable commodity (I used the word intentionally), far more than anything else we produce on our virtual production lines, so it's not unreasonable to resist change without evidence of impact and benefit, its okay to be sceptical until proven otherwise, and change needs to be done in a slow and measured way to ensure we don't unintentionally harm or negatively impact our future workforce.

I covered in an earlier chapter the times when system leaders, heads of schools, governing bodies, and other stakeholders can resist change where the outcome may be a loss of autonomy or authority, and I've covered in the previous chapter where governments often avoid a significant change in favour of smaller tweaks; they can celebrate in their re-election campaigns, but what about as educators? Are you up for innovation and change? I will pre-empt you while you are reading this section and say, "Yes, Al, but if we had some free time and capacity to do it properly," and that would be the fairest (and is the most frequent) defence. The environment and the education system create a workload and pressures that inhibit change whilst simultaneously expecting schools to embrace and model a positive appetite for reflection and development.

Matt Pittman, head of secondary at **Global Village Learning** in Australia, was pretty direct in his perspectives: *"This really is a failure of 'practice what you preach.' When we resist the opportunity to make a change based on the perceived* *notion that we may fail, we accept that we individually, or we as a profession have lost our connection with learning. I believe the education system, despite what some may say, has completely lost its interest in learning and fuels this fear of any kind of substantial change in order to maintain the bureaucracy it serves and the positions of those who make decisions."* What Matt articulated with me was that if the system was designed to cater to those within schools, we wouldn't be asking this question. We would have dynamic and engaging schools that consistently changed with the natural flow of learning. Instead, as he put it, we have robotic processes and systems to align the 1s and 0s.

Research undertaken back in 2005, titled **"Educational change takes ages: Life, career and generational factors in teachers' emotional responses to educational change"** [15], backs up many of the perceptions I have shared, citing that researchers found that teachers often experience emotional responses to educational change, ranging from excitement to fear. The fear often stems from concerns about losing control over their classroom, the potential mismatch between new policies and their teaching style, and the added workload that change can bring. Sound familiar?

2005 must have been a busy research year, as similarly, in a somewhat grandly titled paper **"Teachers' emotions in educational reforms: Self-understanding, vulnerable commitment and micropolitical literacy"** [16], the author discusses how teachers' self-understanding and professional identity are sometimes challenged during reforms or change. When new changes are perceived as threats to their established practices, some teachers exhibit resistance or fear, which impacts their willingness to implement new strategies.

As a follow-up, haven't we all seen a trust rolling out a new strategy, perhaps technology-related and a year later, see that some schools have really progressed and others in the same trust haven't? If all other variables are the same, then there has to be a correlation to teachers' willingness to support and embrace a change, or unsurprisingly, what we see is that, superficially, teachers will support and comply with new policies but, in reality, then continue their old practices behind closed doors.

It would be easy to conclude that I am placing the blame or responsibility firmly at the feet of teachers, but I'm not, as is often the case. Research shows, irrespective of the sector, that people who are less open to new experiences are also often those who feel less supported by their organisation, and it is that influencing factor that makes them more likely to resist change.

Fear of change

What I am trying to recognise and support is that when teachers fear change, it can lead to outcomes that ripple through the educational landscape. They might resist implementing new policies, perhaps, as I've suggested complying on the surface but reverting to familiar practices behind closed doors. This soft, and often unconscious, resistance can seriously undermine the effectiveness of well-intended educational changes. The fear and anxiety associated with constant change, which we have dealt with a lot recently, can also chip away at morale and job satisfaction, affecting not just their wellbeing but also their performance in the classroom. If they are hesitant or feel unprepared to adopt new teaching methods, our students may miss out on the full benefits of these improvements, potentially impacting learning outcomes.

In some cases, the relentless pace of change without adequate support can lead to professional burnout, prompting some teachers to leave the profession altogether. In my earlier chapter on recruitment and retention, we discussed this in much more detail.

However, there's a silver lining or at least a healthy glint of one. We know that with the right support, proper training, beyond the one-hit CPD, and genuine involvement in the change process and genuine co-production, teachers are much more likely to embrace new initiatives. Being part of a collaborative environment where we feel heard and valued can make a world of difference. We all know that this kind of supportive atmosphere helps alleviate fears and fosters a positive attitude towards change, benefitting everyone involved.

So, a fear of change is normally a lack of understanding of the why, a lack of support in understanding and implementing the change, and a lack of leadership that creates the space and environment to deliver. Leadership needs to reflect on themselves before aligning slow adoption with being on the shoulders of their staff, just as teachers do for their students.

My highly advanced formula is therefore:

Poor leadership + Lack of understanding the "why" + Limited capacity = Fear of change

FUNDING LIMITATIONS

Are we chronically under-investing in the resources our schools truly need?

Well, yes. That makes for an awfully short section, so perhaps I should expand. I've already covered some possible ways to mitigate under the recruitment and retention section, from extending the main pay scale to a system reset at circa 15% to realign with other sectors. That all comes at a cost, and while it is less popular to say so, the teacher pension scheme is way above other sectors, so when considered as a whole package, it is much more generous.

We know big pension contributions don't pay the monthly bills, so sensitivities apart, increasing pay grades by 15% and reducing pension contributions by 7.5% would be a more pragmatic approach and compromise (albeit the pension has just been uplifted by almost that amount in England) …but current teachers would absolutely not sign up for the latter, nor would the unions and you can appreciate why. Perhaps, however, for future recruits, a revision that impacts from the bottom up over 20 years would be worthy of further consideration. Many would now see the appeal of a larger salary over a smaller long-term contribution reduction.

It's easy, mind you, to take the view that given 80% on average of a school budget is staff costs, that therein lies the problem. It significantly hides the much bigger issue. On one level, it hides what should but isn't being spent; it hides the lack of capital investment in the school estate, technology, and other resources; and it hides the lack of support staff needed with an ever-growing and complex set of needs for our students. No school or trust accounts scrutiny will help you spot the staff that were needed but couldn't be afforded.

So, do we have funding limitations? Or, more specifically, are we not getting funded enough, or is education just bad at spending? It's an awkward question, but we have all heard the argument in, say, health care, where services are cut, and the stock response is that they waste money on too many administrators and expensive resources. So, what's really the case in education?

I am really mindful of the feedback from people like **Matt Pitman,** who said on the question of are we underfunded: *"It is really hard to say without allowing teachers and students to genuinely have the permission to share what they need to create authentic learning experiences. Needs should never be associated with decisions at the system level; they should come from the ground and be facilitated and met by the system. Unfortunately, it is the other way around and as a result, I'd say we are under-investing by default."* He's right in that in every school, there will be particular needs that differ by setting. In this context, I can only subjectively look at a system level that would, hopefully, fund more yeses to those individual requests.

Global spending

Fortunately, there is plenty of data that others have captured to help shine a bit more light on this topic. The **OECD** [17] shared their **"Education at a Glance 2019– Indicators"** report, which included a summary of the total expenditure on educational institutions per full-time equivalent student [18], by level of education with data from 2016. So, with a note that it's a little bit out of date, they highlighted spending by country as follows (Table 9.2).

We can discount Luxembourg as it's clearly an outlier, and in such a small country, there will be very different economies of scale. We can look at the OECD average and think that it shows us in a better light. However, funding is, of course, heavily linked to the "costs" within the economy, such as average salary costs, cost of living, cost of resources, etc., and so looking to the United States and other European countries is much more realistic.

In 2016, the United Kingdom fared poorly compared to its more typical statistical neighbours, which supports the view that our overall funding allowance is insufficient to compete with other educational systems. For balance, Spain, Italy, and Ireland were all between $8,500 and $9,500 per head, so UK funding is certainly not the worst reported by some margin.

Table 9.2 OECD—Total expenditure on educational institutions per full-time equivalent student, by level of education (2016)

Country	Total expenditure per full-time student
Luxembourg	$19,770
United States	$13,019
Norway	$13,758
Germany	$11,294
Austria	$14,679
United Kingdom	$11,061
OECD average worldwide	$9,271

One thing I know for sure is that everyone has a different way of measuring, so sometimes you have to compare and contrast. The numbers may differ, but hopefully, the methodology for each piece of research will be consistent. In the United States, the **National Center for Education Statistics (NCES)** [19] shared an updated report in 2023 titled **"Education Expenditures by Country"** [20], highlighting that in 2019, the United States' spending had increased to $15,500 per full-time-equivalent (FTE) student on elementary and secondary education, which was 38% higher than the average of OECD member countries at $11,300. In their summary, they showed the UK spending increased to $13,300. That puts us far behind Norway, Austria, Korea, the United States, Australia, Sweden, Germany, and many more.

I will share one more summary from **Statistica**, and their 2023 report reflecting the "Annual expenditure per student on educational institutions in OECD countries for primary, secondary and tertiary education in 2020" [21] as we move increasingly closer to current expenditure levels with each report, we showed in slightly more granular detail that the average spending for primary education was $12,513 and for secondary was $13,695. The United States was $14,321 and $16,018, respectively. There are some real nuances to bear in mind; Germany, for example, spends significantly more than the United Kingdom on secondary education but less on primary education. We also have regional nuance; funding a school in California likely costs significantly more with employment and living costs than in the Midwest, and the same applies when considering inner London and the northeast of England.

So, the devil in the detail will be from lived experience, but all of the available high-level data shows we are below the curve compared to our neighbours in funding in the United Kingdom, and the gradual increase in funding that we have seen in recent years is not happening quicker than anywhere else.

Reflecting on the regional nuance I mentioned, the **Institute of Fiscal Studies (IFS)** [22] published a 2023 report titled **"How does school spending per pupil**

differ across the UK?" [23], with their key findings on how funding across the United Kingdom has changed, reporting that *"after 2010, school spending per pupil fell across all four nations of the UK. Between 2009–10 and 2018–19, school spending per pupil fell by 8%* **in real terms** *in England and by 5% in real terms in Wales. In Northern Ireland, there was a fall of 8% in the shorter period between 2011–12 and 2018–19. In Scotland, there was a fall of 6½% between 2009–10 and 2014–15."* On a slightly more positive note, they also highlighted that since 2018, spending per pupil has largely recovered back to the 2010 levels across England, Wales, and Northern Ireland, with increases in Scotland taking it past the real-term equivalents of 2010.

This may seem like some hint of a light at the end of the tunnel, but with the predicted reduction on student numbers for the next few years, that will still see a bigger squeeze on school budgets and even greater pressures for those with older infrastructure. I should add, with a thank you, that during the pandemic, schools were provided with, in some cases, a significant number of laptops and devices to help mitigate learning loss. We are now in the renewal window for all those devices, and there is no additional funding on the table, so contrary to the national messaging around effective use of technology and embracing appropriate use of AI, in many schools, the conversation is about retiring devices and reducing dependency. What a pickle, and something so easy to predict and with a will, avoid.

Here's another suggestion for a bold politician: How about agreeing that funding for education is treated in the same way as the pensions' "triple lock"? We need to reset the funding level first, but that would be a way of creating a more sustainable and committed funding plan.

WHAT DOES "STRONG AND SUSTAINABLE" LOOK LIKE

In particular, for an education system?

In many ways, it depends on who you ask and how wide a lens they are looking through. At the school level, the narrative is much more around sufficient capacity (people, space, and funding) that allows for a consistently dynamic environment that shifts based on the needs of those within it. It creates space for play, discovery, learning, and autonomy. After all, I was reminded that no generation has the same needs as any before it, so why would we think education could persist unchanged for decades and still serve an entirely purposeful and relevant role in learning? It has to be built with the capacity to adapt and evolve, and one crucial part of that is accessibility and equity, which I am going to cover next. For now, let's zoom out a bit.

You will find summaries like this from the **Department for Educations' "Building strong academy trusts"** [24] guidance on *"Strong academy trusts support school leaders to share and implement the latest evidence-based practice by directing resources through a shared structure. Strong structures (groups of schools) can* *facilitate better professional development and thus better teaching and improvement for pupils.*" This feels quite narrow and curriculum outcomes focused to me, or from the **Confederation of School Trusts (CST)** [25] in their 2021 **"What is a strong trust"** discussion paper [26], where they identify five key domains of strong and effective trusts, namely:

- Expert governance
- Quality of education
- Workforce resilience and wellbeing
- Efficiency and effectiveness
- Public benefit and civil duty

That feels like a really good baseline to build from, and I would encourage you to read their discussion paper; you won't be surprised to see the correlation between this 2021 discussion paper and the 2022 **Department for Education** white paper **"Opportunity for All: Strong Schools with Great Teachers for Your Child"** [27], where they identify the key areas of their "trust quality descriptors" as being:

- Governance and leadership
- High-quality and inclusive education
- Workforce
- Finance and operations
- School improvement

I've ordered them so they best compare, but with the exception of public benefit and civil duty being replaced by school improvement, it is pretty much the same list. Well, at least we have some consistency in the system, and they are sufficiently broad headers that we have a significant amount of nuance around our priorities below them. Bear in mind that this approach of quantifying each of those five categories is how the regional groups identify and assess strong trusts in the context of growth and sponsorship. Under each of those five pillars, they would look for evidence based on three categories, namely:

- Headline metrics to help build their hypothesis and prompt further questions
- Verifiers to provide more in-depth data for a richer understanding of the trust
- Qualitative evidence then enables them to explore areas where data is not easily available or where it does not tell the whole story

I'm using they/them, but as I declared earlier in the book, I also sit on the Regional Directors Advisory board for the East of England, so this is very familiar territory, and I perhaps should say we. The Department for Education guide on **"Commissioning High-Quality Trusts"** [28] is a worthwhile read if you want to broaden you understanding on how the regions groups take decisions about the creation, consolidation, and growth of academy trusts.

Anyway, don't we have to widen our lens one step further and apply the same considerations for strength and sustainability to our national education system, not just at school level, or in the Confederation of School Trusts (CST) context, at the MAT level?

United Nations Children's Fund (UNICEF) [29] reminded us that "Getting all children in school and learning takes strong, innovative education systems," but I think the bigger picture aligns well with United Nations Educational, Scientific and Cultural Organizations (UNESCO's) summary on Education for Sustainable Development (ESD), which explained it as "a process of learning how to make decisions that consider the long-term future of the economy, ecology and equity of all communities. Building the capacity for such future-oriented action is a key education task" [30]. Now, we aren't focused on Sustainable Development goals here, but the same applies to our education system, which we should build to be both strong and sustainable.

I would argue that we need a fusion of the points raised so far, namely:

1. **Oversight and Governance** – the overarching system of check and balance and helping to steer the direction of travel in education at a national level; this has to be best served by a separate semi-autonomous entity whose sole purpose is to continue to build and develop our system, irrespective of political turbulence. A mixed cohort of stakeholders with educational experience and one that rotates so that there is always an inflow of fresh voices at the table.

2. **High-Quality and Inclusive Education** – a reality check that one size doesn't fit all and the need to develop, led by educators, a series of pathways, all equally valued, that foster academic excellence alongside skills acquisition, creativity, innovation, and flexible learning environments that meet each child's developmental needs.

3. **People** – we can call it workforce, but in essence, the system only works if the right people want to be part of it. That is a combination of the right training, in advance and ongoing, a competitive wage with extended opportunities for progression. Reinstating and developing trust and respect for the profession, and where sufficient capacity exists within the role, we are then able to retain experienced people and maximise their skills and the impact they have on our children.

4. **Funding and Efficiency** – often paired to imply the latter is in question and needs to be addressed before the former. As I have covered in the book within a number of interlinked topics, the system needs extensive capital funding to level the playing field nationally with school estates and the equipment and

technology our children have access to. Then the revenue funding needs to cover the reset on teacher pay as well as support the additional staff needed to meet our children's emotional and specialist needs and ensure work and work-life balance allows the system to be sustained.

5. **System Improvement** – Acknowledge, albeit for a plethora of reasons, that our current curriculum and method of assessment have fallen well behind what we really need in 2025. Empower educators who are collaborating together; see examples like the **Foundation for Educational Development**, to shape the changes and transformation needed. Reduce high-stakes assessment, develop trusted routes for equitable continuous assessment, broaden the curriculum so there are suitable pathways for all, and extend the opportunities to acquire skills as alternative credentials that will likely be more valuable for our future cohort.

That's my recipe, and in truth, it's been talked about long before I started writing; I've shaped it based on my writing and research and, most importantly, lived experience at most levels of the education system and the single common thread that will unlock more rapid evolution, is to hand much of this away from the politically influenced sphere. It's like delegating authority to the Bank of England to set the base rate because they know best. Well, let us delegate our curriculum and qualifications to those who know best too.

Is there a disconnect between accessibility and equity with assessment?

And is our current system really fit for purpose?

Now, I am first in the queue to highlight that there are far greater minds than mine when it comes to trying to fathom that sweet spot between the need to undertake assessment and, at the same time, find ways that are fair and accessible for all learners. I don't need to have undertaken a doctorate to know that a rigid standardised text like a General Certificate of Secondary Education (GCSE) will not play to every child's strengths. From my experiences in our schools, I know that for some children, the stress and pressure of that two-hour window to show what they know can be so great they probably highlight a fraction of what they really know.

I know from my time supporting an alternative provision setting that if I sat and chatted with students about a topic, I would glean far more from them than handing them a pen and paper. I also know that how we assign our grades and grade boundaries doesn't pass my sniff test. The concept of waiting until everyone has taken a test and had their paper marked and then defining the grade boundaries has never sat well with me or felt fair. Alternatively, as **Anna Bailey**, the CEO of **Form the Future**, a social enterprise that supports young people as they progress through education into employment, succinctly put it, "*Don't get me started on marking on a curve and the premise that the lowest scores must all be failures...*"

Anyway, I've made the core point: the current assessment process doesn't play to the strengths of some children, and it's not unreasonable to say that continuous assessment is a better way. The subtle and, I think, the awkward point here is that effective continuous assessment would require trusting in the subsequent teacher (TAG)- or centre-assessed grades (CAGs), in part at least.

As we know, the TAG and CAGs during the pandemic resulted in higher awards, and the governments were keen to highlight subsequently, they are back at a lower, pre-pandemic pass rate. Did anyone choose to pause and think that those assessed grades in school were actually more reflective, undertaken by someone who has seen evidence of the child's learning over two or three years? They were just dismissed as overly "generous," but perhaps the current high-stakes testing is "stingy."

A different way

So let's think a bit differently beyond that one-size-fits-all concept. Anna Bailey shared with me: "*I've long thought that I'd like to see testing at school to be more the driver's test. When you feel you've mastered the content and believe you can perform to an acceptable standard, you put yourself forward to be tested. If you don't pass, you continue to learn and improve, and you keep trying until you pass. In this way, some students can pass through a qualification sooner and start to explore more challenging work. Others who aren't yet ready or who are still working in order to pass can keep going. When the test date is set by someone else, it becomes more about their agenda than yours. By letting young people set their own goals and targets, they might be more motivated to learn.*" When we think about accessibility and equity in our system, it's hard to disregard Ann's point.

I also reached out to **Tim Smale**, director of Elevate and a teacher of history at the **Lycée Michel Lucius**, who shared with me some of the current limitations that he faces, explaining, "It definitely creates anxiety, teachers teach to the test, *so it definitely narrows the curriculum. In my history courses at KS4 and KS5 there is no time to play with the subject at the highest level. For example, I have 120 hours to teach 180 hours of content. How can that promote growth? Also, at what other point, other than in education, do we assess competency through an overly time-pressured examination where only one answer is correct?*" Perhaps the most salient point he shared was highlighting that since being a teacher for some 20 years, he has never faced a single time-based examination, yet is still considered competent enough to take on the learning of hundreds of students. There is a very glaring irony in that observation.

He, like many others, has a point. We are happy over three years for our most valuable qualification, a degree, to assign a grade based on three years of essays and checkpoints alongside one final exam to be a valid test, but we can't have similar checkpoints contributing towards an A-level. Is this about an overarching need to "monitor" and a lack of trust in the profession of "self-grading" that somehow doesn't apply to universities?

I am not sure many in the classroom would agree that our current system is fully fit for purpose.

There are different ways of capturing both summative and formative assessment that can be flexed to suit learners. Again, if we look at high-value degree courses, researchers [31] highlight that *"Assessment can be made more inclusive by incorporating a **more diverse range of summative assessment tasks** to assess students' learning. Summative assessments are those which contribute to a student's final qualification."*

There is, of course, lots we can do in the classroom. I have seen some great examples using approaches like the **Universal Design for Learning (UDL)** principle of "Multiple Means of Expression" – aiming to give all students a choice so they choose how they can best demonstrate or express evidence of their learning. **Tim Smale** highlighted the problem perfectly, saying: *"By their very nature, exams unfairly disadvantage students. Let's put the social arguments of monetary wealth aside, do examinations in history, for example, reward those who are best at history or those who are best at sitting history exams? The two are very different and I don't feel that an exam rewards those who are having a bad day, those who have learning needs, those without access to tutors, those with difficult family circumstances etc."*

Surely the more pathways we can provide to support a student better demonstrate their understanding, the more accuracy and credibility we have in our ultimate qualifications.

Kat Cauchi, a former primary teacher, supported the earlier points in this topic: *"Firstly, by using multiple methods of assessment and secondly allowing learners to lead their own learning and choose how best to showcase their understanding. If, for example, a pupil is absolutely brilliant in music but struggles with reading and writing, a written test is not going to be a fair assessment of their skill, but a performance and a conversation with them (that you can record) could paint a much more accurate picture."* This reinforces the need for nuance and classroom and student-specific flexibility in capturing evidence.

You won't be surprised that for this specific topic, I wanted to give more of the words on the page to practitioners; they have the skin in the game on this topic. Going back to **Matt Pitman,** he articulated when I asked him about how excessive testing can narrow the curriculum rather than promote growth: *"Of course it does! There is no better way to limit the potential of a learning area than to reduce its outcomes to a test. What a colossal barrier to deep learning! We don't authentically learn in a vacuum, yet here we are, hoover in hand, expecting our students and teachers to feel enriched and engaged."*

He shared one alternative that very much aligns with my thoughts here, saying, *"Portfolio work provides the freedom to explore a topic of interest and chart an incredible amount of learning and growth while mapping outcomes to the necessary curriculum standards."* As he shared with me, the main change here is that engaging in a portfolio requires ideation, research, collation, and presentation, all processes linked to creative and critical thinking, something exams and high-stakes testing completely miss. Is it a surprise we such a growth in discussions around project based learning?

Measuring success

We have a bigger aim here; we cannot expect to have inclusive schools if the ultimate way we measure success is stacked against some of our cohorts. I can go back to the 1994 **World Conference on Special Needs in Education** in Salamanca, Spain, which concluded that: *"Regular schools with [an] inclusive orientation are the most effective means of combating discriminatory attitudes, creating welcoming communities, building an inclusive society and achieving education for all; moreover, they provide an effective education to the majority of children and improve the efficiency and ultimately the cost-effectiveness of the entire education system."* If we don't acknowledge the need to change or at least vary our assessment model, then all bets are off with our broader inclusive educational ambitions.

So, assuming everyone wants to support change and signs up for this ambition, then looking at a focus on fairness and accessibility, we always need to ensure that the assessment processes are equitable and don't unfairly disadvantage certain groups of students.

All elements come back to one common strand: we need to have multiple pathways of assessment, all valued and recognised as equal and valid, and these often need to be student-directed in what works best for them. **Matt Pittman** echoed this with some words of further wisdom: *"Limiting assessment to a test or an exam is a surefire way to reduce the inclusive nature of any curriculum. What we really need to consider is what is worth learning in this current period of time? Do we need young minds that can succeed through an exam or do we need enthusiastic and curious people who are willing to embrace challenge and dive into a topic with passion?"* Amen to that.

I think to do this we first need to look at how we define success in education and how we can widen this to celebrate many types of success and then we can build in the measures to work with this.

- Kat Cauchi

This section of the chapter was not to provide a magical blueprint for success but to highlight this continuing and very awkward question. The problem is that all of us in our schools, come August each year, will stand up and celebrate the results our students achieve, and rightly so, especially as we have to work within the confines of the current system. Nevertheless, quietly, with that small, grey elephant in the corner of the room, we all know we are celebrating something inherently unfair. We will know that some of our students were destined to feel like failures just because they never had an opportunity to show how amazing they are, fairly.

Some of the primary takeaways for me have to be these:

1. **Rigid assessments don't suit all learners**: Traditional, high-stakes tests like GCSEs don't allow all students to showcase their true abilities. For many, the pressure of a single timed exam prevents them from demonstrating their full knowledge and potential, creating inequity.

2. **Continuous assessment as a fairer alternative**: Continuous assessment, which allows for more regular and diverse evaluations of a student's learning, offers a more accurate reflection of a student's abilities. Trusting teachers to assess students over time, as seen with TAGs during the pandemic, might provide a better balance.

3. **Flexibility in timing and testing**: Offering more flexible, student-led testing models, where students choose when they're ready to be assessed, could reduce anxiety and foster greater engagement. This approach would enable students to set their own goals and pass at their own pace.

4. **Developing a broader range of assessment methods**: Incorporating more inclusive assessment formats like portfolio work, projects, and verbal assessments would allow students to demonstrate their understanding in ways that play to their strengths, rather than being confined to one-size-fits-all exams.

5. **Creating an inclusive and fairer system**: Without changes to assessment, the system risks exasperating inequity. A broader range of assessment pathways, tailored to the needs of learners, is going to be key for building truly inclusive schools and achieving equitable educational outcomes for all.

I've spent many, many months writing all of the chapters in this book, but of all of them, this is the best one to end on. What are we trying to achieve? Why do we care about funding, enough teachers in the classroom, the role of AI, or a long-term plan for anything if we have no intention of actually making the educational journey and outcomes for all our children fair and equitable at every stage?

References

1 C. S. Dweck and E. L. Leggett, "A Social-Cognitive Approach to Motivation and Personality," *Psychological Review*, vol. 95, no. 2, pp. 256–273, 1988.
2 C. S. Dweck, *Mindset: The New Psychology of Success*, Random House, 2007.
3 "National Strategy Needed to End Anxiety of School Admissions Scramble Says School Leaders' Union," National Association of Head Teachers (NAHT), 01 03 2023. [Online]. Available: https://www.naht.org.uk/News/Latest-comments/Press-room/ArtMID/558/ArticleID/1969/National-strategy-needed-to-end-anxiety-of-school-admissions-scramble-says-school-leaders-union

4 N. Roberts, S. Danechi and A. Lewis, "Falling Pupil Rolls in England and School Closures in London," House of Commons Library, 2023.
5 "School Capacity - National, Regional, Local Authority," Department for Education, 02 06 2023. [Online]. Available: https://explore-education-statistics.service.gov.uk/data-tables/permalink/979cf255-eb21-48d0-ff74-08db6354f3ce
6 V. Irwin, T. M. Bailey, R. Panditharatna and A. Sadeghi, "Projections of Education Statistics to 2030," National Center for Education Statistics, 28 02 2024. [Online]. Available: https://nces.ed.gov/programs/PES/section-1.asp
7 "Independent Schools Australia," [Online]. Available: https://isa.edu.au/
8 Independent Schools Australia, "School Enrolment Trends and Projections, ISA Research Report," 2021.
9 U. Parliament, "Nick Gibb Response to Question for the Department for Education," 9 2 2023. [Online]. Available: https://questions-statements.parliament.uk/written-questions/detail/2023-01-11/121149
10 "Schools, Pupils and their Characteristics (Academic year 2023/24)," Department for Education, 06 06 2024. [Online]. Available: https://explore-education-statistics.service.gov.uk/find-statistics/school-pupils-and-their-characteristics
11 "MAT Tracker: Mapping the Country's Multi-Academy Trusts," TES Magazine, 1 7 2024. [Online]. Available: https://www.tes.com/magazine/leadership/data/mat-tracker-multi-academy-trusts-map
12 A. Zickafoose, O. Ilesanm, M. Diaz-Manrique, A. E. Adeyemi, B. Walumbe, R. Strong and G. Wingenbach, "Barriers and Challenges Affecting Quality Education (Sustainable Development Goal #4) in Sub-Saharan Africa by 2030," *Sustainability*, vol. 16, no. 7, 2024. https://doi.org/10.3390/su16072657
13 "SDG 4 "Ensure Inclusive and Equitable Quality Education and Promote Lifelong Learning Opportunities for All"," United Nations, [Online]. Available: https://sdgs.un.org/goals/goal4
14 "10 of the Biggest Problems Facing Education," Concern Worldwide, 12 08 2024. [Online]. Available: https://www.concern.net/news/problems-with-education-around-the-world
15 A. Hargreaves, "Educational Change Takes Ages: Life, Career and Generational Factors in Teachers' Emotional Responses to Educational Change," *Teaching and Teacher Education*, vol. 21, no. 8, pp. 967–983, 2005.
16 G. Kelchtermans, "Teachers' Emotions in Educational Reforms: Self-Understanding, Vulnerable Commitment and Micropolitical Literacy," *Teaching and Teacher Education*, vol. 21, no. 8, pp. 995–1006, 2005.
17 OECD, "Organisation for Economic Co-operation and Development (OECD)," [Online]. Available: https://www.oecd.org/
18 "OECD: Indicator C1. How Much is Spent per Student on Educational Institutions," 2019. [Online]. Available: https://www.oecd-ilibrary.org/how-much-is-spent-per-student-on-educational-institutions_0fdcbb3b-en.pdf
19 "National Center for Education Statistics (NCES)," [Online]. Available: https://nces.ed.gov/
20 "Education Expenditures by Country," National Center for Educational Statistics, 08 2023. [Online]. Available: https://nces.ed.gov/programs/coe/indicator/cmd/education-expenditures-by-country
21 E. H. Dyvik, "Annual Expenditure per Student on Educational Institutions in OECD Countries for Primary, Secondary and Tertiary Education in 2020, by Country," Statistica, 04 07 2024. [Online]. Available: https://www.statista.com/statistics/238733/expenditure-on-education-by-country/
22 "The Institute of Fiscal Studies (IFS)," [Online]. Available: www.ifs.org.uk

23. L. Sibieta, "How does School Spending per Pupil Differ Across the UK?," Institute of Fiscal Studies (IFS), 21 04 2023. [Online]. Available: https://ifs.org.uk/publications/how-does-school-spending-pupil-differ-across-uk
24. "Building Strong Academy Trusts - Guidance for Academy Trusts and Prospective Converters," Department for Education, 05 2021. [Online]. Available: https://dera.ioe.ac.uk/id/eprint/37962/1/Building_strong_academy_trusts_guidance.pdf
25. "Confederation of School Trusts (CST)," [Online]. Available: https://cstuk.org.uk/
26. "What is a Strong Trust? A CST Discussion Paper," Confederation of School Trusts, 2021. [Online]. Available: https://cstuk.org.uk/assets/pdfs/ICE_10102_CST_What_Is_A_Strong_Trust_Discussion%20Paper2.pdf
27. D. f. Education, "Opportunity for All: Strong Schools with Great Teachers for Your Child," 03 2022. [Online]. Available: https://assets.publishing.service.gov.uk/media/62416cb5d3bf7f32add7819f/Opportunity_for_all_strong_schools_with_great_teachers_for_your_child__print_version_.pdf
28. "Commissioning High-Quality Trusts," Department for Education, 06 07 2023. [Online]. Available: https://assets.publishing.service.gov.uk/media/64a676e1c531eb000c64ff2c/Commissioning_High-Quality-Trusts_July_2023.pdf
29. "Strengthening Education Systems and Innovation," UNICEF, [Online]. Available: https://www.unicef.org/education/strengthening-education-systems-innovation
30. "Education for Sustainable Development (ESD) in the UK – Current Status, Best Practice and Opportunities for the Future," UK National Commission for UNESCO, 2013.
31. P. Sotiriadou, D. Logan, A. Daly and R. Guest, "The Role of Authentic Assessment to Preserve Academic Integrity and Promote Skill Development and Employability," *Studies in Higher Education*, vol. 45, no. 11, pp. 2132–2148, 2020.

# Wrapping up

So now we are at the end of our journey through some of these tricky, awkward questions. One thing I have consistently seen and learnt whilst writing this book is that there is never a one-size-fits-all solution. That being said, many of the most challenging issues facing the sector are directly a result of decisions taken outside of education at a high system level. More often than not, the expectation is that education needs to respond more quickly to address the issues we face. Sometimes, that is true, but it's also painfully apparent that it's a convenient deflect from the societal and economic pressures nations face.

Education is unlike any other sector, not only because of the priceless value of those we entrust with our educators or because of the impact they have on our society for generations to come, but perhaps most of all because it is a sector built on sharing and support. There are so many folks around the globe working and collaborating for the betterment of our schools, but sadly, we often miss that final step to achieving political engagement and understanding.

I don't have many of the answers, and in truth, no one person does, but I have tried to amplify the most pressing conversations, those awkward questions, and base the conversation with facts, context, and relevant research to hopefully empower more positive and focused conversations and next steps. I've tried to bring a wealth of trusted voices to the table and signpost many others, the folks who should be at the table when shaping our future education system.

At times, I've battled myself with imposter syndrome; frustration at some of the most obvious problems and solutions at our fingertips, yet seemingly out of reach; and with a desire to not just challenge but to provide support and empathy at every stage. My previous books have all been handbooks and guides on subjects that I know best; this without a doubt has been a fusion of lived experience from my 30 years across education and a willingness to listen and learn.

I hope this sparks conversation and discussion in your school, trust, or district. I hope it connects you with other likeminded individuals and, most importantly of all, I hope the elephant in the room steps out of the shadows and we all feel a little bit more comfortable challenging the status quo.

Al

Acknowledgements

I am hugely grateful to all of these supportive folks from across education who gave up their time to share their insights and experiences with me. They are part of a huge Professional Learning Network that I am proud to be able to support and learn from on a daily basis, and I hope you will reach out and connect with them, too.

Name	Job Title/Organisation
Abid Patel	IT Director, Newham Community Learning Trust
Anne Bailey	CEO, Form the Future CIC
Bonnie Nieves	Founder, Educate On Purpose, Professional Learning Services
Carla Aerts	Independent AIEd consultant, advisor, and thought leader
Clare Flintoff	CEO, ASSET Education Trust
Craig McKee	Former head teacher and founder of SLT AI
Dr. Ian Young	CEO, Peterborough Keys Academies Trust
Dr. Tim Coulson CBE	CEO, Unity Schools Partnership
Dr. Will Van Reyk	Deputy director of innovation, North London Collegiate School, UK
Dr. Helen Price	Executive head, Hampton Academies Trust
Dr. Rachelle Dené Poth	Spanish and STEAM teacher at Riverview School District in Pittsburgh PA; consultant ThriveinEDU LLC
Gary Henderson	Director of IT, Millfield School
John Magee	Managing director and founder of Kindness Matters
John Mikton	Technology for learning coordinator at the International School of Geneva
John Sibbald	Specialist digital leader in education

Kai Vacher	Principal of the British School Muscat and British School Salalah, Oman
Kat Cauchi	Former primary teacher and community engagement lead at NetSupport
Kavitha Ravindran	Former secondary science teacher and co-founder of sAInaptic
Leon Furze	Former secondary educator, consultant, and author, Furze Smith Consulting
Mark Anderson	Former secondary teacher and ICT evangelist
Mark Steed	Former school principal and CEO, and now consulting at Steed Education, UK
Matt Jessop	Head teacher, Crosthwaite C.E. Primary School
Matt Pitman	Head of secondary, Global Village Learning, Australia
Nic Ponsford	Former teacher and founder of the Global Equality Collective
Pete Read	CEO, Persona Education
Philip Murdoch	Specialist design and technology teacher, Rivermount College, Queensland
Phillip Alcock	Former educator, founder of AIxPBL
Professor Bob Harrison	Visiting professor at University of Wolverhampton, former education adviser at Toshiba Northern Europe
Professor Sonia Livingstone OBE	Director, Digital Futures for Children Centre and LSE professor
Sammy White	Former teacher and learning evangelist for Glean
Shemal Rajapakse	Co-founder, Wizzie App
Simon Luxford-Moore	Head of eLearning, ESMS Edinburgh
Tim Smale	Director of Elevate and teacher of history, Lycée Michel Lucius, Luxembourg
Tracey O'Brien	Head teacher, Wallington High School for Girls and author, London

Bibliography

"'I don't really care anymore': Parent apathy on attendance laid bare," Schools Week, 30 August 2024. [Online]. Available: https://schoolsweek.co.uk/i-dont-really-care-anymore-parent-apathy-on-attendance-laid-bare/

"10 of the biggest problems facing education," Concern Worldwide, 12 August 2024. [Online]. Available: https://www.concern.net/news/problems-with-education-around-the-world

"2024 Academies Benchmark Report," [Report]. UHY Hacker Young, 2024.

"21 Million Americans Still Lack Broadband Connectivity," The Pew Charitable Trust, 10 July 2019. [Online]. Available: https://www.pewtrusts.org/en/research-and-analysis/fact-sheets/2019/07/21-million-americans-still-lack-broadband-connectivity

A. Abdulkadiroğlu, P. A. Pathak, J. Schellenberg and C. R. Walters, "Do Parents Value School Effectiveness?" *American Economic Review*, vol. 110, no. 5, pp. 1502–1539, 2020.

"Academies Act," UK Parliament, 29 July 2010. [Online]. Available: https://bills.parliament.uk/bills/642/publications

"Academies Benchmark Report," Kreston UK, 2024. [Online]. Available: https://www.bishopfleming.co.uk/sites/default/files/2024-02/kreston_uk_academies_benchmark_report_2024.pdf

"AI and education: Kids need AI guidance in school. But who guides the schools?," World Economic Forum, 18 January 2024. [Online]. Available: https://www.weforum.org/agenda/2024/01/ai-guidance-school-responsible-use-in-education/

M. Al Jaffa, "Barriers General Education Teachers Face Regarding the Inclusion of Students with Autism," *Frontiers in Psychology*, vol. 13, p. 873248, 2022.

"Alexa – Virtual Assistant," Amazon, [Online]. Available: https://en.wikipedia.org/wiki/Amazon_Alexa

"All Our Futures: Creativity, Culture and Education," [Report]. National Advisory Committee on Creative and Cultural Education, 1999.

P. Allen-Kinross, "Schools with deprived pupils 'still less likely to be judged good', admits Ofsted," Schools Week, 16 December 2019. [Online]. Available: https://schoolsweek.co.uk/schools-with-deprived-pupils-still-less-likely-to-be-judged-good-admits-ofsted/

L. Anderson, D. Krathwohl, P. Airasian, K. Cruikshank, P. Pintrich, R. Mayer, J. Raths and M. Wittrock, *Taxonomy for Learning, Teaching, and Assessing, A: A Revision of Bloom's Taxonomy of Educational Objectives*, Pearson, 2001.

M. Anderson and O. Lewis, *The EdTech Playbook: Your Definitive Guide to Teaching, Learning and Leading with Technology and AI in Education*, John Catt, 2025.

M. Anderson, "The Little Book of Generative AI prompts for teachers," ICT Evangelist, [Online]. Available: https://ictevangelist.com/free-resource-the-little-book-of-generative-ai-prompts-for-teachers/

J. Andrews, "School Performance in Academy Chains and Local Authorities – 2017," Education Policy Institute, 19 June 2018. [Online]. Available: https://epi.org.uk/publications-and-research/performance-academy-local-authorities-2017

P. Armstrong, "Blooms Taxonomy," [Report]. Vanderbilt University Center for Teaching, 2010.

"ASCL analysis shows collapse in creative arts A-level entries," Association of School and College Leaders, 13 August 2024. [Online]. Available: https://ascl.org.uk/News/Our-news-and-press-releases/ASCL-analysis-shows-collapse-in-creative-arts-A-le

S. Baker, "In praise of small MATs: Why bigger doesn't always mean better," Schools Week, 29 April 2023. [Online]. Available: https://schoolsweek.co.uk/in-praise-of-small-mats-why-bigger-doesnt-always-mean-better/

B. Bartanen and K. Andrew, "From Interest to Entry: The Teacher Pipeline From College Application to Initial Employment," *American Educational Research Association*, vol. 60, no. 5, pp. 941–985, 2023.

C. Daniel Batson, *Altruism in Humans*, Oxford University Press, 2011.

M. L. Bernacki and J. Elizabeth, "Exploring the Impact of Service-Learning on Moral Development and Moral Orientation," *Michigan Journal of Community Service Learning*, vol. 14, Spring, pp. 5–15, 2008.

Bett UK (conference) [Online]. Available: www.bettshow.com

D. W. Beuermann, C. K. Jackson, L. Navarro-Sola and F. Pardo, "What is a Good School, and Can Parents Tell? Evidence on the Multidimensionality of School Output," *The Review of Economic Studies*, vol. 90, no. 1, pp. 65–101, 2023.

"Beyond Ofsted," 2023. [Online]. Available: https://beyondofsted.org.uk/

C. Bleakley, "How We've Used AI to Reduce Teacher Workloads," Schools Week, 04 August 2024. [Online]. Available: https://schoolsweek.co.uk/how-weve-used-ai-to-reduce-teacher-workloads/

B. S. Bloom, "The 2 Sigma Problem: The Search for Methods of Group Instruction as Effective as One-to-One Tutoring," *American Educational Research Association*, vol. 13, no. 6, pp. 4–16, 1984.

"Bloom's 2 sigma problem," Wikipedia, [Online]. Available: https://en.wikipedia.org/wiki/Bloom%27s_2_sigma_problem

B. Boileau, L. O'Brien and B. Zaranko, Public spending, pay and pensions, Green Budget 2022, Chapter 4. Insitute of Fiscal Studies (IFS), 08 August 2022. [Online]. Available: https://ifs.org.uk/publications/public-spending-pay-and-pensions

M. Brent, *The Leader's Guide to Managing People: How to Use Soft Skills to Get Hard Result*, FT Publishing International, 2013.

"British Educational Suppliers Association (BESA)," [Online]. Available: https://www.besa.org.uk/

"Building strong academy trusts – Guidance for academy trusts and prospective converters," Department for Education, May 2021. [Online]. Available: https://dera.ioe.ac.uk/id/eprint/37962/1/Building_strong_academy_trusts_guidance.pdf

D. Carter and L. McInerney, *Leading Academy Trusts: Why some fail, but most don't*. John Catt, 2020.

CDT Center for Democracy & Technology, "Off Task: EdTech Threats to Student Privacy and Equity in the Age of AI," September 2023. [Online]. Available: https://cdt.org/wp-content/uploads/2023/09/091923-CDT-Off-Task-web.pdf

"Century – AI powered online learning." [Online]. Available: https://www.century.tech/

"Chaotic government reforms are failing to tackle education inequality," UCL Institute for Education, July 2018. [Online]. Available: https://www.ucl.ac.uk/news/2018/jul/chaotic-government-reforms-are-failing-tackle-education-inequality

"Chartered Collge of Teaching," [Online]. Available: https://chartered.college/
"ChatGPT," OpenAi. [Online]. Available: https://chatgpt.com/
C. S. Chong, "Classroom tips to help integrate soft skills," EtonX, 1 April 2019. [Online]. Available: https://etonx.com/classroom-tips-to-help-integrate-soft-skills/
D. Christodoulou, *Seven Myths about Education*. Routledge, 2014.
D. Clark, "Digital learning in the UK – Statistics & Facts," Statista, 03 July 2024. [Online]. Available: https://www.statista.com/topics/8518/digital-learning-in-the-uk/
"Closing the Attainment Gap,"The Sutton Trust, 2024. [Online]. Available: https://www.suttontrust.com/our-research/closing-the-attainment-gap/
"Closing the Digital Divide for the Millions of Americans without Broadband," U.S. Government Accountability Office, 01 Feburary 2023. [Online]. Available: https://www.gao.gov/blog/closing-digital-divide-millions-americans-without-broadband
R. Coe et al., "What Makes Great Teaching," The Sutton Trust, 2014. [Online]. Available: https://www.suttontrust.com/wp-content/uploads/2014/10/What-Makes-Great-Teaching-REPORT.pdf
J. Collin and E Smith, "Effective Professional Development: Guidance report," [Report]. Education Endowment Foundation, 2021.
"Commissioning High-Quality Trusts" Department for Education, 06 July 2023. [Online]. Available: https://assets.publishing.service.gov.uk/media/64a676e1c531eb000c64ff2c/Commissioning_High-Quality-Trusts_July_2023.pdf
"Confederation of School Trusts (CST)," [Online]. Available: https://cstuk.org.uk/
"Connections Academy by Pearson," [Online]. Available: https://www.connectionsacademy.com/
"Contribution rates – Teachers Retirement System (TRS)," TRS Illinois, 2024. [Online]. Available: https://www.trsil.org/employers/payments/contribution-rates_earnings-limitations
"Convention 108+. Guidelines for the protection of personal data in educational settings," Council of Europe, 2020. [Online]. Available: https://www.europarl.europa.eu/meetdocs/2014_2019/plmrep/COMMITTEES/LIBE/DV/2018/09-10/Convention_108_EN.pdf
A. L. Costa and B. Kallick, *Learning and Leading with Habits of Mind: 16 Essential Characteristics for Success*. ASCD, 2008.
T. Coulson, *The A-Z of School Improvement*. John Catt, 2024.
Council of British International Schools (COBIS). [Online]. Available: www.cobis.org.uk
Council of International Schools. [Online]. Available: www.cois.org
L. Crehan, *Cleverlands: The Secrets Behind the Success of the World's Education Superpowers*. Unbound, 2018.
D. R. Darwin, N. Mukminatien and N. Suryati, "Critical Thinking in the AI Era: An Exploration of EFL Students' Perceptions, Benefits, and Limitations," *Cogent Education*, vol. 11, no. 1, 2024. https://www.tandfonline.com/doi/full/10.1080/2331186X.2023.2290342
"Data Protection Impact Assessment – DPIA," Information Commissioners Office (ICO), 19 May 2023. [Online]. https://ico.org.uk/for-organisations/uk-gdpr-guidance-and-resources/accountability-and-governance/guide-to-accountability-and-governance/data-protection-impact-assessments/
C. Day and L. Smethem, "The Effects of Reform: Have Teachers Really Lost Their Sense of Professionalism?," *Journal of Educational Change*, vol. 10, pp. 141–157, 2009.
P. R. Dene, *How to Teach AI: Weaving Strategies and Activities into Any Content Area*. International Society for Technology in Education, 2024.
J. Dewey, *Moral Principles in Education*. CreateSpace Independent Publishing, 2017.
"Digital Citizenship Education (DCE)," Council of Europe. [Online]. Available: https://www.coe.int/en/web/digital-citizenship-education/the-concept

"Digital Futures for Children," London School of Economics and Political Science. [Online]. Available: https://www.digital-futures-for-children.net

"Digital Poverty Alliance," [Online]. Available: www.digitalpovertyalliance.org

"Do parental involvement interventions increase attainment," Nuffield Foundation, 2013. [Online]. Available: https://www.nuffieldfoundation.org/sites/default/files/files/Do_parental_involvement_interventions_increase_attainment1.pdf

W. Dobbie and R. G. Fryer, "Charter Schools and Labor Market Outcomes," *Journal of Labor Economics*, vol. 38, no. 4, pp. 915–957, 2020.

B. Donovan, "Soft Skills – definition," Encyclopaedia Britannica. [Online]. Available: https://www.britannica.com/money/soft-skills

A. Duckworth, *Grit: Why Passion and Resilience are the Secrets to Success*. Vermilion, 2017.

A. L. Duckworth, "Grit: the power of passion and perseverance," TED Talks, 09 May 2013. [Online]. Available: www.youtube.com/watch?v=H14bBuluwB8

E. Dunkley, K. McGough and H. Agerholm, "Overcrowded specialist schools: 'We're teaching in cupboards'," BBC, 20 Feburary 2023. [Online]. Available: https://www.bbc.co.uk/news/education-64418797

C. S. Dweck and E. L. Leggett, "A Social-Cognitive Approach to Motivation and Personality," *Psychological Review*, vol. 95, no. 2, pp. 256–273, 1988.

C. S. Dweck, *Mindset: The New Psychology of Success*. Random House, 2007.

E. H. Dyvik, "Annual expenditure per student on educational institutions in OECD countries for primary, secondary and tertiary education in 2020, by country," Statistica, 04 July 2024. [Online]. Available: https://www.statista.com/statistics/238733/expenditure-on-education-by-country/

"East of England advisory board," Department for Education. [Online]. Available: https://www.gov.uk/government/publications/east-of-england-advisory-board

"Educate on Purpose," Bonnie Nieves. [Online]. Available: www.educateonpurpose.com

"Education (Scotland) Act," [Report]. UK Parliament, 1872.

"Education Department for Opportunity for all: Strong Schools with Great Teachers for Your Child," March 2022. [Online]. https://assets.publishing.service.gov.uk/media/62416cb5d3bf7f32add7819f/Opportunity_for_all_strong_schools_with_great_teachers_for_your_child__print_version_.pdf

"Education Development Trust." [Online]. Available: https://www.edt.org

Education Endowment Foundation, "A Marked Improvement? – A review of the evidence on written marking," June 2016. [Online]. Available: https://d2tic4wvo1iusb.cloudfront.net/documents/guidance/EEF_Marking_Review_April_2016.pdf?v=1681841884

"Education Expenditures by Country," National Center for Educational Statistics, August 2023. [Online]. Available: https://nces.ed.gov/programs/coe/indicator/cmd/education-expenditures-by-country

"Education for Sustainable Development (ESD) in the UK – Current status, best practice and opportunities for the future," [Report]. UK National Commission for UNESCO, 2013.

Education National Center for The Nation's Report Card. [Online]. Available: https://www.nationsreportcard.gov/

Education Policy Institute. [Online]. Available: https://epi.org.uk/

"Education Reform Act," Department for Education, 1998. [Online]. Available: https://www.gov.uk/government/publications/school-inspection-handbook-eif

Education System in the UK. 2012. [Online]. Available: https://assets.publishing.service.gov.uk/government/uploads/system/uploads/attachment_data/file/219167/v01-2012ukes.pdf

"Educator Pay in America," National Education Association (NEA), 18 April 2024. [Online]. Available: https://www.nea.org/resource-library/educator-pay-and-student-spending-how-does-your-state-rank

M. Egwuekwe, "Opinion: We Must Close the Digital Divide in America,"Government Technology Magazine, 27 Feburary 2024. [Online]. Available: https://www.govtech.com/network/opinion-we-must-close-the-digital-divide-in-america

B. J. Ellis et al., "Beyond Risk and Protective Factors: An Adaptation-Based Approach to Resilience," *Perspectives on Psychological Science*, vol. 12, no. 4, pp. 561–587, 2017.

"England's World Leading Attendance Drive Continues," Department for Education, 10 May 2024. [Online]. Available: https://www.gov.uk/government/news/englands-world-leading-attendance-drive-continues

"English Baccalaureate," Department for Education. [Online]. Available: https://en.wikipedia.org/wiki/English_Baccalaureate

Evaluating Post-Pandemic Education Policies and Combatting Student Absenteeism Beyond COVID-19. OECD Education Policy Perspectives, vol. 101, OECD Publishing, 2024.

"Every Student Succeeds Act," Wikipedia, 2015. [Online]. Available: https://en.wikipedia.org/wiki/Every_Student_Succeeds_Act

"Every Student Succeeds Act (ESSA)," [Report]. U.S. Department of Education, 2015.

"Everything you need to know about SATs," Department for Education, 05 May 2022. [Online]. Available: https://educationhub.blog.gov.uk/2022/05/05/everything-you-need-to-know-about-sats/

"Exceed Academies Trust," [Online]. Available: https://www.exceedacademiestrust.co.uk/

"Explore Teaching as a Career," News South Wales Government, Australia. [Online]. Available: https://education.nsw.gov.au/teach-nsw/explore-teaching/salary-of-a-teacher

P. A. Facione, "Critical Thinking: What It Is and Why It Counts," [Report]. Millbrae, CA: Measured Reasons and The California Academic Press, 1992.

P. E. Facione, "Critical Thinking: A Statement of Expert Consensus for Purposes of Educational Assessment and Instruction," [Report]. The California Academic Press, 1990.

"FACT SHEET: Biden-Harris Administration Announces Improving Student Achievement Agenda in 2024," The White House, 17 January 2024. [Online]. Available: https://www.whitehouse.gov/briefing-room/statements-releases/2024/01/17/fact-sheet-biden-harris-administration-announces-improving-student-achievement-agenda-in-2024/

C. E. Finn Jr., *Assessing the Nation's Report Card: Challenges and Choices for NAEP*. Harvard press, 2022.

D. Fitzpatrick, "7 reasons why we are failing to prepare our kids for the AI world," Linkedin, 15 August 2024. [Online]. Available: https://www.linkedin.com/posts/theaieducator_7-reasons-why-we-are-failing-to-prepare-our-activity-7229788943276265472-7iM4

D. Fitzpatrick, B. Weinstein and A. Fox, *The AI Classroom: The Ultimate Guide to Artificial Intelligence in Education*. TeacherGoals Publishing, 2023.

M. Forehand, "Blooms Taxonomy – From Emerging Perspectives on Learning, Teaching and Technology." 2011. [Online]. Available: https://cft.vanderbilt.edu/wp-content/uploads/sites/59/BloomsTaxonomy-mary-forehand.pdf

"Free Schools – Types of Schools." Gov.uk, 2024. [Online]. Available: https://www.gov.uk/types-of-school/free-schools

M. Friedman, "The Role of Government in Education in Economics and the Public Interest," [Report]. 1955.

M. Fullan, *The New Meaning of Educational Change*. Teachers College Press, 2015.

L. Furze, "Artificial Intelligence and Teacher Workload: Can AI Actually Save Educators Time?" 21 Marh 2024. [Online]. Available: https://leonfurze.com/2024/03/21/artificial-intelligence-and-teacher-workload-can-ai-actually-save-educators-time/comment-page-1/

L. Furze, *Practical AI Strategies: Engaging with Generative AI in Education*. Amba Press, 2024.

"Future of Education and Skills 2030," OECD. [Online]. Available: https://www.oecd.org/en/about/projects/future-of-education-and-skills-2030.html

H. Gardner, *Truth, Beauty, and Goodness Reframed: Educating for the Virtues in the Age of Truthiness and Twitter*. Basic Books, 2011.

J. Gardner, M. O'Leary and L. Yuan, "Artificial Intelligence in Educational Assessment: 'Breakthrough? Or Buncombe and Ballyhoo?," *Journal of Computer Assisted Learning*, vol. 37, no. 5, pp. 1207–1216, 2021.

J. T. Gatto, "The 7-Lesson Schoolteacher," New Society Publishers. [Online]. Available: https://www.newciv.org/whole/schoolteacher.txt

J. T. Gatto, *Dumbing Us Down: The Hidden Curriculum of Compulsory Schooling*, 10th Anniversary Edition. New Society Publishers, 2002.

GESS Dubai (Conference). [Online]. Available: www.gessdubai.com

N. Gibb, "The purpose of education," Department for Education, 09 July 2015. [Online]. Available: https://www.gov.uk/government/speeches/the-purpose-of-education

S. Giraud-Reeves, "The facts of the matter: England is shifting to a 'knowledge-rich curriculum'," Social Market Foundation, 26 July 2021. [Online]. https://www.smf.co.uk/commentary_podcasts/the-facts-of-the-matter-england-is-shifting-to-a-knowledge-rich-curriculum/

Global Equality Collective (GEC). [Online]. Available: www.thegec.education/

D. Goleman, *Emotional Intelligence: Why It Can Matter More Than IQ*. Bloomsbury Publishing, 2020. p. 352.

"Good Career Guidance report," Gatsby, 2014. [Online]. Available: https://www.gatsby.org.uk/uploads/education/reports/pdf/gatsby-sir-john-holman-good-career-guidance-2014.pdf

"Government's approach to teaching reading is uninformed and failing children," UCL/Helen Hamlyn Centre for Pedagogy, 19 January 2022. [Online]. Available: https://www.ucl.ac.uk/news/2022/jan/governments-approach-teaching-reading-uninformed-and-failing-children

J. Gubbels, E. van der Put Claudia and M. Assink, "Risk Factors for School Absenteeism and Dropout: A Meta-Analytic Review," *Journal of Youth and Adolescence*, vol. 48, pp. 1637–1667, 2019.

"Guidance for Generative AI in Education and Research," UNESCO, 16 June 2024. [Online]. Available: https://www.unesco.org/en/articles/guidance-generative-ai-education-and-research

"Guidance on promoting British values in schools," Department for Education, 2014. [Online]. Available: https://www.gov.uk/government/news/guidance-on-promoting-british-values-in-schools-published

"Hallucinations (artificial intelligence)," Wikipedia. [Online]. Available: https://en.wikipedia.org/wiki/Hallucination_(artificial_intelligence)

A. Hamilton, D. Wiliam and J. Hattie, "The Future of AI in Education: 13 things we can do to minimize the damage," [Report]. 2023. https://www.researchgate.net/publication/373108877_The_Future_of_AI_in_Education_13_Things_We_Can_Do_to_Minimize_the_Damage

I. Hamilton and B. Swanston, "2024 Online Learning Statistics," *Forbes*, 31 May 2024. [Online]. Available: https://www.forbes.com/advisor/education/online-colleges/online-learning-stats/#1

A. Hargreaves and I. Goodson, "Educational Change Over Time? The Sustainability and Nonsustainability of Three Decades of Secondary School Change and Continuity," *Educational Administration Quaterly*, vol. 1, no. 42, pp. 3–41, 2006.

A. Hargreaves, "Educational Change Takes Ages: Life, Career and Generational Factors in Teachers' Emotional Responses to Educational Change," *Teaching and Teacher Education*, vol. 21, no. 8, pp. 967–983, 2005.

N. Harper, "Seven Lessons I Teach," *Huffington Post*, 24 June 2012. [Online]. Available: https://www.huffingtonpost.co.uk/nikki-harper/7-lessons-i-teach_b_1622031.html

E. Haves, "Improving schools' performance: Are multi-academy trusts the answer?," House of Lords Library, 11 September 2023. [Online]. Available: https://lordslibrary.parliament.uk/improving-schools-performance-are-multi-academy-trusts-the-answer/

C. Hennessey, "Socialization for Online School Students," Connections Academy by Pearson, 31 March 2022. [Online]. Available: https://www.connectionsacademy.com/support/resources/article/socialization-for-online-school-students/

E. D. Hirsch, Jr., *Cultural Literacy: What Every American Needs to Know*. Random House USA Inc, 1988.

C. E. Hmelo-Silver, "Problem-Based Learning: What and How Do Students Learn?," *Educational Psychology Review*, vol. 16. pp. 235–266, 2004.

L. Hodge et al., "The Features of Effective School Groups report," [Report]. Education Policy Institute, 2024.

T. R. Hoerr, *The Formative Five: Fostering Grit, Empathy, and Other Success Skills Every Student Needs*. ASCD, 2016.

T. N. Hopfenbeck and Gordon Stobart, "Large-Scale Implementation of Assessment for Learning," *Assessment in Education: Principles, Policy & Practice*, vol. 22, no. 1, pp. 1–2, 2015.

T. N. Hopfenbeck et al., "Challenges and opportunities for classroom-based formative assessment and AI: A perspective article," *Frontiers in Education*, vol. 8, p. 1270700, 2023.

"How Homeschooling at Online School Can Help Children With Anxiety," Cambridge Home School Online, Feburary 2021. [Online]. Available: https://www.chsonline.org.uk/blog/homeschooling-at-online-school-can-help-children-with-anxiety

P. Hughes, "What is a Good School?" In *Achieving Quality Education for All: Perspectives from the Asia-Pacific Region and Beyond*. Springer, 2013.

A. Hussain, "How AI is enhancing assessment, reducing workload and improving FE outcomes," FE Week, December 2023. [Online]. Available: https://feweek.co.uk/how-ai-is-enhancing-assessment-reducing-workload-and-improving-fe-outcomes/

B. Hussar et al., "The Condition of Education 2020," [Report]. Institute of Education Sciences, 2020.

ImpactEd Evaluation. [Online]. Available: https://www.evaluation.impactedgroup.uk/

"Improving school attendance by fostering a sense of community belonging," Education Development Trust. 02 April 2024. [Online]. Available: https://www.edt.org/research-and-insights/improving-school-attendance-by-fostering-a-sense-of-community-belonging/

"Independent review of teachers' professional development in schools: Phase 1 findings," Ofsted, May 2024. [Online]. Available: https://www.gov.uk/government/publications/teachers-professional-development-in-schools/independent-review-of-teachers-professional-development-in-schools-phase-1-findings

Independent Schools Australia. [Online]. Available: https://isa.edu.au/

"Inspection Systems: How Top-Performing Nations Hold Schools Accountable," National Center on Education and the Economy (NCEE), 30 May 2018. [Online]. Available: https://ncee.org/quick-read/how-top-performing-nations-hold-schools-accountable/

"Interpreting PISA Results: It's Poverty, Stupid (With a bit of the iPhone)," FairTest. [Online]. Available: https://fairtest.org/interpreting-pisa-results-its-poverty-stupid-with-a-bit-of-the-iphone/

"Introducing ChatGPT," OpenAi, 30 November 2022. [Online]. Available: https://openai.com/index/chatgpt/

V. Irwin et al., "Projections of Education Statistics to 2030," NCES. National Center for Education Statistics, 28 Feburary 2024. [Online]. Available: https://nces.ed.gov/programs/PES/section-1.asp

"Is Education Obsolete? Sugata Mitra at the MIT Media Lab," Civic Media, 16 May 2012. [Online]. Available: https://civic.mit.edu/index.html%3Fp=804.html

B. Jeffreys et al., "School absence fines for parents to rise by £20 in England," BBC, 29 Feburary 2024. [Online]. Available: https://www.bbc.co.uk/news/education-68420275

P. A. Jennings, A. A. DeMauro and P. Misschenko, *Handbook of Mindfulness-Based Programmes*. Routledge, 2019.

P. E. Jennings, *The Trauma–Sensitive Classroom – Building Resilience with Compassionate Teaching*. W. W. Norton & Company, 2018.

J. Jerrim and Sam Sims, "The Teaching and Learning International Survey (TALIS)," Department for Education, June 2019. [Online]. Available: https://assets.publishing.service.gov.uk/media/5f6484c2e90e075a01d2f4ce/TALIS_2018_research.pdf

L. Jin, "Cultural Foiundations of Learning: East and West," [Report]. Cambridge University Press, 2012.

J. T. Gatto. [Online]. Available: https://en.wikipedia.org/wiki/John_Taylor_Gatto

J. P. Johnson, T. Lenartowicz and S. Apud, "Cross-Cultural Competence in International Business: Toward a Definition and a Model," *Journal of International Business Studies*, vol. 37. pp. 525–543, 2006.

P. Kaledio, A. Robert and L. Frank, "The Impact of Artificial Intelligence on Students' Learning Experience." 1 Feburary 2024. [Online]. Available: http://dx.doi.org/10.2139/ssrn.4716747

G. Kelchtermans, "Teachers' Emotions in Educational Reforms: Self-Understanding, Vulnerable Commitment and Micropolitical Literacy," *Teaching and Teacher Education*, vol. 21, no. 8, pp. 995–1006, 2005.

"Key UK education statistics. British Educational Suppliers Association, 11 2022. [Online]. Available: https://www.besa.org.uk/key-uk-education-statistics/

Khan Academy. [Online]. Available: https://www.khanacademy.org/

A. Kingsley, *My Secret# EdTech Diary: Looking at Educational Technology through a wider lens*. Hachette UK, 2021.

A. Kingsley, "6 Considerations For A School District's AI Strategy," *Forbes*, 17 July 2024. [Online]. Available: https://www.forbes.com/sites/forbestechcouncil/2024/07/17/6-considerations-for-a-school-districts-ai-strategy/

A. Kingsley, "Don't fear AI: how to harness its power for good," School News Australia. [Online]. Available: https://www.school-news.com.au/education/the-power-of-ai/

A. Kingsley, "Ignore NAEP. Better Yet, Abolish It," Education Week, 06 June 2022. [Online]. Available: https://www.edweek.org/teaching-learning/opinion-ignore-naep-better-yet-abolish-it/2022/06

A. Kingsley, "Is Knowledge Obsolete?," Forbes Technology Council, 07 March 2022. [Online]. Available: https://www.forbes.com/councils/forbestechcouncil/2022/03/04/is-knowledge-obsolete/

A. Kingsley, *My School & Multi Academy Trust Growth Guide*. John Catt Education, 2023.

A. Kingsley, *My School & Multi-Academy Trust Growth Guide*. Hodder Education, 2023.

A. Kingsley, *My School Governance Handbook: Keeping It Simple, A Step by Step Guide and Checklist for All School Governors*. John Catt Educational, 2022.

R. Kizilcec et al., "Perceived Impact of Generative AI on Assessments: Comparing Educator and Student Perspectives in Australia, Cyprus, and the United States," [Report]. 2024.

https://www.researchgate.net/publication/382625237_Perceived_Impact_of_Generative_AI_on_Assessments_Comparing_Educator_and_Student_Perspectives_in_Australia_Cyprus_and_the_United_States

A. Klein, "Virtual Learning Was Better for Some Kids. Here's What Teachers Learned From Them," Education Week, 18 August 2021. [Online]. Available: https://www.edweek.org/teaching-learning/virtual-learning-was-better-for-some-kids-heres-what-teachers-learned-from-them/2021/08

K. Kristjánsson, "Recent Work on Flourishing as the Aim of Education: A Critical Review," *British Journal of Educational Studies*, vol. 65, no. 1, pp. 87–107, 2017.

"Lack of progress on closing educational inequalities disadvantaging millions throughout life," Institue of Fiscal Studies, 16 August 2022. [Online]. Available: https://ifs.org.uk/inequality/press-release/lack-of-progress-on-closing-educational-inequalities-disadvantaging-millions-throughout-life/

D. Lanier and K. Shelton, *The Promises and Perils of AI in Education: Ethics and Equity Have Entered The Chat*. Lanier Learning, 2024.

S. A. Larsen, "Are Australian Students' Academic Skills Declining? Interrogating 25 Years of National and International Standardised Assessment Data," *Australian Journal of Social Issues*, vol. 21, no. 5, pp. 1–32, 2024.

S. Larsen, "Are the latest NAPLAN results really an 'epic fail'?," The Conversation.com, 14 August 2024. [Online]. Available: https://theconversation.com/are-the-latest-naplan-results-really-an-epic-fail-236782

"Learning about Teaching – initial findings from the measures of effective teaching project," [Report]. Bill & Melissa Gates Foundation, 2010.

M. Lees, "Estonian Education System 1990–2016 'Reforms and their Impact'," 2016. [Online]. Available: https://4liberty.eu/wp-content/uploads/2016/08/Estonian-Education-System_1990-2016.pdf

F. Leon, [Online]. Available: https://leonfurze.com/

LGA, "Better performance for council-maintained schools than academies, says study," Prospect, August 2023. [Online]. https://prospect.org.uk/news/better-performance-for-council-maintained-schools-than-academies-says-study

S. Livingstone and K. Pothong, "Education Data Futures: Critical, Regulatory and Practical Reflections," Digital Futures Commission, 5 Rights Foundation, 2022. [Online]. Available: https://educationdatafutures.digitalfuturescommission.org.uk/

S. Livingstone and G. Shekhawat, "AI and Children's Rights." 29 May 2024. [Online]. Available: https://www.norrag.org/ai-and-childrens-rights/

Local Government Association. [Online]. Available: https://www.local.gov.uk/

L. Loewus, "Teaching Force Growing Faster Than Student Enrollment Once Again," Education Week, 17 August 2017. [Online]. Available: https://www.edweek.org/leadership/teaching-force-growing-faster-than-student-enrollment-once-again/2017/08

C. Long, "What can we really learn from the 2022 PISA test results?," neaToday, January 2024. [Online]. Available: https://www.nea.org/nea-today/all-news-articles/pisa-2022

T. Loveless, "The NAEP proficiency myth," Brookings Institute, 13 June 2016. [Online]. Available: https://www.brookings.edu/articles/the-naep-proficiency-myth/

R. Luckin, Machine Learning and Human Intelligence: The Future of Education for the 21st Century. UCL IOE Press, 2018.

W. B. MacLeod and M. Urquiola, "Is Education Consumption or Investment? Implications for School Competition," *Annual Review of Economics*, vol. 11, pp. 563–589, 2019.

P. Main, "Social Learning Theory – Bandura," Structural Learning, 24 October 2022. [Online]. Available: https://www.structural-learning.com/post/social-learning-theory-bandura

J. Mannion and K. McAllister, *Fear Is The Mind Killer: Why Learning to Learn Deserves Lesson Time – And How to Make it Work for Your Pupils*. John Catt, 2020.

J. Mannion and N. Mercer, "Learning to Learn: Improving Attainment, Closing the Gap at Key Stage 3," *The Curriculum Journal*, vol. 27, pp. 1–26, 2016.

J. Manyika et al., "Jobs Lost, Jobs Gained: Workforce Transitions in a Time of Automation," McKinsey Global Institute, December 2017.

K. Martin et al., "Supporting the recruitment and retention of teachers in schools with high proportions of disadvantaged pupils: Understanding current practice around practice review," [Report]. Education Endowment Foundation, 2023.

"MAT Tracker: Mapping the country's multi-academy trusts," [Online]. TES Magazine, 1 July 2024. [Online]. Available: https://www.tes.com/magazine/leadership/data/mat-tracker-multi-academy-trusts-map

H. McCormack, "The over-subscription of specialist schools: Too many children are being failed," SEND Network, 23 Feburary 2023. [Online].

D. McLean, "An image problem," National Foundation for Educational Research, 05 June 2024. [Online]. Available: www.nfer.ac.uk/blogs/an-image-problem

L. Meakin, "AI and assessment: Rethinking assessment strategies and supporting students in appropriate use of AI," Chartered College, 13 May 2024. [Online]. Available: https://my.chartered.college/impact_article/ai-and-assessment-rethinking-assessment-strategies-and-supporting-students-in-appropriate-use-of-ai/

"Mental health is main cause of rising absences in England, say headteachers," *The Guardian*, 14 June 2024. [Online]. Available: https://www.theguardian.com/education/article/2024/jun/14/mental-health-anxiety-absences-pupils-schools-covid-pandemic-headteachers

Ministry of Education and Culture Finland, "Reflections on Competences for Human Flourishing," December 2023. [Online].

S. Mitra, "Hole in the Wall Education Project," [Online]. Available: https://www.hole-in-the-wall.com/

S. Mitra, "Kids can teach themselves," TED Talks, Feburary 2007. [Online]. Available: https://www.ted.com/talks/sugata_mitra_kids_can_teach_themselves?subtitle=en

A. Molnar, "Virtual Schools in the U.S. 2019," University of Colorado. May 2019. [Online]. Available: https://nepc.colorado.edu/sites/default/files/publications/Virtual%20Schools%202019.pdf

R. Montacute and E. Holt-White, "Views on the ground from parents, providers and teachers," [Report]. The Sutton Trust, 2021.

"More MATs pooling GAG and reserves to look after 'financially weaker schools'," FE News, 05 March 2024. [Online]. Available: https://www.fenews.co.uk/education/more-mats-pooling-gag-and-reserves-to-look-after-financially-weaker-schools-or-target-additional-resource/

"Multi-academy trusts: Benefits, challenges and functions," Ofsted, July 2019. [Online]. Available: https://www.gov.uk/government/publications/multi-academy-trusts-benefits-challenges-and-functions

"National Assessment Program – Literacy and Numeracy," Australian Department for Education. [Online]. Available: https://www.education.gov.au/national-assessment-program/national-assessment-program-literacy-and-numeracy

National Association of Head Teachers (NAHT). [Online]. Available: https://www.naht.org.uk/

National Center for Education Statistics (NCES). [Online]. Available: https://nces.ed.gov/

"National Curriculum," Department for Education, 2014. [Online]. Available: https://www.gov.uk/government/collections/national-curriculum

National Education Association (NEA). [Online]. Available: https://www.nea.org/

National Education Union (NEU). [Online]. Available: neu.org.uk

National Foundation for Educational Research (NFER). [Online]. Available: https://www.nfer.ac.uk/

"National strategy needed to end anxiety of school admissions scramble says school leaders' union," National Association of Head Teachers (NAHT), 01 March 2023. [Online]. Available: https://www.naht.org.uk/News/Latest-comments/Press-room/ArtMID/558/ArticleID/1969/National-strategy-needed-to-end-anxiety-of-school-admissions-scramble-says-school-leaders-union

NCFE. [Online]. Available: https://www.ncfe.org.uk/

NetFlix. [Online]. Available: https://www.netflix.com/

"NetSupport – Award Winning Education Solutions," [Online]. Available: www.netsupport-software.com

"New report shows practical strategies for MAT growth," *Education Business*, 07 Feburary 2023. [Online]. Available: https://www.educationbusinessuk.net/news/07022023/new-report-shows-practical-strategies-mat-growth

"No Child Left Behind (NCLB) Act," [Report]. U.S. Department of Education, 2002.

"No Child Left Behind Act," Wikipedia, 2001. [Online]. Available: https://en.wikipedia.org/wiki/No_Child_Left_Behind_Act

"NORRAG Global Education Centre," Geneva Graduate Institute. [Online]. Available: https://www.norrag.org

"Number and percentage of students enrolled in degree-granting postsecondary institutions, by distance education participation, location of student, level of enrollment, and control and level of institution," National Center for Educational Statistics (NCES), 2021. [Online]. Available: https://nces.ed.gov/programs/digest/d22/tables/dt22_311.15.asp

T. O'Brien, *Rethinking School Inspection: Is there a better way?* John Catt Educational Limited, 2023.

T. O'Brien, *School Self-Review – A Sensible Approach: How to Know and Tell the Story of Your School.* John Catt Educational Ltd, 2022.

"OECD and Pisa tests are damaging education worldwide," *The Guardian*. [Online]. Available: https://www.theguardian.com/education/2014/may/06/oecd-pisa-tests-damaging-education-academics

OECD, "Future of Education and Skills 2030," [Report]. 2019. p. 5.

OECD, "Learning Compass 2030," 2019. [Online]. Available: https://www.oecd.org/content/dam/oecd/en/about/projects/edu/education-2040/1-1-learning-compass/OECD_Learning_Compass_2030_Concept_Note_Series.pdf

OECD, Organisation for Economic Co-operation and Development (OECD). [Online]. Available: https://www.oecd.org/

OECD, PISA High Performing Systems for Tomorrow (HPST). [Online]. Available: https://www.oecd.org/en/about/projects/pisa-high-performing-systems-for-tomorrow-hpst.html

OECD, Programme for International Student Assessment (PISA). [Online]. Available: https://www.oecd.org/en/about/programmes/pisa.html

OECD Yearbook 2014: Better Policies for Better Lives. [Report]. OECD, 2014. p. 46. ISSN 0029-7054.

"OECD: Indicator C1. How much is spent per student on educational Institutions," 2019. [Online]. Available: https://www.oecd-ilibrary.org/how-much-is-spent-per-student-on-educational-institutions_0fdcbb3b-en.pdf

M. Oliver, "It's not true that academies care more about money than pupils," Schools Week, 05 July 2018. [Online]. Available: https://schoolsweek.co.uk/its-not-true-that-academies-care-more-about-money-than-pupils/

Online Education & E-Learning Statistics UK. Oxford Learning College, 2023. [Online]. Available: https://www.oxfordcollege.ac/news/online-education-statistics/

S. Oreg, "Personality, Context, and Resistance to Organizational Change," *European Journal of Work and Organizational Psychology*, vol. 15, no. 1, pp. 73–101, 2004.

"Parental Engagement Toolkit," Education Endowment Foundation (EEF). [Online]. Available: https://educationendowmentfoundation.org.uk/education-evidence/teaching-learning-toolkit/parental-engagement

Parliament UK, "Nick Gibb response to question for the Department for Education," 9 2 2023. [Online]. Available: https://questions-statements.parliament.uk/written-questions/detail/2023-01-11/121149

H. Patel, "Five policies to make AI-enabled learning safe and equitable," Schools Week, 23 Feburary 2024. [Online]. Available: https://schoolsweek.co.uk/five-policies-to-make-ai-enabled-learning-safe-and-equitable/

E. Peirson-Hagger, "Salman Khan's third attempt to change the world of education," TES Magazine, 12 August 2024. [Online]. Available: https://www.tes.com/magazine/analysis/general/salman-khan-how-ai-can-transform-education

E. Peirson-Hagger, "The scale of the teacher retention crisis revealed," TES Magazine, 21 June 2024. [Online]. Available: https://www.tes.com/magazine/analysis/general/teacher-retention-scale-crisis-revealed-dfe-data

M. K. Pennington and J. Trinidad, "Nuance in the Noise: The complex reality of teacher shortages," [Report]. Bellwether Education Partners, 2019.

M. Perkins et al., "The Artificial Intelligence Assessment Scale (AIAS): A Framework for Ethical Integration of Generative AI in Educational Assessment," *Journal of University Teaching and Learning Practice*, vol. 21, no. 6, 2024.

J. Perryman et al., "Beyond Ofsted – Final report of the inquiry," [Report]. National Education Union (NEU), 2023.

"Persistent absence and support for disadvantaged pupils – Report Summary," UK Parliament, 27 September 2023. [Online]. Available: https://publications.parliament.uk/pa/cm5803/cmselect/cmeduc/970/summary.html

Peterborough Keys Academy Trust. [Online]. Available: www.pkat.co.uk

"PISA 2012 Results: What Makes Schools Successful? – Volume IV," [Report]. OECD, 2013. p. 54.

M. Pitman, *The Connection Curriculum: Igniting Positive Change in Schools Through Sustainable Connection*. Amba Press, 2024.

N. Plaister, "The current state of play for MATs", FFT Education Data Lab, 10 July 2024. [Online]. Available: https://ffteducationdatalab.org.uk/2024/07/the-current-state-of-play-for-mats/

N. Ponsford, "Labour must rethink schools' whole relationship with data," 22 August 2024. [Online]. Available: https://schoolsweek.co.uk/labour-must-rethink-schools-whole-relationship-with-data/

Public First. [Online]. Available: www.publicfirst.co.uk

"Public School Leaders Report 90 Percent Average Daily Student Attendance Rate in November 2023," NCES, 18 January 2024. [Online]. Available: https://nces.ed.gov/whatsnew/press_releases/1_18_2024.asp

Public Schools Act. UK Parliament, 1868. [Online]. Available: https://en.wikipedia.org/wiki/Public_Schools_Act_1868

"Pupil absence in schools in England," Department for Education, 2020. [Online]. Available: https://explore-education-statistics.service.gov.uk/find-statistics/pupil-absence-in-schools-in-england/2018-19

"Pupil attendance in schools – Headline facts and figures," Department for Education, 08 August 2024. [Online]. Available: https://explore-education-statistics.service.gov.uk/find-statistics/pupil-attendance-in-schools

"Review of best practice in parental engagement," Department for Education, 2011. [Online]. Available: https://www.gov.uk/government/publications/review-of-best-practice-in-parental-engagement

N. Roberts, S. Danechi and A. Lewis, "Falling pupil rolls in England and school closures in London," [Report]. House of Commons Library, 2023. CDP-0115.

K. Robinson and L. Aronica, *Creative Schools: The Grassroots Revolution That's Transforming Education*. Penguin Books, 2016.

K. Robinson, "Changing education paradigms," TED Talks, October 2010. [Online]. Available: https://www.ted.com/talks/sir_ken_robinson_changing_education_paradigms

T. Robinson, "Reimagining Alternative Education," Edutopia, 02 August 2021. [Online]. Available: https://www.edutopia.org/article/reimagining-alternative-education/

J. Rudolph, S. Tan and S. Tan, "ChatGPT: Bullshit Spewer or the End of Traditional Assessments in Higher Education?," *Journal of Applied Learning and Teaching*, vol. 1, no. 6, pp. 342–363, 2023.

N. Runyon, "Why "power skills" is the new term for soft skills in the hybrid work world," Thomson Reuters, 18 February 2022. [Online]. Available: https://www.thomsonreuters.com/en-us/posts/legal/power-skills-rebranding/

A. Saavedra, M. Polikoff and D. Silver, "Parents are not fully aware of, or concerned about, their children's school attendance," Brookings Institute, 26 March 2024. [Online]. Available: https://www.brookings.edu/articles/parents-are-not-fully-aware-of-or-concerned-about-their-childrens-school-attendance/

S. Sandhu "Sir Kevan Collins: What the education tsar wanted for the school catch-up plan versus what children will get," *The i newspaper*, 03 June 2021. [Online]. Available: https://inews.co.uk/news/education/sir-kevan-collins-education-tsar-wanted-school-catch-up-plan-versus-children-get-1033137

"Scaling up digital learning and skills in the world's most populous countries to drive education recovery. UNESCO, 20 04 2023. [Online]. Available: https://www.unesco.org/en/articles/scaling-digital-learning-and-skills-worlds-most-populous-countries-drive-education-recovery

H. G. Schmidt and J. H. C. Moust, "Factors Affecting Small-Group Tutorial Learning: A Review of Research," In *Problem-Based Learning*. Routledge, 2000. pp. 19–51.

"School attendance crisis: One in four secondary students persistently absent," *SecEd Magazine*, 30 January 2024. [Online]. Available: https://www.sec-ed.co.uk/content/news/school-attendance-crisis-one-in-four-secondary-students-persistently-absent/

"School capacity – national, regional, local authority," Department for Education, 02 June 2023. [Online]. Available: https://explore-education-statistics.service.gov.uk/data-tables/permalink/979cf255-eb21-48d0-ff74-08db6354f3ce

"School Enrolment Trends and Projections, ISA Research Report," [Report]. Independent Schools Australia, 2021.

"School Inspection Handbook," Ofsted. [Online]. Available: https://www.gov.uk/government/publications/school-inspection-handbook-eif

"School Performance in Academy Chains and Local Authorities – 2017," Education Policy Institute, 19 June 2018. [Online]. Available: https://epi.org.uk/publications-and-research/performance-academy-local-authorities-2017/

"School teachers' pay and conditions," Department for Education. [Online]. Available: https://www.gov.uk/government/publications/school-teachers-pay-and-conditions

"School workforce in England – reporting year 2023," Department for Education, 06 June 2024. [Online]. Available: https://explore-education-statistics.service.gov.uk/find-statistics/school-workforce-in-england

"Schools, pupils and their characteristics (Academic year 2023/24). Department for Education, 06 06 2024. [Online]. Available: https://explore-education-statistics.service.gov.uk/find-statistics/school-pupils-and-their-characteristics

Schoolsweek, "White paper: What academy shakeup means for trusts, councils and schools," 28 March 2022. [Online]. Available: https://schoolsweek.co.uk/white-paper-what-academy-shakeup-means-for-trusts-councils-and-schools/

SDG 4, "Ensure inclusive and equitable quality education and promote lifelong learning opportunities for all," United Nations. [Online]. Available: https://sdgs.un.org/goals/goal4

M. Sellars et al., "Conversations on Critical Thinking: Can Critical Thinking Find Its Way Forward as the Skill Set and Mindset of the Century?," *Education Sciences, vol. 8, no. 4, p. 205, 2018.

"SEND review: Right support, right place, right time," Department for Education, March 2022. [Online]. Available: https://www.gov.uk/government/consultations/send-review-right-support-right-place-right-time

"Shape the Future: How educational system leaders can respond to the provocations of artificial intelligence," [Report]. Educate Ventures, 2024.

L. Sharma, *Building Culture: A Handbook to Harnessing Human Nature to Create Strong School Teams*. John Catt Education, 2023.

"Shifting career motivations are not to blame for worsening teacher shortages," NFER, 18 July 2024. [Online]. Available: https://www.nfer.ac.uk/blogs/shifting-career-motivations-are-not-to-blame-for-worsening-teacher-shortages/

J. Sibbald, "Greater Manchester's MBacc: What digital skills education could look like," AQi, 12 October 2023. [Online]. Available: https://www.aqi.org.uk/blogs/greater-manchesters-mbacc-what-digital-skills-education-could-look-like/

L. Sibieta, "How does school spending per pupil differ across the UK?," Institute of Fiscal Studies (IFS), 21 April 2023. [Online]. Available: https://ifs.org.uk/publications/how-does-school-spending-pupil-differ-across-uk

L. Sibieta, "School spending in England: A guide to the debate during the 2024 general election," Institute for Fiscal Studies, June 2024.

J. Silberg and J. Manyika, "Notes from the AI frontier: Tackling the bias in AI (and in humans)," [Report]. McKinsey Global Institue, 2019.

D. C. Simmons and E. J. Kameenui, "A Focus on Curriculum Design: When Children Fail," *Focus on Exception Children*, vol. 28, no. 7, pp. 1–16, 1996.

Sir Ken Robinson. [Online]. Available: https://www.sirkenrobinson.com/

Siri. Apple Corporation. [Online]. Available: https://www.apple.com/uk/siri/

A. Smolansky et al., "Educator and Student Perspectives on the Impact of Generative AI on Assessments in Higher Education," [Report]. 2023. https://dl.acm.org/doi/10.1145/3573051.3596191

"SMSC in Education: Everything you need to know," Votes for Schools, 2024. [Online]. Available: https://www.votesforschools.com/blog/smsc/

"Social Science Research Network," SSRN. [Online]. Available: https://www.ssrn.com/index.cfm/en/

Sophia High School. [Online]. Available: www.sophiahigh.school

P. Sotiriadou et al., "The Role of Authentic Assessment to Preserve Academic Integrity and Promote Skill Development and Employability," *Studies in Higher Education*, vol. 45, no. 11, pp. 2132–2148, 2019.

SPARX Learning. [Online]. Available: https://sparx-learning.com/

SRI International. [Online]. Available: https://en.wikipedia.org/wiki/SRI_International

L. Stanford, "Charter Schools Are Outperforming Traditional Public Schools: 6 Takeaways From a New Study," Education Week, 06 June 2023. [Online]. Available: https://www.

edweek.org/policy-politics/charter-schools-are-outperforming-traditional-public-schools-6-takeaways-from-a-new-study/2023/06

M. Stevenson, "Education for Human Flourishing," [Report]. OECD, 2023.

D. Stipek, Motivation to Learn: Integrating Theory and Practice. Allyn & Bacon, 2002.

"Strengthening education systems and innovation," UNICEF. [Online]. Available: https://www.unicef.org/education/strengthening-education-systems-innovation

"Superannuation for teachers and education workers," NGS, 01 July 2024. [Online]. Available: https://www.ngssuper.com.au/articles/news/super-teachers-education-worker

"Sure Start Centres," Wikipedia, 1998. [Online]. Available: https://en.wikipedia.org/wiki/Sure_Start

"TALIS 2018 Results (Volume II): Teachers and School Leaders as Valued Professionals," [Report]. Paris: OECD, 2020.

A. Tang, The Leader's Guide to Resilience: How to Use Soft Skills to Get Hard Results. FT Publishing International, 2021.

F. W. Taylor, "Taylorism," Wikipedia. [Online]. Available: https://en.wikipedia.org/wiki/Frederick_Winslow_Taylor

TeachAI, "AI Guidance For Schools Toolkit," 2024. [Online]. Available: https://www.teachai.org/toolkit

"Teacher pay scales 2024–25: What will your salary look like?," TES Magazine, 29 July 2024. [Online]. Available: https://www.tes.com/magazine/analysis/general/teacher-pay-scales-how-much-are-teachers-paid-england#Main%20UK

"Teacher Salaries 2024," Department of Education, Western Asutralia, 2024. [Online]. Available: https://www.education.wa.edu.au/teacher-salaries

"Teaching and Learning Toolkit," Education Endowment Foundation. [Online]. Available: https://educationendowmentfoundation.org.uk/education-evidence/teaching-learning-toolkit

"The AI Educator," Dan Fitzpatrick. [Online]. Available: https://www.theaieducator.io/

"The Association of British Schools Overseas (AoBSO)," [Online]. Available: www.aobso.uk.

"The EBacc 10 years on: should it stay or should it go?," National Association of Head Teachers (NAHT), 2019. [Online]. Available: https://www.naht.org.uk/News/Latest-comments/Thought-leadership/ArtMID/590/ArticleID/786/The-EBacc-10-years-on-should-it-stay-or-should-it-go-Case-study-three

"The Education Act," UK Parliament, 1870. [Online]. Available: https://www.parliament.uk/about/living-heritage/transformingsociety/livinglearning/school/overview/1870educationact/

"The Education Act (Balfour Act)," [Report]. UK Parliament, 1902.

The Education Company. [Online]. Available: http://www.educationcompany.co.uk/

"The Features of Effective School Groups," Education Policy Institute, 16 April 2024. [Online]. Available: https://epi.org.uk/publications-and-research/the-features-of-effective-school-groups/

The Foundation for Education Development (FED). [Online]. Available: https://fed.education/

"The Future of Jobs Report 2020," World Economic Forum, 20 October 2020. [Online]. Available: https://www.weforum.org/publications/the-future-of-jobs-report-2020/

The Huffington Post. [Online]. Available: https://www.huffingtonpost.co.uk/

The ICT Evangelist. Mark Anderson. [Online]. Available: https://ictevangelist.com/

The Institute of Fiscal Studies (IFS). [Online]. Available: www.ifs.org.uk.

"The National Association of School-Based Teacher Trainers," NASBTT. [Online]. Available: https://www.nasbtt.org.uk/

"The National Center for Fair and Open Testing," FairTest. [Online]. Available: https://www.fairtest.org

The National Center on Education and the Economy (NCEE). [Online]. Available: https://ncee.org/

"The NEU case against academisation," National Education Union, 12 August 2022. [Online]. Available: neu.org.uk/advice/your-rights-work/academisation/neu-case-against-academisation

"The state of popular education in England. Vol.1," [Report]. H.M. Stationary Office, 1861.

"The True Teacher," *Texas Heart Institue Journal*, vol. 37, no. 3, pp. 334–335, 2010.

"The Vital Role of Extracurricular Activities for SEND pupils," Huntingdon Research School, March 2024. [Online]. Available: https://researchschool.org.uk/huntington/news/secondary-case-study-the-vital-role-of-extracurricular-activities-for-send-cohorts

"These 3 charts show the global growth in online learning," World Economic Forum, 27 January 2022. [Online]. Available: https://www.weforum.org/agenda/2022/01/online-learning-courses-reskill-skills-gap/

"Total enrollment and enrollment in exclusively distance education courses of the 120 largest degree-granting postsecondary institutions, by selected characteristics and institution: Fall 2021," National Center for Educational Statistics, 2021. [Online]. Available: https://nces.ed.gov/programs/digest/d22/tables/dt22_312.10.asp

A. Tricot and J. Sweller, "Domain-Specific Knowledge and Why Teaching Generic Skills Does Not Work," *Educational Psychology Review*, vol. 26, no. 2, pp. 265–283, 2013.

M. Trucano, *AI and the Next Digital Divide in Education*. Brookings Institute, 10 July 2023.

A. Turing, "The Turing Test," 1950. [Online]. Available: https://en.wikipedia.org/wiki/Turing_test

U.S Government Accountability Office. [Online]. Available: www.gao.gov

"Understanding Attendance: Findings on the drivers of pupil absence," ImpactEd Evaluation, January 2024. [Online]. Available: https://www.evaluation.impactedgroup.uk/research-and-resources/understanding-attendance

Unity Schools Partnership. [Online]. Available: www.unitysp.co.uk

"Updates to contribution rates," Teachers Pensions, 09 April 2024. [Online]. Available: https://www.teacherspensions.co.uk/news/employers/2024/02/updates-to-contribution-rates.aspx

"Use of Artificial Intelligence in Education Delivery and Assessment," UK Parliament, 23 January 2024. [Online]. Available: https://post.parliament.uk/research-briefings/post-pn-0712/

"Vision 2030 – Education in Saudi Arabia," HMC, 29 March 2022. [Online]. Available: https://www.hmc.org.uk/blog-posts/vision-2030-education-in-saudi-arabia/

"Warm Data Labs," The International Bateson Institute. [Online]. Available: https://batesoninstitute.org/warm-data-labs/

A. Webb, *The Big Nine: How the Tech Titans and Their Thinking Machines Could Warp Humanity*. PublicAffairs, 2019.

R. Wegerif and L. Major, *The Theory of Educational Technology: Towards a Dialogic Foundation for Design*. Routledge, 2023.

"What is a strong trust? A CST Discussion Paper," Confederation of School Trusts, 2021. [Online]. Available: https://cstuk.org.uk/assets/pdfs/ICE_10102_CST_What_Is_A_Strong_Trust_Discussion%20Paper2.pdf

"What is AI (artificial intelligence)?," McKinsey & Company, 03 April 2024. [Online]. Available: https://www.mckinsey.com/featured-insights/mckinsey-explainers/what-is-ai

"What is digital citizenship? – A guide for teachers," Future Learn, 03 September 2021. [Online]. Available: https://www.futurelearn.com/info/blog/what-is-digital-citizenship-teacher-guide

"What is the average graduate salary?," Institute of Student Employers (ISE), 10 November 2023. [Online]. Available: https://insights.ise.org.uk/attraction-and-marketing/blog-what-is-the-average-graduate-salary/

"What is the Impact of Artificial Intelligence on Students?," eSchool News, 05 Feburary 2024. [Online]. Available: https://www.eschoolnews.com/digital-learning/2024/02/05/what-is-the-impact-of-artificial-intelligence-on-students/#:~:text=Overall%2C%20the%20positive%20impact%20of,dynamic%20and%20adaptive%20educational%20experience

"What the Research Says on Socialization," Coalition for Responsible Home Education. [Online]. Available: https://responsiblehomeschooling.org/research/summaries/homeschooling-socialization/

F. Whittaker, "Fact check: Do council schools really outperform academies?," Schoolsweek, 03 August 2023. [Online]. Available: https://schoolsweek.co.uk/fact-check-do-council-schools-really-outperform-academies/

"Why Is Project-Based Learning Important? The many merits of using project-based learning in the classroom," Edutopia, 19 October 2007. [Online]. Available: https://www.edutopia.org/project-based-learning-guide-importance

M. Williams and M. Davies, "Mental health cited for pupils missing school," BBC, 27 May 2024. [Online]. Available: https://www.bbc.co.uk/news/articles/cd11g7jz92ro

D. T. Willingham, *Why Don't Students Like School?: A Cognitive Scientist Answers Questions About How the Mind Works and What It Means for the Classroom*. Jossey-Bass, 2021.

J. Winslow, "America's Digital Divide," The Pew Chaitable Trust, 26 July 2019. [Online]. Available: https://www.pewtrusts.org/en/trust/archive/summer-2019/americas-digital-divide

"Working together to improve school attendance," Department for Education, 07 March 2024. [Online]. Available: https://www.gov.uk/government/publications/working-together-to-improve-school-attendance

"Workload challenge: Analysis of responses," Department for Education, 06 February 2015. [Online]. Available: https://www.gov.uk/government/publications/workload-challenge-analysis-of-teacher-responses

J. Worth and S. Tang, "Next government needs long-term pay strategy that will help teacher supply challenge," National Foundation for Educational Research, 14 May 2024. [Online]. Available: https://www.nfer.ac.uk/blogs/next-government-needs-long-term-pay-strategy-that-will-help-teacher-supply-challenge/

D. Wyse and A. Bradbury, "Reading Wars or Reading Reconciliation," *Review of Education*, vol. 10, no. 1, pp. 1–53, 2022.

J.-Y. Yen et al., "Social Anxiety in Online and Real-Life Interaction and Their Associated Factors," *Cyberpsychology, Behavior and Social Networking*, vol. 15, no. 1, pp. 7–12, 2012.

W. J. Yin, "Will Our Educational System Keep Pace with AI? A Student's Perspective on AI and Learning," Educause, 24 January 2024. [Online]. Available: https://er.educause.edu/articles/2024/1/will-our-educational-system-keep-pace-with-ai-a-students-perspective-on-ai-and-learning

A. Zickafoose et al., "Barriers and Challenges Affecting Quality Education (Sustainable Development Goal #4) in Sub-Saharan Africa by 2030," *Sustainability*, vol. 16, no. 7, p. 2657, 2024.

M. Ziegler, "Maps of school teacher salary averages for 2024," Fox news, 26 May 2024. [Online]. Available: https://www.livenowfox.com/news/school-teacher-salary-average-map-2024-how-much-paid-state

Index

Pages in *italics* represent figures and **bold** indicates tables in the text.

Academies Act (2010) 57
academy schools 57
Aerts, Carla 84, 103, 114–115
"Agency in the Anthropocene" 11
"AI and Children's Rights," NORRAG Global Education Centre 97
"AI and the next digital divide in education," Brookings Institute 100
AI assessment scale (AIAS) 106–107
Alcock, Phillip 103, 115; "Does AI change the role of the teacher?" 83
Alexa 33, 87
alternative provision (AP) school 127–129
"America's Digital Divide," Pew Charitable Trust 146
Anderson, Mark 105, 111
Aristotle 13
Artificial General Intelligence (AGI) 111
artificial intelligence (AI) 33, 41–42, 82–83, 171–172, 174, 197; AI assessment scale (AIAS) 106–107; and assessment 104–106, 109; bad prompt *vs.* good prompt in **90**; benefits of AI in education **98**; bias mitigation, strategies for 117; black box 114–116; challenges and concerns 94–101; as collaborator 102–104; common generative tasks *87*; data privacy and security 94; decision-making, strengths in 117; definition of 85; digital divide conversation 99–100; education, ethics in 113–118; educator perspectives on 111–113; equity and access of tools 99; ethical use of 101, 109; generative/non-generative AI 87–88; human connection 109–111; international perspectives on 83–85; opportunities and benefits 87–94; personalised learning 92, 94, 109; PREP framework 90–91; principles for use in education 93; prompting *91*; skills development, impact on 98; strategies 101–102; terms and their descriptions of 86–87; visibility 116–118
Artificial Superintelligence (ASI) 111
Asian countries, respect for educators in 162
attendance of school children, improving: absenteeism/absent rates 124–125; causes of disengagement 132–133; changing spaces 129–132; fines 134–135; hybrid and online schools 126–129; parental disconnect 133–135; parents, role of 136–138
Australia 15–16, 84, 128, 157, 196

Bailey, Anna 207–208
Baker, Sarah 75–76
Balfour Education Act 30
Bandura, Albert 187
Barton, Geoff 132, 134

Batson, Daniel, *Altruism in Humans* 187
Beyond Ofsted 10, 14
Blair, Tony 57
Bleakley, Charlotte, "How we've used AI to reduce teacher workloads" 89
Bloom, Benjamin, "2 Sigma Problem" 174–175, *175*
Bousted, Mary 67
British Educational Suppliers Association (BESA) 61, 68
Brookings Institute 100, 133
Burnham, Andy 38

CAMHS (Child and Adolescent Mental Health Services) 134–135
Carter, David, *Leading Academy Trusts* 72
Cauchi, Kat 108, 127, 161, 209–210
Center for Democracy and Technology (CDT) 94
centre-assessed grades (CAGs) 208
CENTURY tool 92–93
"Charter schools and labour market outcomes," *Journal of Labour Economics* 17
"Charter Schools Are Outperforming Traditional Public Schools," *Education Week* 17
ChatGPT 13, 82, 92
China 42, 114, 162
Christodoulou, Daisy, *Seven Myths about Education* 40, 107
Clarke, Arthur C. 174
"Classroom tips to help integrate soft skills," EtonX 48
"Closing the Digital Divide for the Millions of Americans without Broadband," U.S. Government, Accountability Office 145–146
Collins, Kevan 166
community-focused school 65, 70
Confederation of School Trusts (CST) 60, 68; "What is a strong trust" 205
continuous assessment 207–208, 211
Coulson, Tim 20, 23, 69–70, 75, 77
Coursera learning platform 142
Crehan, L. 42

critical spirit 45
critical thinking 45–46, 50
"Critical thinking in the AI era: An exploration of EFL students' perceptions, benefits, and limitations," *Cogent Education* 99
"Cultivating Awareness and Resilience in Education" (CARE) 50
curiosity, human 42–43, 49–50, 181–182, 184
"The current state of play for MATs," FFT Education Data 57
curriculum, balanced 4–5, 32, 35–41, 44–46, 52, 176–178, 186, 188; and assessment 102; current 32–34, 43, 126, 128, 207; curriculum and outcomes 66; hidden 170–172

Data Protection Impact Assessment (DPIA) 97
Department for Education (DfE) 124–125, 154, 180, 197; 2014 Workload Challenge 88; absence rates of school children 124; "Building strong academy trusts" 204; "Commissioning High-Quality Trusts" 206; "The Increase in Homeschooled Children" 143–144; "Opportunity for All: Strong Schools with Great Teachers for Your Child" 59; "Pupil Attendance in schools" 144; "review of best practice in parental engagement" 8; "School workforce in England" 158; "Working together to improve school attendance" 126
Derbyshire, Caroline 65
Dewey, John 187
digital citizenship 146–147, 183
Digital Citizenship Education (DCE) 147
digital divide conversation 99–100
digital equity 142, 145–147
digital literacy 53, 183–184
digital poverty 145
Digital Poverty Alliance 101, 145–146
Di'Iasio, Pepe 156; "ASCL analysis shows collapse in creative arts A-level entries" 5

"Don't fear AI: how to harness its power for good," *School News Australia* 95

"Do parental involvement interventions increase attainment?", Nuffield Foundation 8

"Do parents value school effectiveness?", *American Economic Review* 17

Dorrell, Ed, "Attendance: Another fine mess the government's got us into" 134

dropouts, school 124, 161, 165

Duckworth, Angela, *Grit: Why passion and resilience are the secrets to success* 52

Dweck, Carol 193

early career teachers (ECTs) 127, 157, 161

EBacc (English Baccalaureate) 5

EdTech (technology within education) 95, 117–118, 147, 149

The Education Company 58, 60

The Education Development Trust 126

Education Endowment Foundation (EEF) 88, 160, 167; Parental Engagement Toolkit 8

Education for Sustainable Development (ESD) 206

education, health and care plan (EHCP) 124, 156

education inspection framework (EIF) 10

Education Policy Institute (EPI) 70–71; "The Features of Effective School Groups" 74

Education Reform Act (1998) 4

efficiency *vs.* turnover, teacher 76

Elementary Education Act (3) of 1870. *see* Forster's Education Act

11 Child Rights Principles 95, *96*

emotional dependence 172

empathy 50–51, 163, 167, 186–188, 199, 215

"England's World Leading Attendance Drive Continues" 125

Estonia, education system in 22

"Every Student Succeeds Act (ESSA)" 14, 177

Exceed Academies Trust 89

"Fact check: Do council schools really outperform academies?", *SchoolsWeek* 67

Falcone, "Critical Thinking: What It Is and Why It Counts" 45–46

Federal Communications Commission 145

feedback mechanisms 8, 22–24, 77–79, 93, 104–106, 129, 132, 160, 162, 202

finance/financial factors 62–63, 74–76

Finn, Chester E., Jr, *Assessing the Nation's Report Card* 15

FirstPass platform 93

Fischer Family Foundation (FFF) 57–58

Fitzpatrick, Dan, "The AI Educator" 90–91, 171–172

"Five policies to make AI-enabled learning safe and equitable," *SchoolsWeek* 100

fixed mindset *194*; *see also* growth mindset

Flintoff, Clare 92, 103

Forster's Education Act 30

Foundation for Education Development (FED) 179, 189, 207

free schools 57, 63

"From Interest to Entry: The Teacher Pipeline From College Application to Initial Employment" 155

Fullen, Michael, *The New Meaning of Educational Change* 176

Furze, Leon 84, 103, 114; *Practical AI Strategies: Engaging with Generative AI in Education* 91

GAG (general annual grant) pooling 68–69, 166

Gatto, John 170–172; *Dumbing Us Down: The Hidden Curriculum of Compulsory Schooling* 172

General Certificate of Secondary Education (GCSE) 5, 20, 32, 207

general education (GE) 127

generative AI 87–88, 94, 104, 106; *see also* non-generative AI

GESS (Global Educational Supplies and Solutions) conference 164

Gibb, Nick 39, 59–60, 186; "The Purpose of Education" 180

global education 141–142
Goleman, Daniel 184
"Good Career Guide," Gatsby Foundation 7
good schools 10, 22–24, 165; elements of 24–25
Gove, Michael 32–33
Government Technology Magazine 146
grit 52–53
group work 49
growth in education system 193; accessibility and equity with assessment 207–208; barriers of 197; fear of change 198–201; funding limitations 201–204; global spending 202–204, **203**; LAs estimated number of pupils **196**; school places, increase in 194–197; strong and sustainability 204–207; system growth 197
growth mindset 49, 181–182, 184, 193, *194*; *see also* fixed mindset
Grundy, Mark 93–94
"Guidance for Generative AI in Education and Research," UNESCO 88

Halfpenny, Susan 146
Hamilton, Arran, "The Future of AI in Education: 13 things we can do to minimize the damage" 108
Harper, Nikki 172
Harrison, Bob 19, 31, 35
Hattie, John, "The Future of AI in Education: 13 things we can do to minimize the damage" 108
Henderson, Gary 113–114, 150
Herbert, Fred, "The True Teacher" 109
"Here's how many hours a week teachers work," *EducationWeek* 154
higher education 104–105, 142–143
High Performing Systems for Tomorrow (HPST) project 12–13; "Education for Human Flourishing" 13
Hirsch, E. D., *Cultural Literacy: What Every American Needs to Know* 41
Hoerr, T. R., "The Formative Five: Fostering Grit, Empathy, and Other Success Skills Every Student Needs" 51–52

Hollis, Emma 154
homeschooling 131, 143, 145, 172–173
human-to-human interaction 110, 142, 144
Hussain, Aftab 93
hybrid schools 128–129, 131, 182
hypothetical scenarios 49

"Improving school attendance by fostering a sense of community belonging," Education Development Trust 133
"Improving schools' performance: Are multi-academy trusts the answer?", House of Lords 71
inclusivity 6, 193
independent learning 48–49
Independent Schools Australia (ISA) 196
"In praise of small MATs: Why bigger doesn't always mean better," *Schools Week* 75
"Inspection Systems: How Top-Performing Nations Hold Schools Accountable," NCEE 14
Institute for Education, University College London 70
Institute for Fiscal Studies (IFS) 156–157, 203
intellectual dependence 172
isolation, social 62, 148, 150, 187
"It's not true that academies care more about money than pupils," *Schools Week* 75

Jaffal, Al, "Barriers general education teachers face regarding the inclusion of students with autism" 127
Japan 42
Jessop, Matt 20–21, 47, 77, 84–85, 112
Journal of Educational Change 177

Keegan, Gillian 59, 76, 88, 125
Khan, Sal 110–111
Kingsley, Al: "6 Considerations for A School District's AI Strategy" 101; *My School and Multi-Academy Trust Growth Guide* 57; *My Secret #EdTech Diary* 97

large language models (LLMs), AI 93
Larson, Sally, "Are the latest NAPLAN results really an 'epic fail'?" 15–16
leadership 75–76, 78, 84, 159–160, 164, 201; leadership transitions 63, 69; and management of school 4, 9; and quality 150; supportive 25
"Learning Skills Curriculum," Chartered College of Teaching 33
Leonard, Dave 97
Litmus test 2, 15, 32
Livingstone, Sonia 95, 97
Local Authorities (LAs) schools 57, 62–63, 66–68, 70–71, 73–74, 77, 126, 129, 132, 177, 195; decision making in 77–79; LAs estimated number of pupils **196**
Local Government Association (LGA) 67
Luckin, Rose, *Machine Learning and Human Intelligence: The future of education for the 21st century* 42
Luxford-Moore, Simon 20, 114

Maclean, Dawson 159
mainstream school 59, 126–128, 131
"A Marked Improvement," EEF 88
MAT Financial Insights survey (2023) 68
"MAT Tracker: mapping the country's multi-academy trusts," *TES Magazine* 59
McBride, Melissa 149
McGee, Craig 112, 116
Meier, Deborah, *Achieving Quality Education for All* 17
mental health: and home pressures 135; and inclusion 53
"Mental health cited for pupils missing school," BBC 133
Mikton, John 92, 111, 116, 179
mistakes and failure, embracing 49
Mitra, Sugata: and Clarke 174; "Hole in the Wall" 174; "Is Education Obsolete?" 110, 174
moral education 186
"More MATs pooling GAG and reserves to look after 'financially weaker schools' or 'target additional resource'", *FE News* 69

Moynihan, David 60
Muijs, Daniel 67
multi-academy trusts (MATs) 57–64, **58**, *58*, 66–67, 69, 71, 73–75, 89, 101, 197; advantages and drawbacks 71; larger/smaller MATs 74–76
Murdoch, Phillip 84

"The NAEP proficiency myth," Brookings Institute 15
The National Advisory Committee on Creative and Cultural Education (NACCCE) 35
National Assessment of Educational Progress (NAEP) tests 14–16
National Assessment Program–Literacy and Numeracy (NAPLAN) 15–16
National Center for Education Statistics (NCES) 125; "Education Expenditures by Country" 203; "Projection of Education Statistics" 195
National Center for Fair and Open Testing (FairTest) 11; "Interpreting PISA Results: It's Poverty, Stupid (With a bit of the iPhone)" 12
National Centre for Education and the Economy (NCEE) 14
National Curriculum in England and Wales 4, 39
National Education Association (NEA) 157
National Education Union (NEU) 68, 70; case against academisation 70
National Foundation for Educational Research (NFER) 159, 164, 167
"The Nation's Report Card". *see* National Assessment of Educational Progress (NAEP) tests
natural language processing (NLP) 93, 112
Netflix 87
newly qualified teachers (NQTs) 127
"New report shows practical strategies for MAT growth," *Education Business* 69
new schools, opening of 63

Nieves, Bonnie 91
non-generative AI 87–88; *see also* generative AI
"Nuance in the Noise: The Complex Reality of Teacher Shortages" 155

O'Brien, Tracy 20
OECD (Organisation for Economic Co-operation and Development) 37; "Education at a Glance 2019–Indicators" 202; "Evaluating post-pandemic education policies and combatting student absenteeism beyond COVID-19" 125; "Future of Education and Skills 2030" 34; "High-Performing School Systems" 10–11; OECD Learning Compass 34; PISA (*see* Programme for International Student Assessment (PISA))
"Off Task: EdTech Threats to Student Privacy and Equity in the Age of AI," CDT 94
Ofsted rating (Office for Standards in Education, Children's Services and Skills) 2, 129, 160, 162; "Independent review of teachers' professional development in schools: phase 1 findings" 4; school inspection 64; "Schools with deprived pupils 'still less likely to be judged good,' admits Ofsted" 9–10
Oliver, Martyn 75
one-size-fits-all education 5, 20, 130–131, 208
online colleges 142–143
online learning 129–131, 143, 149–150; digital equity 142, 145–147; school age 143–144
"Online School as an Agent of Socialisation," Connections Academy 148–149
online schools 129–131, 148–150
OpenAI 82
operational efficiency 66, 68
outdoor learning 47, 53

"The over-subscription of specialist schools: Too many children are being failed," SEND network 127
Oxford Learning College 143

parental and community involvement 7–8
Patel, Abid 115
Patel, Hamid 100
perception, power of 69–70
personal development 6
personalised learning 92, 94, 109, 130–131, 175
Pitman, Matt 128, 134, 161, 165, 199, 202, 209–210
play-based learning 182
PLN (professional learning network) 117
political change and educational reforms 175–179
Ponsford, Nic 18–19, 77
Poth, Rachelle Dené 108
power skills 35–37, 47, 53, 183, 185
Price, Helen 66
primary schools 57, 69, 71–72, 99, 112, 114, 124, 195, 197; guide for primary schools, QCA 37
problem-based learning (PBL) 38–39
problem-solving skills 49–50
Programme for International Student Assessment (PISA) 11–12, 57, 125
project-based learning 44, 50, 176, 181–183
provisional self-esteem 172
Public First 134
pupil outcomes, measures of 7
pupil referral units 128

Qualifications and Curriculum Authority (QCA) 37

Rajapakse, Shemal 39
Ravindran, Kavitha 117
Read, Pete 37, 44
recruitment and retention of teachers 64–65, 153–155, 195; challenges 166–167; compensation and respect 163–166; delta strategy for modelling

teacher pay 164–165; extra funding for education 156; first-year earnings comparison *157*; funding, increase of 166; international respect for teachers 162–163; misconceptions 162; pension 164; progression, opportunities for 158–159; rebuilding perception of teaching 163; respect for profession 166–168; salary gap 164; starting salary for ECT 157–158; undervalued perception of teaching 159–163; workload and pay 155–156, 160, 162–163

reflection and continuous improvement, evidence of 9

"Reflections on Competences for Human Flourishing" 13–14

Regional Schools Advisory Board 64

"Reimagining Alternative Education," Edutopia 129

Revised Code of Regulations (1872) 31, **31–32**

Reyk, Will Van 112, 116

"Risk Factors for School Absenteeism and Dropout: A Meta-Analytic Review" 124

Robinson, Ken 144; *Creative Schools: The Grassroots Revolution That's Transforming Education* 33–34

role-play 49

Rollett, Steve 67

"The Royal Commission on the Public Schools" 30

Runyon, Natalie, "Why 'power skills' is the new term for soft skills in the hybrid work world" 36

Saffron Academy Trust, Essex 65

Saudi Arabia, transformation of education in 178–179

"The scale of the teacher retention crisis revealed," *TES* magazine 153–154

"Scheme of Delegation" 70

Schleicher, Andreas 12, 34, 173

school boards 30

"School Performance in Academy Chains and Local Authorities," Education Policy Institute 67

school–pupil relationships 133

"Schools Inquiry Commission" 30

school teachers' pay and conditions document (STPCD) 157–158

secondary schools 24, 38, 57, 63, 70, 124, 133, 144, 195, 197

self-reflection 49

"SEND review: right support, right place, right time" 6

Senior Leadership Team (SLT) 126, 137

"Seven Lessons I Teach," *Huffington Post* 171

Shekhawat, Gazal 97

shortages of teacher 128, 131, 155, 159

Shulman, Lee 38–39

Sibbald, John 38, 47

Singapore 10, 167

single-academy trusts (SATs) 57, 59, 73

Siri 33, 87

Smale, Tim 20, 208–209

"SMSC in Education: Everything You Need to Know," Votes for Schools 6

SMSC (spiritual, moral, social, and cultural development) measures 6

social and emotional learning (SEL) programmes 185

social, emotional, and mental health (SEMH) 52, 124–125, 128, 131, 148, 166

socialisation 147–150

social learning 182, 187

Social Science Research Network (SSRN) 99

societal consensus and goals of education 179–188; adaptability and lifelong learning 184; balancing specialisation with broad-based skills 185–186; cultural competence 185; future career, preparation for 183, 188; love for knowledge and learning 180–182, 188; moral character 186–188; play and creativity 182; social and emotional

skills 184–185, 188; technological competence 183–184
soft skills 46–48; development in classrooms 48–49
South Korea 167
SPARX tool 93
Special Educational Needs (SEN) 64, 124
Special Educational Needs and Disabilities (SEND) 6, 127, 131–133, 135, 147
Special Educational Needs and Disabilities Coordinator (SENDCO) 50
specialisms 64–65
specialist school 127
standards of school 63
Steed, Mark 160
student-led testing models 211
Sure Start centres 132
surveillance, AI-powered 172
Sutton Trust 3, 7, 148; "10-point plan for closing the Attainment Gap" 7; "Views on the ground from parents, providers and teachers" 148; "What Makes Great Teaching?" 3

Tarn, Rob 126
"A Taxonomy for Learning, Teaching and Assessing" 44
"Taxonomy of Thinking Skills" 44
teacher-assessed grades (TAGs) 208
Teaching and Learning International Survey (TALIS) 154–155, 166
"Teaching and Learning Toolkit," Education Endowment Foundation 3
teaching quality of school 3
technological literacy 183
"The EBacc 10 years on: should it stay or should it go?", NAHT 5
"The Impact of Artificial Intelligence on Students' Learning Experience," SSRN 99
TLRs (teaching and learning responsibilities) 159
Toomey, Heather, "Turning data into insight and why data sharing is as vital as it is concerning" 97

traditional schools, social elements of 147–150
trust board 73, **73**, 78
Tucano, Michael 100
"2024 Online Learning Statistics," *Forbes* 142

"Understanding Socialisation," Coalition for Responsible Home Education 148
UNESCO (The United Nations Educational, Scientific and Cultural Organization) 88, 99
UNICEF 206
United Arab Emirates 164
The United Kingdom 40, 131, 143, 155, 157–158, 202–203; undervalued perception of teaching 160–163
The United States of America 14, 125, 155, 157–158, 203
Universal Design for Learning (UDL) principle 209
"Use of Artificial Intelligence in Education Delivery and Assessment" 88

Vacher, Kai 161–163
virtual learning. *see* online learning
"The Vital Role of Extracurricular Activities for SEND Pupils," Huntingdon Research School 6

Ward, William Arthur 109
warm data 19
Webb, Amy, *Big Nine* 114
Wemyss, Matthew 104
"What can we really learn from the 2022 PISA Test results?", neaToday 11–12
"What is a Good School, and Can Parents Tell? Evidence on the Multidimensionality of School Output" 16
"What is AI (artificial intelligence)?", McKinsey & Company 85
"What is the Impact of Artificial Intelligence on Students?", *eSchoolNews* 98–99

Whiteman, Paul 132
White, Sam 35–36
Wiliam, Dylan, "The Future of AI in Education: 13 things we can do to minimize the damage" 108
Willingham, Daniel 41; *Why Don't Students Like School?* 43, 129
World Conference on Special Needs in Education (1994) 210
World Economic Forum 101, 183; "AI and education: Kids need AI guidance in school. But who guides the schools?" 93; "These 3 charts show the global growth in online learning" 142

Yates, Lorriane 132
Yeats, William Butler 94
Yongpradit, Pat 98
Young, Ian 19, 70, 75

Zahawi, Nadhim 59

For Product Safety Concerns and Information please contact our EU
representative GPSR@taylorandfrancis.com
Taylor & Francis Verlag GmbH, Kaufingerstraße 24, 80331 München, Germany

www.ingramcontent.com/pod-product-compliance
Lightning Source LLC
Chambersburg PA
CBHW062137160426
43191CB00014B/2308